D1127151

The Children in Our Lives

SUNY Series, Feminist Theory in Education

Madeleine R. Grumet, Editor

The Children in Our Lives

Knowing and Teaching Them

Jane Adan

State University of New York Press

Cover photo courtesy of Suzanne Adan.

Permission to quote has been generously given by the following:

From "Gratitude to the Unknown Instructors," by W. B. Yeats. Reprinted with permission of Macmillan Publishing Company from *The Poems of W. B. Yeats: A New Edition*, edited by Richard J. Finneran. Copyright 1933 by Macmillan Publishing Company, renewed 1961 by Bertha Georgie Yeats.

From "Dinosaur Spring," by Marilyn Nelson Waniek. Reprinted with the permission of Louisiana State University Press from *Mama's Promises*. Copyright 1985 by Marilyn Nelson Waniek.

"Mother's Song," translated by Willis Barnstone. From *A Book of Women Poets from Antiquity to Now* edited by Aliki and Willis Barnstone. Copyright © 1980 by Schocken Books, Inc. Reprinted by permission of Schocken Books, a division of Random House, Inc.

From "Looking at Henry Moore's Elephant Skull Etchings in Jerusalem During the War," by Shirley Kaufman. Reprinted from *From One Life to Another*, by Shirley Kaufman, by permission of the University of Pittsburgh Press © 1979 by Shirley Kaufman.

From "A Complaint About Exile," by Máiri MacLeod, translated by Joan Keefe. Reprinted from *The Penguin Book of Women Poets*. Copyright © Carol Cosman, Joan Keefe, and Kathleen Weaver, 1978, by permission of Joan Keefe.

From *Henry and Beezus* by Beverly Cleary. © 1952, 1980 by Beverly Cleary. William Morrow and Company, Inc./Publishers, New York. Used by permission of the publisher.

Four lines quoted at the end of Doris Dana's comments on "Lagar." From *Selected Poems of Gabriela Mistral*, translated by Doris Dana. Copyright 1961 by Doris Dana. Reprinted by permission of the Joan Daves Agency.

From "I Years Had Been From Home," by Emily Dickinson. Reprinted by permission of the publishers and the Trustees of Amherst College from *The Poems of Emily Dickinson*, Thomas H. Johnson, ed., Cambridge, Mass.: The Belknap Press of Harvard University Press, Copyright 1951, © 1955, 1979, 1983 by the President and Fellows of Harvard College.

An earlier version of Chapter one of the present work appeared as "The Child David" in *Phenomenology + Pedagogy* V, no. 1, (1987):22–34 and is reprinted by permission of the journal.

Many thanks to the children whose photographs appear in this book. The photographs appearing at the opening of each chapter are not of the children who are the subject of the chapter.

Published by State University of New York Press, Albany

© 1991 Jane Adan   All rights reserved   Printed in the United States of America

No part of this book may be used or reproduced in any manner whatsoever without written permission except in the case of brief quotations embodied in critical articles and reviews.

For information, address State University of N.Y. Press, State University Plaza, Albany, N.Y. 12246

Production by Christine M. Lynch   Marketing by Bernadette LaManna

Library of Congress Cataloging-in-Publication Data

Adan, Jane, 1947–The children in our lives : knowing and teaching them / Jane Adan.
    p. cm. — (SUNY series, feminist theory in education)
    Includes bibliographical references (p.) and index.
    ISBN 0-7914-0811-6 (alk. paper). — ISBN 0-7914-0812-4 (pbk. : alk. paper)
    1. Children and adults.   2. Child psychology.   3. Intergenerational relations. I. Title. II. Series.
HQ772.5.A23 1992
305.2—dc20

                                  90-22958
                                  CIP

10   9   8   7   6   5   4   3   2   1

For my children

All things hang like a drop of dew
Upon a blade of grass.

W. B. Yeats
"Gratitude to the Unknown Instructors"

Contents

A Sierra Nevada stream in summer, after the snow melt.

Foreword

In the mid-sixties when I was having babies, I spent a lot of time with my friends, Barbara Oder and Margaret Anderson and Judy Engerman and their babies. While the kids scattered Legos under the furniture or played in the park, we would talk about them . . . for hours . . . as we nibbled on their leftover chocolate chip cookies. We talked about their sleeping habits and their language. We talked about their fathers and their grandparents. We talked about other mothers and their kids. Later we talked about their teachers and coaches. And now we talk about their lovers, employers and friends. Soon we will talk about their children.

These conversations, centering on the most mundane and domestic of topics, were—and are—utterly compelling, far-reaching in their insights and implications. Trusting each other, at times only so far, we would bring (almost) everything we had ever known, read and thought about to the interpretation of what we and they were doing. Our disagreements were subtle but terrifying, for they touched our childhoods as well as those of our children.

During the years that I taught in high school, before the kids were born I would talk like that about students with Kathy Burkman and Barbara Oder (she was there too) and again, years later, when I read and wrote and taught educational theory with John Burns and Joan Stone. I remember these talks of parents and teachers, their range and scope, and have searched in vain for a discourse in education that would capture the vivid specificity and attachment as well as the inquiry and deep reflection that informed those discussions. *Children in Our Lives* is such a text.

This book should be read by anyone who wishes to raise, educate or know young children. If this book were well read by the students who would be teachers, I would be greatly assured that they had been exposed to the kind of inquiry into the lives of children that teaching requires.

When I first read Jane Adan's essay, "The Child David" (Chapter I) as a reviewer for the journal, *Phenomenology and Pedagogy*, I was awed by the sweep of her theory. Set in the daily life of children and their families, laid out on the picnic table among the hotdogs and hamburgers, it reached to the philosophical discourse of idealism and then curved back again to challenge judgments and accommodations enacted by the adults both for the children and for themselves. Never had I found theoretical discourse and an account of everyday life both so alive and well and thriving in one text. Adan provides detailed analyses of children in very conventional and mundane settings and situations. In education we have tended to bring this exquisite attention only to descriptions of pathology, as if the story of children's everyday lives were not filled with the magic, terror and illumination that Jane Adan reveals.

As Jane speaks to us about the children—about David, about Mark and Laura, about Daphne and finally about herself—it all comes together. The care, specificity, detail and candor of this text combine to provide the seamless world we share with children. The story of each child unfolds like a mystery. That's the way Adan sets it up. Line by line, page by page the description gets fuller, the picture gets clearer. Nevertheless, for all of its suspense the narrative never abandons us to an inevitable denouement. Adan knows what and how she wants us to see and she intervenes and intercedes so that we will remember that we as well as she have responsibility for our readings of these children. To reconstruct the child's view is to imagine or recover a way of seeing the world that most of us have relinquished. Adan recreates these views so that once again we can sense and feel their plausibility. And even as we comfort the children and return with them to family and classroom, we are grateful that those shelters can never fully protect us from sharing their glimpse of the full terror of mortality and the wonder of existence.

At conferences my colleagues talk about their kids for hours in the coffee shops, but rarely talk about children, theirs or anyone else's at the podium. In classrooms and lounges, teachers hardly ever talk about theory. In each place, either P.S. 42 or the university, wisdom regularly surrenders to the politics and rhetoric of gender. In each place the critical and creative tension of the discourse sags because part of it has been categorically exiled to the other place, even though that part is the dialectical, if systematically and discursively repressed, ground of what is being spoken. Talk about kids and lessons in P.S. 42 is carried on the tides of developmental theory and learning theory; it rides on unspoken assumptions about how to constitute a civil society, the limits and possibilities of democracy and the relation of cultural difference to a common curriculum. At the university or in the meeting rooms at the Sheraton, discussions of critical pedagogy, teacher empowerment, qualitative evaluation and testing resonate with gossip from the old neighborhood, the talk around the kitchen table, and echoes of the relations that bound us as children to mothers, fathers and teachers still bind us to each other.

Though informed by psychology this text rescues its children from the clichés of classification that trap them in closed systems. In the seventies we began to speak about child development as if children were a separate species. Reinforced by reductionistic understandings of Piagetian research, attempts to render and understand the world of children become either clinical or patronizing. Adan refuses both stances. She works to depict the child's standpoint, but as she peels back each layer, moving from what is apparent to what is actual, both the adult and the child are revealed as constituting and constituted by each other's worlds.

The continuity that this text creates between private and public life as well as between practical and theoretical knowledge realizes the social and methodological goals of both curriculum theory and feminism. During the last decade I have been convinced that curriculum theory's interest in bringing the language of teaching and educational theory into one discourse cannot be accomplished unless we also address theory's repression of female enterprise and interests. As editor of this Feminist Theory in Education series, I seek texts that address the elision of female experience from teaching and theory as well as examples of practice and discourse that accomplish the synthesis that is the aspiration of both feminism and curriculum theory.

Adan's studies are the finest examples I know of curriculum theory, for they move from the particular moment, wedged right in the middle of the family picnic, or of bathtime, or of playing dress-up to an interpretation that has a sweep as wide and broad as any that philosophy, social science, and literature can offer us. For centuries we have denigrated local knowledge, preferring statistics, curves, and commissions to the nagging truths that linger in Adan's backyard. In these narratives we hear the story of an educational community, composed of parents, friends, family, teachers. The intricate connections and manipulations of these caregivers unwind in narratives that go right to the heart of the national concern about the welfare of children. In their specificity and sensitivity these narratives exemplify the kind of attention that children need to flourish.

This study *does* what we all say our books, and research, and teaching should do. "Dip your line deep in the stream" Virginia Woolf tells us as she urges the writer to grasp the felt life. Adan dips and trawls. She grasps fragile, even poignant detail, yet never gets so fascinated by specificity that she abandons a sense of a community, a system of meaning. If one of the enduring problems for education is the tension between the individual and the community, Adan's text addresses that issue, in form as well as content, in style as well as ideology. She shows us that to think carefully enough about an individual child is to think about the world that we provide for that child and for each other.

Preface

Early one July morning in 1984, while rummaging through a trunk full of family papers, I discovered a skeleton resting quietly in a sheaf of pink business triplicates that had been neatly folded and tucked into a white legal-size envelope. Because describing the nature of the skeleton with anything approaching accuracy is beyond the scope of a preface and because I am bringing up the skeleton not so that I can tell its story but so that I can acknowledge its generative power in relation to other stories, let me simply say that like most skeletons, mine raised the issues of trust and betrayal. Let me also say that eventually my discovery proved disturbing enough to touch off a period of upheaval during which I took a long look at my past and present life and at the familiar faces that filled it, particularly with respect to the relation between vulnerability and power, a look without which I could not have written the six chapters that form this book.

I had gone to the trunk initially to search for a letter from the late seventies evaluating my performance as a part-time college instructor. About to begin work on a high school teaching credential, I wanted to include the missing letter, along with some others I had dug up, in a personnel file I was compiling. My hope was that a credential would allow me to do something I took pleasure in while at the same time allowing me to increase the family income and gain a sense of economic independence. In turn I hoped that the added income would make me feel less guilty about the time I had been spending writing children's fiction that no one wanted to publish. Shaken by the appearance of the skeleton but also determined to move forward with my plans to teach, I told myself that though at some point I was going to have to come to terms with the skeleton and that this was almost certainly going to require a great deal of attention and energy, the skeleton would simply have to wait its turn.

With one notable exception that I did not pay much attention to at the time, my plan to postpone attending to the skeleton seemed to work relatively well until I began my student teaching, at which point the skeleton began to plague me. Feeling increasingly as if I were a pane of compressed glass that must shatter unless I took action, I made an appointment with a therapist, exited my student teaching, and turned my attention fully to the skeleton.

Although at the time I did not understand why the pressure began when it did, I now think that the skeleton had been with me from the moment I discovered it in the trunk. A main reason I hadn't felt plagued immediately was that until I started teaching my schedule had left me enough time to begin coming to terms with the skeleton metaphorically, through writing. As early as the CBEST (California's test of basic skills for teaching candidates), which I coincidentally had taken the Saturday after my rummage through the trunk, I was asked to write a personal essay. In it I recalled an experience from first grade that dealt with the child's experiencing of the teacher's powerfulness. And when I began the course work that preceded my teaching, there were more writing assignments, all lending themselves to an exploration of the relationship of the child's or young person's experiencing of adult power. In addition, when I was not focusing on my course work, I was writing in private, not only the children's fiction I had experimented with before returning to school, but a whole host of other things as well—sketches, poems, a journal of miscellaneous observations—all touching on power and vulnerability.

When I began to teach, however, two things happened that I believe contributed to my feeling plagued. One was that the demands of teaching left me no time for the personal writing projects with which I had become so involved. In other words, the skeleton, to which I had been devoting hours without realizing it, was abandoned the instant I began to teach. Another was that teaching required me to exercise power at a time when my feelings about power were in total disarray and in a place (the public high school classroom) fraught with the complex consequences of years and years of warped relations between vulnerability and power.

As soon as I stopped teaching and returned to a schedule that left time for writing, my feeling that I was about to shatter began to subside. In fact, shortly after I quit teaching, I experienced a surge of energy and commitment to self that prompted all sorts of rash acts (rash for *me*—and in the sense of impractical, undutiful, frightening, and exciting), three of which are pertinent here. The first was to enroll in a creative writing class; the second was to take some time to follow my nose and sit in on courses and take on projects that appealed to me at the moment; and the third was to submit a personal essay to *Phenomenology + Pedagogy*, a journal I had only just met when I made the submission.

That the discovery of the skeleton, the upheaval, and the three rash acts were experiences essential to my well-being is as clear to me today as anything has ever been. Though the upheaval did estrange me from my plans to teach and did return me, in the eyes of many, to the status of lowly housewife and Sunday writer wandering aimlessly about a university campus at a time when more and more women (most much younger than I) were achieving economic independence through clearly defined goals leading to visible careers, it is also true, as I have said, that without the upheaval I would not have written the six chapters that form this book.

Chapter 1, set off as Part I, introduces a group of children and adults and a number of issues that will be focused on at greater length in Parts II and III. A revision of the essay referred to above, Chapter 1 appeared in *Phenomenology + Pedagogy* in 1987 and was originally written for an unorthodox educational psychology class I took on returning to school. Like later chapters, it explores, through first-person narrative and reflection, an unsettling experience in the life of a real child known personally to me and the potential for discrepancy between the child's experience and the adult's interpretation of it.

On the one hand, the autobiographical focus facilitates one of my central aims (to depict adult-child relationships with a concrete specificity made possible by long intimacy) and reflects the urgency I felt, during my period of upheaval, about questioning the quality of the grass in my personal sphere. On the other hand, this focus has meant that my book explores a comparatively privileged landscape, a place, that is, in which each child written about has a home address and is at least one generation removed from the material poverty that constricts the lives of so many children in our culture. It is also a place where the children focused on do not have to face the flagrant bigotry or the subtler expressions of prejudice that our culture continues to heap, day in and day out, year after year, from one century to the next, on its racial minorities.

That some readers will find such a landscape frivolous and controversial is undeniable. That these readers will almost certainly focus on Chapter 1, with its spring picnic and its two little boys squabbling over hamburger and hot dog buns, is also undeniable. And yet, as I wrote the book, my intent from start to finish was to attend not just to the children I know best but to all children by exploring a complexity of nurture, a narrowness of traditional, dominant, or mainstream values, and a potential for discrepancy between the experiencing of children and of adults that extends beyond the life of any one child, race, or class. In addition, because my book takes a critical perspective, it seemed appropriate to focus on a community of children and adults who could be termed my "doorstep." Finally, though I take great pleasure in life and want all of us to have an opportunity to do the same (and, of course, to have the food, clothing, shelter, health care, and education that every human being by definition deserves), I also think that we need to keep in touch with the potential of material plenty to obscure a narrowness of vision that can impair our ability to know and teach children.

As for the gaps left by my book, one way to look at them would be as silences created by an individual writer's limitations. Which is not to say that a writer cannot expand into the territory of her own silence but simply to suggest that new voices enlarge us all and that the very persistence of inequity means that there is no shortage of human beings capable of placing in our midst the personal stories and intimate imagery of children and adults that I have not provided. Here, given my interest in literature, I think of voices in poetry and fiction who have already spoken, for example, of Claribel Alegría's voice in "Small Country" (1980), Angela Figuera Aymerich's in "Women at the Market" (1979), Christopher Gilbert's in "Saturday Morning at the Laundry" (1984), the anonymous Native American's in "I'd Run About" (1980), Simon J. Ortiz's in "Canyon de Chelly" (1977), Margaret Walker's in "Childhood" (1979), and Jamaica Kincaid's in her novel *Annie John* (1986) as well as of Helen Joseph's in her non-fiction journal documenting South African oppression, *Tomorrow's Sun* (1967). I also think of Gerald W.

Barrax's (1980) voice, which I discovered just today while roaming the library stacks, and of his poem "Narrative of a Surprising Conversion," which dramatizes the narrowing of a black American high school student's horizon through aptitude testing.

Another controversial aspect of Chapter 1 is its clap of thunder at the adult world for perceived oversights in relation to children, a clap that is louder (more urgent and less compromising) than that of later chapters. One factor here is that though over the years my experience as a public school volunteer, a parent, and a part-time teacher of introductory and preintroductory college composition has taught me how difficult it can be to nurture children and young people, I at the same time recall vividly the pain of childhood and am of the opinion that the nurturer's difficulty and the child's pain could both be eased if we would explore the roots of our culture's dominant values. Another factor is that Chapter 1 was a breakthrough piece for me and has less narrative and "plot" to temper the thunder (and also the analysis and reflection) than later chapters have. A third is that I wrote Chapter 1 shortly after discovering the sheaf of business triplicates referred to earlier (in other words, during a period of personal upheaval), whereas I wrote Chapters 2 through 6 several years later. Later chapters, too, however, are filled with a mix of emotions, including those often labeled "base."

Actually, all six chapters, and not just Chapter 1, differ in various ways, and I think this is because the book took shape as I wrote it rather than being fully grasped from page 1. For me, writing is like conversation, or travel, with discovery occurring along the way, discovery that both sobers and exhilarates because it testifies at one and the same time to our awesome capacity for blindness and our awesome capacity to see. Present discoveries reflect on earlier ones, earlier on present, so that the possibility of a new slant, or a bigger picture, exists so long as there is more to touch, taste, hear, see, smell—which it seems there always is. And yet in some sense each discovery I made while writing this book also struck me as autonomous, as deserving of respect in its own right, if only as a record of what one human being was able to perceive—and, equally important, not perceive—at given moments in her life. My aim, then, has not been to seek answers but rather to invite others to converse about the experiencing of children and of the adults who would know and teach them. In this same vein, and because there is a lot of the know-it-all in me, I have tried to remember the great pitfall as well as the great strength of the first-person point of view. The pitfall is that as readers and writers we sometimes experience first-person narrative as omniscient, which, of course, no narrative can ever be; the great strength is that first-person narrative can encourage conversation by saying to readers, "I've spoken up in my own voice and so can you speak up in yours."

Chapters 2 through 6 were written between 1987 and 1990 in response to series editor Madeleine Grumet's interest in Chapter 1. Because each chapter focuses on a conflict in the life of a real child, because some of the children preferred not to be identified by their given names, and because a degree of distance seemed in order, I have used pseudonyms throughout (except for myself) and have changed a detail here and there. And I have done this even though all but one of the conflicts are the kind our culture would tend to term trivial or mundane and even though, as in the case of my own two children, some identities are clear despite the pseudonyms. Though I know that such changes are routine in various contexts (the case studies of clinical psychology come to mind) and though I accept them as necessary in the present context, I came to realize while writing the book that these changes have a potential to distort far beyond what we typically anticipate. In fact, the changes have made me feel claustrophobic at several points by obscuring issues in need of address. I also feel, however, that when moving towards some perceived destination, in this case greater openness, we need to consider present reality and make a judgment, inescapably subjective, about the distance we can travel in any one leg of the journey. And so I have made the changes, at the same time viewing them as a compromise about which I feel an ambivalence that is simply there.

An even greater compromise I have made is to tell the children's stories at all. Though I am convinced that the experiences of women and children (and, in a slightly different sense, also of men) need to be more openly shared if the world and all of us who live in it are to approach wholeness and though today I have few reservations about sharing my own experiences, I also would argue that sharing personal stories with the public can have a negative as well as positive impact on one's life, an impact with which the children, though they have all given me permission to write their stories, have no experience and to which they may be vulnerable in unforeseeable ways.

I do realize that some of the hurt we suffer arises from granting others, including the public, a power over us we have the capacity to refuse. And I realize that by refusing to grant others this power we can minimize their ability to cripple our spirits and spoil our lives. But I also know that it took me years and years to learn this and that I am still learning it. For me to assume, therefore, that the children I have written about will themselves already have grasped and so be strengthened by a truth I did not discover until after I myself had become an adult would be wishfully optimistic and self-serving.

As my daughter made clear to me when she exploded, only a few nights ago, at my suggestion about how she could handle the return of a defective video rental, though I may have reached a point in my life where I could view the power of the other (in this case, the video store owner) in a way that would enable me to handle the return according to my suggestion, this did not mean that she had reached that point. To put it a little differently, my daughter brought home to me that she was still struggling with the legacy of her culture and of my early years of mothering. In particular, she emphasized that any knowledge I may have gained in recent years about how to act in the face of the other's power had not automatically freed her from the influence of those earlier years, years in which I had passed on to her my oversensitivity to this power. In short, my daughter was reminding me that readiness is a complex matter and that hers could not be guaranteed by mine.

And so, because I respect my daughter's insight and suspect that it applies to other mothers and daughters as well as to adults and children involved in all the various nurturing relationships, I tell these stories not only with the sense that such telling is necessary but also with some reservation. Or perhaps it would be more accurate to say that I tell them with the knowledge that there are no guarantees and that I cannot know in advance where the telling may lead. Will one or more of the children at some future point regret the telling and say to me, "You were the adult, the mother, you should have known better"? Will those who read the stories and gain the reader's power treat the children who have shared them with the care and respect they deserve? No, to the first question; yes, to the second—these are the answers I would choose. They are not, however, the answers I will necessarily get. Anything can happen.

And yet to postpone speaking because I cannot guarantee the future would, in my view, be to forget that venturing in advance of final answers is essential to the spiritual growth of human beings. Yes, we need to consider the implications of our actions, but if we allow ourselves to be silenced by the fact that we do not know for certain what lies around the curve, we will never venture in those ways that can make and keep us whole. Nor will we ever set the venturer's example for our children.

Johnny the Clown, a toy handed down by an old family friend
to David and Laura's father.

Acknowledgments

To acknowledge all who have made a difference would take many pages. The students, teachers, and staff that I met on returning to school in 1984 and to whom I am grateful include Rosalee Storz, Marianne Gatheral, Judy MacDonald, and Vincent Crockenberg. Also important was therapist and writer Hanna Bauer, who opened a door for me one morning by stating that hers was not the business of raising good daughters. Others associated with my return to school include the teachers and teaching assistants whose courses I audited or took for credit between 1985 and 1988, most of whom do not know me from Eve—among them Stephanie Shields, Thomas Natsoulas, Cindy Litman, Karen P. Ericksen, and William Bossart. Influential teachers from earlier years include Miriam Young, Robert Miles, Lindsay Mann, Charles Gregory, Bud Gardner, and Victor Comerchero.

I also want to thank series editor Madeleine Grumet for her enthusiastic support throughout my long engagement with the manuscript and for the generosity of her commentary, editor-in-chief Lois Patton for her introduction to the publishing process and for her discerning attention through some sensitive revision, SUNY's reviewers for the thoughtful comments that helped me bring the manuscript to its final form, and all those others associated with the press who helped my manuscript become a book, particularly production editor Christine Lynch.

Three friends I want to thank are George Yonge, for assigning the essay that became Chapter 1, for inviting me to sit in on his graduate courses, and for the scope of his critical feedback; Sandra Marquiss, for materializing out of the blue one day, for spontaneously taking up a conversation interrupted years before, and for the warm composure of her commentary; and Jac O'Casey, for all the gal-pal talk.

Thanks, finally, to the children who shared their stories and to all of my family, especially to my husband and to our two children, who not only supported my decision to write the book when it was a job, and not a book, that we had all expected to emerge from my return to school but who also supported me through the daily work of writing. I will not forget the day my daughter lent new substance to my decision to attempt the book by declaring, in a personal essay for her French class (and sandwiched in among observations about her father's quick temper and my irksome sense of logic), that "Ma mère, elle est écrivaine." It jarred my tentativeness to hear so weighty a voice state so matter-of-factly that her mother was a writer, and it also made me feel again something I had felt many times before, which is that a mother's "occupation" can loom large for children these days. Nor will I forget the day my husband set off in his pickup and hauled home a slab of wood from his art studio to enlarge the surface area of my desk or the day my son became my teacher when I switched midway in my writing from a typewriter to a computer. They have stamina, their souls are keen, they gave me room, these three human beings to whom I extend my thanks.

I

Taking Shape

A preschool girl approaches a goose in the park where
Mark and David had their picnic.

1

A Sky-Blue, Orange-Warm Picnic

Just now I took my baby out of his crib
and teetered on the edge of the vortex.
I saw millions of hands imploring,
mouths open, eyes his.

I fell into a universe of black, starry water,
and through that into monstrous love
that wants to make the world right.

Marilyn Nelson Waniek,
"Dinosaur Spring"

Comparisons are odious, says Cervantes' Don Quixote. And so, at
one time or another, say most children I have met. In agreeing with
Don Quixote, however, these children sometimes find themselves
in disagreement with the world at large. Take David, for instance,
whose anger I witnessed one spring afternoon (David was about
seven at the time) when the adults in charge of a picnic ruled in
favor of another child.

As I remember the day of the picnic, it brought ideal weather.
Blue sky held an orange sun that shone warm through scrub oaks
onto green-brown knolls where people chattered and played together
around barbecues and redwood tables. Jays and squirrels and children inhabited the trees, baseball games sprung up as spontaneously as weeds, ducks dove for bread crumbs in the pond that
separated the picnic grounds from a nature preserve, and a trail led
down the hill from the tables to a river where rafters navigated an
easy current and steelhead fingerlings grew towards the sea.

As I remember David's anger, it burst forth when the adults at
the picnic let eight-year-old Mark transform a traditional hamburger
into a hamburger–hot dog hybrid. Specifically (and it will help if
you can exercise your adult patience in the face of *child*-crisis), they let

Mark eat a rectangular hamburger patty on a rectangular french roll instead of a round hamburger patty on a round kaiser roll or a typically shaped hot dog on a rectangular french roll, the latter two choices being the only ones David deemed acceptable.[1] That David was my son and that I, his mother, had been the one to rule against him only added to his fury.

Furthermore, David stayed angry long after I made my ruling, long enough, in fact, to find himself cast out socially on the grounds that he was, among other things, an unreasonable and unimaginative child. Mark, in contrast, was perceived as both reasonable and imaginative. As responsible adults sharing the world with children, I think we might ask ourselves what could have motivated David, who loved picnics as much as any child, to spoil his own good time and threaten the prevailing harmony of the outing. Why would a child of seven have gone to such lengths to align himself with Don Quixote, especially over a comparison as negligible as that between a hot dog and a hamburger? What, in other words, made David such an uncooperative, difficult child?

Perhaps a partial answer can be found in the specifics surround–ing David's anger. Background information includes the fact that David's family hosted the picnic, that such occasions were quite special rather than routine, and that the rectangular rolls were origi-nally intended for the hot dogs and the round ones for the ham-burgers, mainly because that was the way his family ate hamburgers and hot dogs at home. In contrast, Mark had a home history of eating hamburgers on rectangular rolls and of not eating hot dogs at all. As for the crisis, it emerged as the two boys first noticed that the picnic table had been spread with food and as they, eager for a closer look, abandoned their play and moved towards the table to survey the food, talk over their range of choices, and select those items that would, when the adult call "Let's eat!" was heard, become their picnic lunch.

Before describing the crisis itself, however, I want to pause for a moment to remind myself of something that my absorption in the adult world often removes me from, which is that children exist in the world at large, including the world of home, and not just the world of school, essentially as learners and that the world of home predates the world of school. In other words, I want to remind myself that home (in all its considerable variations) is the child's original or primary "schoolhouse," and I want to follow up by adding that as an adult present with the child in the home world, I have an opportunity and also a responsibility (insofar as is humanly possible) to guide the child-learner as the need arises (Langeveld 1958, 53–54).

In the setting of the picnic, my reminder helps me see that when David and Mark turned their attention from their play to the table spread with food and to the choices that it offered, they were not simply behaving as picnickers but were also evidencing the human capacity for learning about and for shaping their world. They were, in other words, also demonstrating their capacity to sense the world around them (in this case not the world of the classroom, with its chalky smell, its rows of desks, and its ringing bells, but the world of a picnic in the park), to single out and attend to some aspect of that world (to the array of food spread out on the picnic table), to perceive the aspect as a whole, to analyze its several parts, and to synthesize and shape, interpret, or "create" the aspect in a way that expressed a personal point of view (that is, to shape an individual lunch on the basis of perception and analysis [Straus 1963]). Because it acknowledges that human beings exist essentially as learners and creators, my reminder also encourages me to pay a broad attention to David and Mark, an attention that opens itself not only to those moments that our culture has formalized as "educative" (the school day, for example, or the homework hour) but also to those educative moments that materialize outside such designated boundaries (at a spring picnic, for example).

Thus encouraged, I want to turn my attention to the emerging conflict as revealed through David and Mark's conversation over the picnic table:

David: There's hamburgers—I helped make them—and hot dogs, potato chips, macaroni salad, Mountain Dew—I told Mom to buy it because you and me like it best—Pepsi Cola, iced tea, and beer and wine for the grown-ups. For dessert, we made a chocolate cake. I don't like the frosting, but Mom says I can peel it off. For lunch I'm having a hamburger, chips, and Mountain Dew. Laura [David's sister] wants a hot dog. She doesn't like hamburgers. Not ever. She thinks they're sickening. And we got the kind of rolls Laura likes. For the hot dogs. French ones that are kind of like big hot dog buns. But I'm not having a hot dog. Even though I like them. I'm having a hamburger.

Mark: I'm having a hamburger, too. On one of those french rolls Laura likes. And Mountain Dew. And chips. And salad.

David: No, Mark. You can't have a french roll for a hamburger. It wouldn't fit right. They're for the hot dogs.

Mark: But I like hamburgers on french rolls. I always have them that way at home.

David: It doesn't matter. You still can't have one. They're for the hot dogs. If you want a hamburger, you have to have it on a *round* roll.

Mark: But I don't like this kind of round roll. I've never had it before. And they look funny on top. I like the french rolls that Laura likes.

David: Then have a hot dog. They're good. I have them sometimes.

Mark: I don't want to. I don't like them.

David: Then have a hamburger on a round roll.

Mark: I told you, David. I don't like *round* rolls. Don't you listen?

David: Yes I listen. And you do too like *round* rolls.

Mark: I do not. So don't say I do.

David: You eat round rolls at Burger King [Mark's favorite fast-food restaurant].

Mark: That's different, David. They only have round rolls at Burger King.

David: Well, that's the only kind we have, too, for hamburgers. See—the hamburgers are all wrapped up on that platter. I helped make them. And they're round. So you have to have a round roll if you want a hamburger. Or the hamburger won't fit.

Mark: I don't care what you say. You're not the boss. I'm going to ask my mother if I can have the roll I want.

David: Go ahead. Ask her. And I'll ask my mother not to let you have one.[2]

Though the conversation could be interpreted from many angles, and though I don't believe we could ever exhaust all that such a conversation has to tell us, I want to interpret it from the view of an adult interested in understanding rather than in censuring David. First, David seems proud to be part of the hosting family. Cataloguing the food, he carefully points out his and his family's attempts to anticipate the tastes of others. He refers to the problem of shape repeatedly, and he also mentions that he himself has helped shape the hamburger patties, the first mention as evidence that he has exerted himself in preparing for the guests (in other words, the first as evidence that he is moving towards a sense of responsible participation in his world), and the second mention as an attempt to get Mark to finally recognize that the *roundness* of the hamburger makes it critical that it be eaten on a *round* roll. David also intends to shape or "synthesize" a meal that exactly suits his tastes (hamburger on a round roll, his favorite soft drink, and chocolate cake with the *frosting peeled off*).

In general, then, David's conversation with Mark suggests that David wants to host the picnic according to some plan that he has been developing, perhaps through dialogue with himself and with his family, a plan tied to the concrete preparations for the picnic, but which David has personalized to some extent through his imagination. In his role of host, David might be compared to a composer working out a variation on the well-known picnic theme, or perhaps to the director of a play who is turning over from various angles how best to realize the essentials of a given script. And at this point in his directorship, he is perhaps not particularly innovative; he would probably costume Hamlet in gear reflecting the dress of Elizabethan England or the Denmark of *Hamlet*'s setting and would probably object to any flexibility of direction that would dress Hamlet as, say, a contemporary business executive, or, even more outrageously, given David's traditional point of view, send Hamlet on stage nude.

Regardless of the degree of David's innovativeness, however, his pleasure in the picnic appears clearly tied to his power as a host to please his guests and at the same time actualize his image of what this particular picnic ought to be. And I should add that David seems to want to exercise the power of the host as well as the privilege of the guest. David, then, could be viewed as a child in the process of learning gradually to exercise freedom responsibly and as having some difficulty moving from the intoxicating freedom of

exercising power with little or no regard for the other's equal human dignity to the sobering freedom of exercising power responsibly, with full regard for the other's equal human dignity. Like most
children, then, David is experiencing tension between the person he
is at the moment and the person he is seeking (if only on a vague
and inarticulate level) to become.

But what of Mark's feelings about the picnic? And how far
apart are they from David's? In light of their conversation, Mark
seems to be a happy guest, to appreciate the food that has been
provided, and to be eager to discuss the possible choices with his
host. Once the conflict emerges, however, he is no more willing to
be a gracious guest than David is to be a gracious host. Instead, he
immediately sees himself as someone who should be accommodated.
And why not? Haven't David and his sister, Laura, as members of
the hosting family, managed to accommodate their personal tastes
by influencing my purchases at the grocery store? From this perspective, Mark only seeks an equal footing with the other children,
only seeks to exit the social role of cooperative, grateful guest and
demand his equal rights as an individual child. Furthermore, both
boys seem determined that their picnic lunch will be traditional,
that is, will be as much as possible like the meals they eat at home.
David wants a hamburger on a round roll, just the way he eats
hamburgers at home. And Mark wants a hamburger on a rectangular
roll, just the way he eats hamburgers at home. Neither boy, then, is
showing much imagination in his choice of a main course. And
neither has a very expansive concept of a picnic. In other words,
both are determined to satisfy their usual preferences.

The above interpretation, however, differs from that of the majority of adults at the picnic. Let's pick up the story as the two boys
approached their mothers with opposite requests. After hearing
David's objections to Mark's request for a rectangular roll, I acknowledged that the hamburger patties were indeed round, that
David had indeed helped make them, that, no, they wouldn't fit
very well on rectangular french rolls, and that, yes, the french rolls
had in fact been bought to use with the hot dogs. And I should add
that all the while I was doing this acknowledging I felt an urge to
gloss over Mark's request as whiney and spoiled and rule in favor
of my own child.

In keeping with the spirit of a picnic as a special occasion marked
by the relaxed, hospitable, and harmonious atmosphere that can
foster openness to possibilities at the moment they arise, however,

and resisting the urge to discount Mark's request, I said that since there happened to be plenty of both kinds of rolls, everyone could have a choice. Taking her cue from me, in my role as her hostess, Mark's mother told Mark that he could have a french roll for his hamburger and also suggested that they reshape one of the round patties into a rectangular one to fit the french rolls. Mark marched off in triumph to transform one of the round patties *David had helped make* into a rectangular one, and David proceeded to alternate conspicuous pouting with equally conspicuous attempts to reopen the discussion, probably hoping to change the adult verdict before Mark's rectangular hamburger hit the barbecue grill and roundness was transformed for keeps into rectangularity.

David's unpicniclike behavior eventually caught the attention of most of the adults, who at first found his behavior an annoyance—a disruption of their adult conversation—but who finally focused on it as an opportunity to express various attitudes towards children and upbringing. After a "discreet" discussion in which David and Mark were compared in some detail,[3] the majority of adults concluded that David's behavior was essentially dictatorial, antisocial, inhospitable, uncooperative, rigid, and unimaginative, whereas Mark's behavior was seen by these same adults as involving an easily accommodatable request that arose from his imaginative perception of a hamburger as something that could be either rectangular or round. Becoming a sort of hero of the moment, Mark ate his hamburger with understandable gusto, whereas David, becoming a sort of social outcast, ate next to nothing. And the adults, interpreting David's behavior as calling for labeling and censure rather than as an appeal for guidance, overlooked an opportunity to positively influence both children, and may also have impressed on both boys that one person's freedom must exist at another's expense.

The question of whether David's behavior was really dictatorial, antisocial, inhospitable, uncooperative, rigid, and unimaginative is easily answered. His behavior was to some degree all of these things—especially dictatorial in its perception of Mark as a subordinate who must conform to his, David's, wishes. Rather than resting satisfied because the labeling of David was, on its face, accurate, however, and accepting his casting out on the basis of this labeling, it might be more productive to explore a question raised earlier. What made David such a difficult child? Or, in short, what was his motivation?

I think it is possible to argue that David was motivated, in part, at least, by a desire to defend his definition of a hamburger as something distinct from a hot dog, as something distinct to some degree on the basis of shape—a shape that David himself had helped impart—as something that had value because it was distinct, as something whose value made it worthy of respect, and as something that was, at least on the level of concrete survival, most truly respected when allowed to retain its individual essence. In other words, David's objection to Mark's choice of rolls could have been David's way of asserting, with Don Quixote, that comparisons are odious because they violate the items compared by depriving them of (or threatening to transform) their essence, a deprivation that young children could be especially sensitive to because their own sense of identity tends to be so tenuous or raw.

And here, for those who may not share my sense of terms, I should add that for me the relationship between identity, comparison, and transformation is typically intimate and often also fluid. In terms of intimacy, I mean that a comparison typically involves the grasping of identity and a transformation the grasping of a comparison (for example, on a relatively simple and clear-cut level, to compare a pumpkin and a coach requires some knowledge of both, and to transform the pumpkin into a coach, as Cinderella's fairy godmother does, suggests the perception of enough similarity between the two items to provide a basis for the transformation). By fluid, however, I mean that the boundaries between the three categories can be less than solid and that an identification can tend towards, hint at, or have its source in a comparison, or can have one "foot" in each category, so to speak (for example, to say that David is dictatorial can tend towards saying that he *is* a dictator or perhaps towards comparing him to some historical dictator, and, to reverse the direction, to compare him to a specific dictator can tend towards the more abstract observations that he is dictatorial or a dictator). Similarly, a comparison can tend towards a transformation.

Also worth noting is that the grasping of identity, comparison, and transformation is not always self-aware (I doubt, for instance, that Mark was aware of or "registered" the comparison between a mother and a boss implied in his dialogue with David that I quoted earlier). Nor is the grasping necessarily always reflective or cerebral but instead can sometimes be visceral and intuitive (as, say, Huck's largely is regarding Jim's fully human stature in *Huckleberry Finn*). The grasping can, of course, also be somewhere in between the two extremes. In the present context, this intimate, fluid relationship and this variation in the quality of the grasping mean that when I speak of the transformation of a traditional hamburger into a hamburger–hot dog hybrid, I am assuming that a comparison and a perception of identity are integral to or "mingled in with" the transformation and that David, though he on some level grasped, comprehended, or "lived" all three, would not necessarily have been able to talk about or reflect on his comprehension beyond his few observations to Mark about the shape of the hamburger patties and the rolls. A last point to keep in mind is that my focus here is on *David* (as the indignant person) and on his perception of the comparison and of the transformation. Even though Mark, the "offender," was the one who "made" the comparison or brought the "odious" comparison to David's attention by choosing the rectangular roll, David's response was independent of any grasping of the comparison on Mark's part.

If David's anger at the picnic was indeed rooted in his indignation at a comparison that he experienced as odious in its ability to violate an identity that he valued, then the "fuss" he made at the picnic (although ill-timed from the adult point of view) could suggest a developing sense of moral or spiritual courage, the sort of courage it is an adult's responsibility to nurture, and which also sometimes involves a child's selective disobedience or rebellion, which it is to some extent an adult's obligation to endure (live through). The challenge is to find a way to nurture the child's sense of courage without at the same time promoting a disregard for the rights of others. Above all, that which is seeking growth (and here I mean *seeking* to encompass a vague groping as well as a clearly defined directedness) in a child's motivation and behavior needs to be acknowledged. Otherwise, an opportunity to affirm the child's inclination towards maturity is lost.

Unfortunately, the adults at the picnic, or adults anywhere, cannot meet the challenge of nurturing David, or any child, by focusing on behavior and ignoring motivation. How then might such adults be convinced to at least consider an alternative argument? How, in other words, might these adults, and, for that matter, all the rest of us, be convinced to entertain the possibility that a mention of children, hot dogs, hamburgers, Don Quixote, individual essences, comparisons, the recognition of true values, and moral courage all in one breath is not necessarily as ludicrous as it sounds? Perhaps a reminder that even as adults we frequently find ourselves in situations parallel to David's would help. Perhaps by seeing the "David" in ourselves, we would be more sympathetic to his plight. Perhaps we would offer our hand to this seven-year-old outsider, to this child who finds himself so at odds and full of anger, and help him find a place for himself once again within the group.

Beginning with myself, I can say that although I am an adult who does not care what shape of roll a person chooses for a hamburger, I do experience indignation when people use comparisons that violate the essence of certain words, words that I, as a lover of language, have come to value. For example, when I hear an advertisement for Thunderbird wine or a Thunderbird automobile, I am tempted to shoot a letter off to the manufacturer of these products informing them that the word *thunderbird* is essentially beautiful in the context of Native American creation mythology and that advertisers violate its essence when they slap it on a label for cheap wine or emblazon it in chrome across the grill of an expensive car.[4] Even observations by friends and family that my indignation is essentially impotent and idiosyncratic do not sway me from my stance. And in my adult indignation at a comparison I regard as debasing, in my rigid resistance to the violence of metaphor, in my reluctance to attribute through the use of my imagination the power of the Native American thunderbird to a bottle of wine or a car, in my refusal to accommodate the world at large, *in my essential willfulness*, I am like the child David.

Nor am I alone. If I seek adult company in my selective indignation at comparison—in my right to reject comparisons that debase my sense of value—I have only to look as far as the next room, where my husband sits listening to the Blues and grading high school student art. A sculptor who works in wood and values tools, he has on occasion become indignant when our two children and their friends have attempted to transform a finely crafted spoon gauge or some chisel with a purpose all its own into a "stick" for digging in the mud or stirring jars of poster paint.

And from my husband in the living room, I could move into the world outside our home, where I would discover adults everywhere exercising David's prerogative on every imaginable level: I would find a housewife who became indignant when some less than sensitive sleeper transformed a strictly decorative bedspread into a quilt for keeping warm; I would find a chef at a fine restaurant who became indignant when a diner transformed a masterpiece into a travesty by asking for the ketchup; I would find a neighbor-

hood naturalist who became indignant when the recreation department transformed a patch of wood into a tennis court; I would find
a secretary who became indignant when her boss transformed her
into his personal domestic by directing her to scrub and polish his
false teeth; I would find a public school teacher who became indignant when a school board transformed her into a second-class citizen
by denying her the right to march for civil rights; I would find a
husband who became indignant when his wife transformed him
into a cuckold by engaging in sexual intercourse with his best friend;
I would find a father who became indignant when another day of
futile searching for the job that would feed his family transformed
him into a failure in their eyes; I would find a single mother of
small children who became indignant when an income lost to illness
transformed her into one of America's homeless; I would find a
surgical nurse who became indignant when an anesthesiologist
transformed his female patient into an object for sexual gratification
by appropriating her body for an act of fellatio while she was under
anesthetic;[5] and I would find a policeman who became indignant
when evidence pointed to a live-in boyfriend's having transformed
a living child into a heap of stinking char by burning the child alive
in the kitchen oven in the presence of his girlfriend, who was also
the child's mother, reportedly citing as his justification that the child
was the devil Lucifer in disguise.[6]

Now that we adults have had an opportunity to see ourselves
as people who routinely deny comparison, as people who exercise
our imaginations in the context of our values, now that we have
interpreted David's behavior as possibly motivated by something
other than mere arbitrary "difficultness," some of us might begin to
feel confident enough to respond to David in his particular
situatedness, to offer him the guidance that he needs. I think, however, that such an offer would be premature. I think that before we
can qualify as truly ready to offer David anything substantial in the
way of guidance, we must first question ourselves about our reac-
tions to atrocity that perpetrators defend by invoking metaphor. We
might ask ourselves, for example, some questions, admittedly unsettling, about a live-in boyfriend like the one described above. Do
we as human beings admire such a boyfriend's imaginative solution
to the problem of the child as a nuisance? And, assuming her assent, is the girlfriend of such a man, the mother of such a child, to
be spared consequence on the ground that she was an appreciative
audience, one that was sensitive and receptive to her boyfriend's

creativity? Do we tell a policeman who bags the child's remains that he stifled creativity when he attempted to intervene regarding behavior that he knew was criminal?

These questions are absurd, some adults are likely to respond. Absurd and an offense to human dignity, others are likely to chime in. Too obvious to merit a response, still others will object. And yet I ask the questions anyway. Though I want these adults to be right. Though I want each one of us without exception to stand and answer that we do not applaud such a boyfriend or such a mother, that we weep for them instead, and for the murdered child, and further, that in our weeping we discover our capacity for sorrow in the face of loss and also recognize our obligation (an imperative) to defend the dignity of human beings from those who would debase it through the monstrous perversion of the imaginative power of comparison—though I want these adults to be right—I cannot bring myself to sentimentalize my view of human nature, to accept as truth these noble human utterances, without at least one backward glance at human history.

And so I exercise my memory by recalling a past that includes the Spanish Inquisition and the Salem witch trials, the decimation of America's great diversity of native tribes, the seizure of African people to provide slave labor for America's economy of privilege, the killing of huge numbers of Armenians in Turkey, the liquidation of Russian kulaks by deportation to remote areas of Siberia, the internment of Japanese-Americans during World War II, the institution of apartheid in South Africa, and the systematic slaughter of the Jews. And by exercising my memory, I make a start towards answering my own question about a boyfriend's burning of a child and a mother's tolerance of such an act. I answer from the historical perspective that some of us will stand in protest (deny the boyfriend's right to employ his imagination as he has), some of us will participate in the slaughter (actively support through word or deed—in my opinion from some deeply rooted cowardice—his right to employ his imagination as he has), some of us will watch (affirm his right by being unprotestingly present to his act), and some of us will look the other way (will tolerate his perversion by pretending not to see it, perhaps because we secretly appreciate it or because we are simply too busy with our own lives—too self-absorbed). And all of us, I think, will make our decision to some extent on the basis of our particular situatedness when the atrocity occurs. The mother could be more committed to her boyfriend than to her child.

The adults at the picnic could be more committed to bandying superficial explanations of "childishness" than they are to understanding a given child. And these commitments, as absorptions, could distance both the mother and the adults from personal compromises of which they feel ashamed.

In refusing to attend to history and its relevance to rearing children in the present day, then, we adults are susceptible to adopting a perspective that is by definition superficial in its deficient involvement with the world as it actually exists and is accessible to us. Such refusal can hamper our ability to guide our children, first, because it means we will lead the child towards a less than adult— less than comprehensive—point of view, and, second, because it can promote an overconfidence in which we hold too tightly to our own perspective and so ignore the child's. More specifically, and from a historical perspective, just as the Spanish Jews at Cádiz were seen as difficult by the Spanish monarchy and the Catholic church, so were the monarchy and the church seen as difficult by the Jews; again specifically, and this time from the perspective of the picnic, just as David's behavior was seen as difficult by the majority of adults, so was the adults' behavior seen as difficult by David. Ideally, then, when we seek to help a child we need to see ourselves as the child sees us, and we also need to see the child as the child sees him- or herself. In other words, children need adults who understand them, who have the courage and ability to shift perspectives without losing sight of the main goal, which is to guide a child towards the fullest sort of adulthood, to support a creative tension that enables the child to retain an individual essence within the context of the group.

And David, for all his negative behavior, was no exception. Hands in pockets, eyes downcast, circling an oak tree, kicking at the grass, not speaking when spoken to, muttering to himself, he was, following his casting out, an obviously miserable child. So miserable, in fact, that in recalling the afternoon of the picnic, it has occurred to me that it would have been a perfect occasion to have played God—lots of adults do it—and resurrected the Rumanian-born French sculptor Constantin Brancusi from the dead. My one condition—as God I could have been as conditional as I liked— would have been that he appear to the adults at the picnic in his maturity, that he appear, in other words, as an aging adult artist wearing his long white robe and sporting his long white beard, an artist covered from head to foot with the fine white dust of carved

Carrara marble, an artist flanked by his two white dogs and armed with the white washbasin into which he pours, from the bottle he has brought, the white milk with which he nourishes them.[7] And when he stood before the adults at the picnic, I would have asked him, graciously, of course, because, though God, I would also have been his host and he my guest, to tell the adults at the picnic what he once told his young apprentice, Isamu Noguchi: "Who is no longer a child is no longer an artist" (Noguchi 1976, 29) were Brancusi's words. And although what Brancusi really meant, I can never know for sure, I would have been just impertinent enough in my superhuman role to have speculated that, for Brancusi, the act of creation originates in the artist's ability to reach back through time and space at will and grasp the essence of beginnings, the essence of potentiality and possibility: in other words, the essence of the child. "Who is no longer a child is no longer an artist" is a statement, then, that could apply as readily to the teacher as to the artist, if by teacher is meant an adult who is able to meet the child in his or her distinct and specific situatedness and guide the child gradually from a sort of infantile chaos to a new and orderly adult reality.

As a human being and no god, however, I lack the power of resurrection, and so, on the day of the picnic, could not have called Brancusi back, even if I had thought of it. Instead, on the day of the picnic, I sought a human solution to David's "crisis" by calling on the help of a fellow human being, David's father, who, instead of encountering the adults, encountered David in his loneliness and took him for a walk along the riverbank. They talked about the shape of things, about what makes a hamburger really a hamburger, about what makes a hot dog really a hot dog, about what it means to be a host and what it means to be a guest, about the thoughtlessness of some adults, about how much it can hurt when friends do not appreciate our efforts, and, eventually, about the rights of Mark. David's father, then, encouraged David to see the conflict with Mark in its totality, and then helped him to understand, as best he could, the conflict in its various parts, finally helping his son to resynthesize the conflict into a more harmonious, less discordant lived experience than the experience as first lived through by David. Intervening both acceptively and correctively, David's father helped him separate out that which was good in his experience and let go the rest. When David returned to the picnic table, he sat down with Mark, accepted from me, his mother—the very same woman who had betrayed him earlier by ruling in favor of another child—a piece of chocolate cake, and peeled the frosting off. David was once again an individual child capable of existing in a group.

My final task in coming to grips with David's "difficultness" is to face a second time the fact of Don Quixote, but this time I must see him in light of Constantin Brancusi. Can Don Quixote's belief that comparisons are odious stand beside the comparison implicit in Brancusi's observation that "Who is no longer a child is no longer an artist"? And what of all the comparisons I myself have made throughout my argument? In my first paragraph I compared difficult, disagreeable children to Don Quixote. Later, in a note, I compared the anesthesiologist Miofsky to the adults at the picnic. And just now I have compared a teacher to an artist. Am I to be denied these comparisons by some fictional knight who exists between the covers of a book written in Spain in 1604? Must I tolerate a perspective so far removed from my own here and now, especially one that seems not quite to fit my argument, not in its beginnings, perhaps, but as it has developed?

"Don Quixote does not belong; throw Don Quixote out," shouts some true believer in consistency who would help me solve my problem. And yet I like my aging knight much too much to cast him out. Besides, there is no need. For the man who is referred to by his neighbors as "plain Señor Quixana," a man nearing fifty who eats his meals alone and spends his evenings reading romance, transforms himself, through the power of comparison, into Don Quixote de la Mancha, the Knight of the Sad Countenance.[8] Though Don Quixote denounces comparisons as odious, he at the same time lives metaphorically. In my opinion, he possesses the artist's imagination: he simultaneously grasps two seemingly contradictory perspectives; he manages to maintain artistic tension without feeling compelled to reach out towards the comfort of consistency or resolution.[9]

I would be a fool to cast Don Quixote out. Don Quixote *is* my argument (And yes, I know that I have just indulged in yet another metaphor). He comes to know, through lived experience, that comparisons are both odious and sublime, that comparisons have the power to overwhelm as well as the power to actualize. Instead of an aging man who lives alone and reads romance, Don Quixote becomes a seeker of adventure in the world at large. And I would like to add, lest there be some among us who are as yet reluctant to perceive love as adventure, that Don Quixote seeks love as much as anything.

Through the power of comparison, Don Quixote gives direction
to his individual essence. And we as adults in charge of children
would be wise to acknowledge his accomplishment. For if we lose
our sense of direction, if we define our world only in relation to
ourselves, if we cannot from our subjective vantage point sustain
the tension between the child's point of view and the adult's, if we
define the child as *other* than he or she actually is, if we try to love
the child as that other, then we indulge in the odious sort of comparison that deprives a child of the right to be him- or herself. In
other words, when we as adults lose our way, we know not where
to lead the child. And the child, sensing that the guide is lost, begins
inevitably to cry. Impatient in the face of crying we cannot quiet,
deaf to it as a signal of distress—as a cry that says, "I love your
adultness. I want you *not* to be lost. I need you to help me find my
way"—we as adults label our children difficult and cast them out
when we should most embrace them as our touchstones. As much
as anything, and certainly as much as any lack of creativity or bent
towards tyranny on David's part, it was an adult failure of imagination that was the source of David's difficulty. We as human beings
can make comparisons that truly illuminate only if we have the
imagination to grasp individual essences. This is a bottom line for
me. It is the reason I would not want to push a child too fast
towards flexibility, even flexibility that is creative, and the reason I
would have to be convinced by someone I have yet to meet of the
value of flexibility that is facile. It is also the reason I find myself in
sympathy, not only with the child Mark and with a whole wide
world full of children I will never personally know, but also with
the child David, whose anger burst forth so willfully one spring
afternoon to disrupt the harmony of a sky-blue, orange-warm picnic.

II

The Children in Everyday Places

Wings of clay frame a young boy at his grandparents' house.

2

Mark at Preschool

If snow falls on the far field
where travelers
spend the night,
I ask you, cranes,
to warm my child in your wings.

Anonymous, "Mother's Song"
(translated from Japanese
by Willis Barnstone)

Mark, the same Mark I introduced as an eight-year-old in Chapter
1, began preschool on the first day of a new session, when he was
between three and four years old. Among the children attending
with him, some were also beginning preschool for the first time,
some were making transitions from other preschools, and some
were continuing students from previous sessions. Among these
continuing students was Laura, also mentioned in Chapter 1, who
carpooled with Mark to school.

The setting of the school was a nearly equal mix of country and
city, commercial and residential. As well as asphalt and cement and
cyclone fences, there were trees and flower beds and lawns and
hedges, split-rail fences, vacant lots, irrigated pastureland, and open,
unkept fields where purple vetch, wild grass, and thistle grew. A
river ran through county parkland about ten bicycle minutes from
the preschool, and those who liked the feel of country within the
proximity of city, and could afford it, had moved increasingly into
the area. The school, which was private and relatively expensive,
drew its students mainly from these mobile upper-middle-class
families, but also from a number of less well-off families who sought
a quality preschool education for their children and who eased the
expense by choosing a two- or three-day school week instead of the
traditional five-day week. Looking more like someone's house than

a school, the school building itself was unpainted redwood. The classroom offered a well-maintained and generous assortment of books and toys—the kind generally termed "educational"—as well as a kitchen area supplied with a pitcher, glasses, napkins, a sponge and dish towels, and a vegetable peeler and small paring knife for the children to use in preparing and cleaning up after such snacks as celery, carrots, crackers, and fruit juice. Out the back door of the classroom was the playground, where each school day began with a short before-school playtime.[1]

On Mark's first day, as on other days, not all of the fifteen or so children on the playground stopped playing immediately when their teacher, Rita, called them in. They did, however, soon break away from their involvements with the slide, the sandbox, the jungle gym, and the horse that grazed on the other side of the playground fence so that in a minute or two all of the children, including Mark, were heading toward the classroom. But when they reached the open door and the time came to step through into the classroom, Mark refused. Rita, who valued autonomy and preferred that the children enter the classroom under their own power, went over to Mark and tried to convince him to step inside while the assistant teacher tended to the other children. Laura, who had been walking with Mark, stopped walking when he stopped, as friends are wont to do, and so as a matter of course was witness to his refusal.[2]

Although I know from Laura that Rita's effort was gentle and concerned, I did not witness Mark's refusal myself and so do not know what Rita said to him.[3] Nonetheless, on the basis of my experience at the school on other days, I want to describe the form Rita's effort probably took. As I see it, Rita would have knelt down beside Mark and pointed out that the classroom had been designed especially with children in mind and that though he was new to it, the school had lots to offer him, if he would only give it a chance. She might then have pointed out various areas and objects in the classroom that were visible to both of them through the open door. For example, she might have pointed to the open area on the carpet and explained that Mark and the other children would start their morning with the fun of songs, games, and informal talk while they sat together in a circle. Then she might have pointed out a place on the job shelf,[4] just inside the door, where a small basket of bright orange marbles sat beside a larger basket filled with modules of various shapes that could be interlocked like puzzle pieces, but in a variety of combinations, to form a passageway of tunnels, slides, and bridges through which he could send the marbles rolling, single file.[5] After that, she might have pointed to the child-size table and chair sets where he would be able to work at a job of his choice, either by himself or with other children. She might also have pointed to the stack of carpet squares that could be used to define a personal work space when he preferred working on the floor to working at a table. And as Rita talked to Mark, she might have paused a time or two to gauge his mood and suggest that they go inside and begin their circle time.

Given the Rita described above, I think it would be fair to say that she did pretty much what any one of us has done at one time or another when faced with a reluctant person, which is to try to get the person to adopt our perception of the landscape.[6] In other words, I am suggesting that interwoven with Rita's gentleness and concern, whose authenticity I am not questioning, there was an attempt to get Mark to adopt an "official" perspective on the school as a place designed especially for children that he need not resist. Furthermore, in Rita's effort as I have depicted it, she did not establish or maintain a distinction between the objects in the classroom (for example, the child-size furniture and the space for circle time) and the "official" meaning or connotation of these objects (that child-size furniture will please children, that circle time is fun). Instead, as most of us have done at one time or another, she "confused" or "poured together" the objects and the meaning, even though, if she had paused to think about it, perhaps to recall situations from the past in which she had been the reluctant other, she would very likely have discovered that one object can have many connotations and that it is invariably the connotation of an object that the reluctant other resists. That such a confusion of object and meaning can narrow the confuser's perception and blind him or her to alternative meanings would be no more likely to occur to the Rita I have been describing than it would to any one of us in similar circumstances.

However, though my sense is that this pouring together did occur in the case of Rita and Mark, I do not know for sure that it did. Nor do I know for sure—if the pouring did occur—whether it had any impact, immediate or eventual, on Mark's attitude towards preschool. All I do know with certainty is that whatever form Rita's effort took, Mark would have none of it. Instead of entering the classroom, he continued to refuse until, finally, Rita picked him up around the waist, body facing outward, arms and legs free, and carried him screaming and thrashing into the classroom.[7] Once inside, Mark further refused, according to Laura, to sit in the circle with her and the other children. Rita's response was to accept the refusal and suggest that he sit down behind Laura, a suggestion with which Mark complied and a sitting-behind that became routine until one day—Laura does not remember how long it took but only how wonderful it was when it did occur—Mark joined the circle of his own accord and voluntarily participated in whatever song or activity the class was involved in that day.[8]

Although Mark's refusal to enter the classroom as described above dramatically illustrates his intense and active resistance to preschool, and although this refusal was not his first refusal (I will describe his first refusal shortly), active and intense resistance was not his initial response towards the prospect of preschool. Actually, intense resistance constituted only one facet of his attitude towards the preschool, and his refusal to enter the classroom on the first day was only one incident in the history of that attitude.[9] The history also included two previous visits to the preschool as well as much adult discussion of his intense resistance once it did emerge. To begin with, Mark's parents had decided to send him to preschool mainly because they lived in a neighborhood where there were few children for him to play with, because his mother had her hands full caring for Mark and his younger brothers, the youngest having been born when Mark was not quite three, and because his mother was perceived, by herself as well as her husband and the other adults in her world, myself included, as overprotective. And his parents decided to send him to the same preschool as Laura because her father and I were very satisfied with it, because Laura herself had loved the school from her first visit there, because the general opinion was that Laura's presence would help Mark "break the ice" at preschool, and because Mark's mother and I could form a carpool.

In relation to her overprotectiveness, Mark's mother says that one of her biggest worries was that Mark would fall and break (*break* is her word). Hovering anxiously about him, she would clear his path of anything that had the potential to upset his balance. And she was tireless when it came to assisting Mark or retrieving him and redirecting his attention when he approached objects not easily moved (say, a bed or a couch) that she feared he might climb up on, or any expanse of flooring that was not quite level (for example, the expanse where living room carpet and kitchen linoleum met). Her memory is that he never suffered even scratches or a skinned knee while in her care. Another of her worries was that

Mark would choke on his food. Long after other children his age began to handle quarters of toast and sandwiches and child-size bites of fruit, meat, and vegetables, she continued to cut his food into tiny pieces. Even given these precautions, she says that she still feared he would choke and that she would think about administering first aid if he so much as coughed while eating.[10]

When Mark's parents introduced the idea of preschool to him, he did not respond with eager anticipation or with active resistance but with profound tentativeness or uncertainty.[11] On the one hand, the idea seemed to interest or intrigue him; on the other, he seemed wary of it. One way to further characterize his attitude would be to say that he seemed pleased, perhaps even a little flattered, to be deemed qualified or worthy of preschool, preschool being something he would have known that other children attended (Laura, for instance) but that he perhaps had never thought of as a possibility for himself. And one way to further characterize his wariness would be to say that he was awed and a little frightened by the discovery of this new possibility and perhaps also startled or even insulted that his parents would be willing to part with him. If he had been older and more capable of verbalizing his attitude, and if he had not grown too self-conscious or too "sophisticated" or masculine to voice his feelings, he might have said, "Preschool? Me? You mean I could go to preschool? But isn't preschool just for other children?" As for his wariness, he might have verbalized it by saying, "It felt really good to find out that I am a child who has the same potential for preschool as other children, but I'm not sure I really need to go to preschool. Maybe I'd better think about it." In addition, I suspect that his "thinking" about his need to go would have included such questions as "What would happen to me at preschool? Would people be nice to me? Would I be safe there? How come Mama and Daddy want me to go to preschool anyway? Don't they like me as much as they used to? If I do go, what will Mama and my brothers be doing while I'm away?" Mark was not older, however, and his verbalization of his attitude towards preschool was confined mostly to answering his parents' queries with nods of the head, shrugs of the shoulder, and monosyllables. In respect to any interior monologue about preschool, I expect it would have taken the form of a fluctuating complex of feelings and images or fantasies with a minimum of verbal dialogue or captioning.

Mark's tentativeness persisted until his first visit to the preschool on orientation day, which he attended with Laura and me while his mother stayed at home with his two brothers. The decision that I, and not his mother, take him to the school itself requires comment. Although in looking back Mark's mother has said that she probably had been relieved not to have to take him to orientation day, it is also true that the decision was made not so much by Mark's mother as by her many "helpful" advice givers, including myself, who felt that Mark would cling to her if she took him. That such clinging could be detrimental to a child was something that many of us accepted in that time and place in much the same way that many of our mothers had accepted that babies should be on a strict feeding schedule and that bottle feeding was as good as or better than breast feeding.[12]

However, though this and other such decisions are often intertwined with the popular psychology and medical opinion of the day and so are easy to justify and feel confident about, I think that the entwinement allows us to pursue unarticulated motives and that I slipped easily into the role of the know-it-all who would intervene and fix everything at Mark's house. In other words, the prospect of performing competently was so pleasurable that I did not think about how my behavior robbed Mark's mother of an opportunity to demonstrate her own competence and broaden her relationship with her son, an opportunity that in every sense belonged to her and not to me.

Orientation day was held a week or so before the first official day of the new session described in the introduction, and my most vivid memory of it is of Mark's change from a child who had been uncertain about preschool to a child who actively resisted it. When I picked him up at home, he came along without protest. There was no last-minute change of heart, which I had not expected anyway, since Mark had come along with me on lots of outings, with and without his mother, and we seemed in general to get along fine. On the ride to the preschool, he and Laura talked together. Although I can't remember the topic of their conversation, Mark did at some point during this period develop an imaginary friend whose great size (twenty feet tall) and great powers (omnipotent and omniscient as well as omnipresent, although idiosyncratically in that, according to Mark's own memory, his friend rode to the preschool with him but did not enter the classroom because "he did not like it") were a recurring topic of conversation on our rides to school and may have been discussed by Mark and Laura on the way to orientation.[13] When we arrived, Mark got out of the car without any visible hesitation, but when Laura and I walked him to the classroom, which Laura was going to show him around, Mark refused to enter.

Not expecting Mark's refusal, I did not immediately take it in for what it was. At first I felt I must have missed something— perhaps he had left something in the car, had gotten a rock in his shoe, or had spotted something outside that he wanted to examine. And when I understood that what he wanted was *not* to enter the classroom, I concluded that he had "butterflies" and that the pull of the school and the other children would soon draw him in. When he remained adamant, however, I was taken aback. Although I would not have been surprised if Mark had objected, say, to being dropped off at orientation day and picked up a little while later, or if he had not wanted to go into the classroom while Laura and I visited some other part of the school, I could not understand his refusal to enter the classroom with Laura and me beside him.[14] I was further taken aback when he would not walk through the gate at the side of the school to explore the playground. As it turned out, during our entire visit, the most he would venture was to let me lift him up so that he could get a glimpse of the playground over the fence.

After his glimpse, and while those around us, adults as well as children, including Laura, went about the business of exploring the playground and classroom and being welcomed by the teachers, Mark and I sat on a bench amidst some shrubbery in front of the school. Teachers passing by smiled and said hello, and one of the assistant teachers introduced herself and asked Mark if he would like to see more of the school, but, except for jerking his head no in an emphatic way he had, he ignored her. Nor did he initiate any talk with me. Instead, he sat on the bench, gripping its edge with his fingers, agitated and alert, a prototype of anxiousness. Before long I found myself wishing that Laura would return from whatever it was she was doing so that we could go home.

There were many reasons for my wanting to leave. For one thing, Mark's behavior was socially awkward: he was *supposed* to be orienting himself to the school, not quaking beside me on a bench in the shrubbery. And it was personally threatening: my hope was that no one at orientation day, not the teachers, the visiting adults, or even the preschoolers themselves, would mistake *me* for the mother of this inflexible and anxious little boy. Furthermore, it was egotistically disappointing: Mark was rejecting a preschool that I regarded as an altogether superior sort of school, one that I myself would like to have had a chance to attend as a young girl, a school where Laura was thriving, and a school that I had had no doubt would charm him out of his tentativeness about preschool and transform it into enthusiastic anticipation. Mark's refusal also meant I would have to be the bearer of bad news. Instead of returning Mark to his mother triumphantly, with the news that he had loved the preschool and that she could stop worrying, I was going to have to tell her that Mark had spent the orientation visit sitting with me on a bench outside the school.[15] Powerful as all of these considerations were, however, I do not think they can entirely explain my desire to escape the school. Instead, I think Mark's anxiety disturbed the peace of things in a very essential way, deranged the space in which we sat, and was so nakedly intense that it threatened to unnerve me, making me want to be rid of him.

As the person who lived with Mark day in and day out, his mother was the one who had to struggle with the aftermath of his orientation visit to the school.[16] Despite the frequent talks they had about the school, about the playground and the classroom, the children he would meet there, and the likelihood that he would make friends he would look forward to being with at school and inviting home to play, Mark remained adamant about not going to preschool. And at some point in most of their talks, or at odd moments during the day, he would place himself squarely before his mother and announce, always using the same five words, "I don't like that place!" Usually, the announcement was accompanied by a shaking of the finger, not the vertical shaking I associate with a person who is scolding another, but a horizontal shaking that seemed bent on eliminating once and for all any possible doubts his parents may have had about where he stood in relation to the prospect of preschool. As for the vagueness of the word *like* in his "I don't like that place!" its use was connected, in my opinion, not only to his limited ability to verbalize but also to an effort to compress a multitude of feelings into one short pronouncement. The five feelings I suspect were compressed into his pronouncement are conviction ("I *know* that place is wrong for me."), frustration ("Why can't you, who are my mother, accept my conviction?"), anger ("How dare you thwart my conviction by sending me to preschool in spite of my opposition!"), desperation-resignation ("Even though I know I am right and you are wrong, it doesn't matter. You have all the power, and, should you decide that I must go, I don't know what I can do to stop you."), and hope ("Until you actually deliver me to the preschool and drive away there is still a chance that you will relent and let me stay at home with you.").[17]

In addition to making herself available for talks with Mark about preschool, Mark's mother also took Mark to the preschool for a second orientation visit at a time when they would be able to observe the class he was scheduled to attend. His mother's hope was that she would be able to get a better understanding of his resistance by being there at the school with him and also that the visit might compensate for the possibility that Mark would have benefited from her presence on his first orientation visit. Although Mark was not eager to go back to the school, he did go with his mother, and once they got there, he did accompany her into the classroom. According to his mother, however, he did not attend to what they had come to see. Anxious and alert, he was basically removed from the fact that the room was full of fifteen or so children close to his own age as well as all sorts of equipment and playthings—even his favorite Legos were present—designed to invite a child to explore. Nor did Mark gradually relax and settle into the situation as the visit progressed but remained anxious throughout. Bringing Ernest Schachtel's ([1959] 1984) theory of perception to bear, we might say that Mark's attitude towards preschool was not allocentric but autocentric: that is, his attitude was not marked by openness and receptivity, and he was not perceiving the school in terms of the question characteristic of Schachtel's allocentric mode, which is "Who or what are you who are part of this same world of which I am a part?" (222)[18] Instead, Mark's attitude seemed marked by alarm or worry. He seemed to be perceiving the school in terms of a question characteristic of the autocentric mode, which is "How can I protect myself from you?" and to be too preoccupied with this particular question even to ask another question characteristic of this mode, which is "How can I use you?" (218–224).[19]

That Mark's resistance persisted to include his first day as an official preschool student we know from the introductory description of his having to be carried forcibly into the classroom. Something we do not know, however, is how the adults in Mark's world were making sense of his resistance. Although they had been aware of Mark's tentativeness, they had not expected the extreme behavior that developed. Their response was to remind themselves that preschool was unfamiliar to Mark and that he was very dependent on his mother, and they vocalized the view that she was responsible for this dependence (and therefore also for his apprehension about

preschool) because she overprotected him. Another opinion common among the adults was that Mark would be fine if his mother
would just leave him alone, and they also tended as a group to
think that she would be making a terrible mistake if she gave in to
Mark's pleas and postponed or altogether canceled preschool instead
of standing firm and insisting that he continue. If we wanted to
describe their view in language that has found its way, in varying
degrees, into the general vocabulary by way of mainstream social
science, we might say that the adults in Mark's world felt he was
suffering from separation anxiety or from the anxiety of encountering
a strange situation.[20]

Among these generally concurring adults, of which I was one,
Mark's mother held the most divergent view. Though she did agree
that Mark needed a place where he could be free from her attempts
to prevent all mishap, she also felt that her overprotection had become a convenience to friends and family in that whenever Mark's
behavior confounded their understanding, they attributed it to her
overprotectiveness. Furthermore, even though she intended to stand
firm about preschool, she did not feel that anxiety in the face of a
strange situation, even a situation as "strange" as preschool, could
in itself encompass what her son was experiencing.[21] Another way to
express her sense that a discrepancy existed would be to say that
separation anxiety, as she understood it and had, up until orientation
day, seen it operate in Mark's life, possessed an emotional hue that
was qualitatively different from that of his response to preschool.

As the overprotective or blameworthy mother, however, she
was also the adult whose divergent view was least likely to be
taken seriously, and for any number of reasons. In the first place,
and even taking into account our culture's token veneration of
mothers and motherhood in the abstract, mothers are susceptible to
being dismissed or regarded as lightweights when it comes to
knowing their own children, perhaps in part because of the traditional and still operative stereotype of women as less cognitively
capable than men and perhaps in part because of the stereotype of
mothers, at least mothers who do not have careers or work outside
the home (as Mark's mother did not), as less cognitively capable
than other women. Another facet of this degradation of a mother's
capacity for knowledge of her own children is probably tied to our
conception of the mother-child relationship as physical, intuitive,
and emotional as opposed to rational, scientific, and objective. A
second obstacle to an *overprotective* mother's credibility is that she

risks automatic classification as a person we are even less obligated to take seriously or "hear out" than we would a "normal" mother. Though a normal mother is on occasion in a position to be taken seriously on the basis of our concept of women's intuition, the over-protective mother forfeits her claim even to this source of authority and is susceptible to being viewed as delusionary rather than intuitive. Third, if she is overprotective of a *son*, a mother risks being regarded as a thief, as one who robs the son of his right to become a man and, perhaps even worse, robs society (those "in charge") of its right to put his manhood to work in the interest of the society's perpetuation. Finally, as the villain in the script, an overprotective mother is not only *guilty* of wrongdoing but is also subject to being seen as someone who is looking for a theory (in the sense of a rationale) that will explain her child's behavior in terms other than her own overprotectiveness—in the case of Mark's mother, for a theory that would account for Mark's negative response to preschool so that she would not have to take the blame, the responsibility, for the thrashing, screaming, timid, embarrassing, disruptive child-nuisance *she* had created. And so, as a result of such cultural views as these, a mother's sense that her son's reluctance to venture in the world has been misperceived would be easily dismissible as more overprotectiveness or as an attempt to shirk responsibility or as both. I should add in passing that all of this is not to say that mothers are incapable of destructive relations with their children but rather that we are capable of abusing a mother's potential for a destructive relationship by using it as an excuse to deny her a fair hearing and to save ourselves the time and effort of exploring the specific situatedness of a child whose behavior disconcerts us or disrupts the social order.[22]

Given her awkward position—that she was perceived as over-protective and that she had no concrete alternative theory to offer but only a vague intuition or sense of puzzlement—it is not surprising that Mark's mother did not stand up for her divergent perspective. Nor is it particularly surprising, given her role as guilty person and also the seven-day-a-week demands of mothering, that she did not make any sustained, reflective, systematic, or overt effort to discover the concrete specificity that as a rule forms the ground from which vague feelings rise. Even so, it seems to me that as human beings we possess a creative core, a willful core, a core that couples with perplexity in silence and thrives beyond the boundaries of the cautionary tales the masters tell. It further seems to me that this core has the power to continue working on the puzzles we would appear to outsiders, including the outsider in ourselves, to have abandoned, and that this was what happened to Mark's mother.[23] Despite her apparent deference to the other adults, she did one day make a connection that gave substance to her feeling.[24] It was one of those connections that create order out of chaos, that make all that has been a puzzle fall into place for the person who has made it, and Mark's mother did not hesitate to share it.

The connection was that the house she and her family lived in was built of cement block whereas Mark's preschool was built of unfinished redwood. At first mention, the connection will probably appear no connection at all but merely a contrasting of the construction materials of two buildings in a child's landscape. But if we also know the story "The Three Little Pigs" and that over a period of months Mark had developed a highly emotional—in looking back, I would even say a highly passionate—relationship with this story, then it seems to me that the connection immediately "lights up" or becomes graspable. "My God," we might say, if we were to verbalize the connection, "Mark's mother is suggesting that for Mark the cement-block house he lives in is the third little pig's house of bricks,[25] that the redwood preschool is the second little pig's house of sticks, and that the big bad wolf is going to blow the preschool in, capture all the little children-piggies, including child-piggy Mark, and roast them in the oven." Furthermore, it seems to me that the connection is highly imaginative and therefore has an imaginative aura—a shimmering or texture—that will attract some of us as intensely as it will repel others. In fact, I would be surprised if some members of the audience did not disclaim or pull back from the connection even as they grasped it, that is, if some of them did not resist it as "farfetched" even as its import dawned on them, perhaps resist similarly to the way in which children at school occasionally resist as "dumb" or "stupid" or "scary" some activity the teacher suggests that does not appeal to them or that they dread. On the other hand, I would also be surprised if some members of the audience did not embrace or acclaim the connection spontaneously as "insightful" or "inspired" and begin to spin out its implications even before the next word appeared to them from the page, perhaps embrace it in much the same way that children at school might grab the chalk or the ball, so to speak, and delve right into an activity the teacher suggests that appeals to them or that they are good at.

As for my own view, I would tell those readers who are still within earshot that the connection felt right to me as soon as Mark's mother communicated it. There is always the chance, however, that this "feeling right" could have been a mistaken intuition on my part. For example, it could have arisen because the connection had touched some inarticulated aspect of my own life history, prompting me to assume or project that something important had been revealed about Mark when actually something important had been revealed about me. Or the intuition could have been nothing more than an expression of my desire to be swept off my feet or dazzled by the novel quality of the connection.[26] And so, though I am certainly drawn towards further exploration by my very feeling of "rightness," I am also drawn by the call to support intuition through investigation.

Several additional reasons encourage exploration. For one thing, the making of the connection strikes me as integral to Mark's story and so hardly seems something I could ignore, even if it had felt farfetched or scary instead of "right." Second, my feeling is that the boundary between home and school can fracture a child's sense of relationship or integration by estranging the various aspects of the child's life, one from the others. For instance, the parent can be estranged from the child as school-child, the teacher from the child as home-child, the parent from the teacher, the home-child from the school-child, and so on. Consequently, I felt validated by the fact that Mark's mother's connection could only have been made by someone who had access both to Mark's home world and to his school world, in other words, by someone who had crossed the boundary we ask our children to cross every school day but that many of us have not, since our own childhoods, often found the time to cross ourselves, except perhaps as required to get our children to and from school and to discharge such duties as parent conferences, parents' night, or open house.[27] Third, I was also one of two adults—and also a mother—who had crossed the boundary between Mark's home world and the preschool world, witnessed his resistance on orientation day (as well as afterwards in his home), and been thoroughly upset by it. Nevertheless, I had pulled back from my agitation and settled for a recipelike, standardized perspective on his resistance, a perspective that, though plausible and doubtless to a degree accurate, did not explore beyond the labeling of Mark as anxious, the situation as strange, and his mother as overprotective.[28] And so it seems fitting that I pay attention to her connection and explore in some detail its potential for helping make sense of what Mark may have been experiencing when he began preschool. In addition, though the impact that the cement-block and redwood building materials could have had on Mark's experiencing of preschool are my ultimate concern, I want to provide a background description of Mark's involvement with "The Three Little Pigs," and I also want to explore a number of tasks that I think constituted his involvement and that Mark could have been in the midst of when he was introduced to preschool.[29]

When Mark was still an infant, he had been given a book titled *Great Children's Stories: The Classic Volland Edition* (1972). Introducing the selections as "the classic stories which for generations have constituted the heritage of children" and cautioning adults not to overlook the delight the stories have over the years brought to children (5), the collection was one of the many books his parents eventually read to him, and it included a version of "The Three Little Pigs" (hereafter referred to as the Volland edition or version) with which he was almost certainly familiar.[30] In addition to the Volland version, Mark also at some point received the Walt Disney recording of the story, a recording that includes the song "Who's Afraid of the Big Bad Wolf" and describes the song, on the jacket cover, as "that loveable classic."[31] Although Mark would have known the story in book form before he knew it in record form, it was with the record version that he became so passionately involved. Having a portable child's phonograph that was kept in the open within his easy reach, as were his records, Mark played his records pretty much wherever and whenever it suited him. In the months before his parents introduced the idea of preschool to Mark, he had come increasingly to single out "The Three Little Pigs."

By orientation day, his involvement with the record had become a matter of routine, with Mark spending several intervals almost every day listening to the record, usually playing it more than once at each sitting and becoming so occupied with it that he hardly seemed present.[32] Intense talk about the record was common, as was fantasy play centering around the characters, and the record generally seemed to leave him feeling slightly intoxicated or feverish. Even when he appeared to have turned his attention elsewhere, he might "out of the blue" (at least out of the blue from the standpoint of those observing the overt Mark) introduce the topic of the story. When playing, he would initiate games in which he and his playmates took the roles of the little pigs and the wolf, and at home he would sometimes wear a "tail"—a belt tied to the back loop of his jeans so that it hung down behind him—and would display it to visitors and explain that it was a wolf's tail. During the time of his involvement with the story and the overlapping time in which he began preschool, he created, as I mentioned previously, an imaginary friend whose character evolved according to the demands of various situations and whom Mark recalls as being a wolf. Although aspects of his involvement may sound endearing or "cute," overall it was not the sort generally expected from a child delighting in a loveable classic. Instead, his involvement had an overwrought quality, and he could be glowering or genial by turns, sometimes eagerly sharing his involvement with others and sometimes crankily protesting another's broaching of the subject.[33]

Keeping in mind Mark's involvement as described above, I want to suggest that the story "The Three Little Pigs" had engaged him, through time, in a labyrinth of enormously complex tasks, each one sufficient in itself to challenge a three-year-old child, and each one compounding in difficulty as the other tasks appeared before him. Insofar as I can manage it, I want to separate some tasks out from this labyrinth, a separating that will require me to touch on tasks peripheral to those on which I want to focus and that, unfortunately, will undercut their interwovenness. As I see it, Mark's first task, the one that must have involved him for the other tasks to appear at all, was to comprehend the Volland version of "The Three Little Pigs" as a story, and I mean in the sense of a story as a highly complex cultural object for the child in that a story comprehends any number of objects in any number of relationships revealing themselves in a specific narrative sequence (Schachtel [1959] 1984, 260).[34] My picture is of Mark engaging in this task at bedtime (the bedtime story became a tradition very early in Mark's life). All tucked in, perhaps propped up against his pillows, his three-year-old consciousness would have been gathered together in a concerted effort to grasp "The Three Little Pigs" as it was read to him, a grasping that adults, with their years of experience with stories and their abstract way of grasping, could hardly conceive of (Schachtel [1959] 1984, 260).[35]

Given the image of Mark tucked into bed trying to grasp the Volland edition of "The Three Little Pigs," I want to introduce the Walt Disney recording of the story into Mark's world. Even acknowledging the difference between hearing a story read by an adult who is physically present and hearing a story narrated by a strange voice on a record—Sterling Holloway's in the case of Walt

Disney's "Three Little Pigs"—I expect that theoretically, or in certain circumstances, listening repeatedly to a record of a story could facilitate the child's grasping of it. But if we accept that changing the content of a story will thwart the child's effort to grasp it and that such change "is about as upsetting to the child as it might be to an adult to discover that overnight the table in the living room had changed its shape" (Schachtel [1959] 1984, 260–261),[36] and if we know that the Volland version differs dramatically from the Walt Disney version, then I think there is a good chance that the Disney record would throw into question—create chaos of—whatever comprehension Mark had achieved prior to its introduction. In fact, though I don't know the exact circumstances under which Mark received the record (given the workings of Mark's household, his father could have brought it home after work, his mother could have bought it on a shopping trip, or Mark could have chosen it while he was at the record store with his parents or a relative or friend), I picture him, when he did receive the record, taking it out of the jacket and placing it on the turntable expecting to hear the same story that he had been read. Instead, he heard a story that was different, not only in that some of the narrative had become a song and that the various characters' parts were read by different voices, but also in that the text had been cut as well as elaborated so that, even though there were three little male pigs, a house of straw, a house of sticks, a house of bricks with a fireplace, and a big bad wolf, the story differed in many ways as well, some of which are listed below:

1. The Volland edition begins with a mother pig (no mention of a father pig) who is poor and forced to send her three son pigs out to seek their fortunes, and it ends with the third little pig and his mother—just the two of them—living happily ever after together in the house of bricks; the Disney version eliminates the mother pig and begins with three little pigs who have been living happily (parentless and houseless) in an Edenlike valley when a change in the weather prompts them to build houses. It ends with all three little pigs living together in the house of brick.

2. The Volland edition depicts two brick or bricklike houses (the illustrator has drawn the mother pig's house as built of red brick with a light gray chimney of squared-off stone); the Disney version includes just the one brick house built

by the third little pig. In addition, the Volland version refers to the third little pig's house as a house of brick, whereas
the Disney version refers to the third pig's house as a house
of brick and stone.

3. Though the Volland version includes a mother pig, the
Disney version eliminates her and introduces three new
characters—three little wolves who are nephews to the big
bad wolf and one of whom is a "good little wolf" who
helps the three little pigs escape from traps masterminded
by the big bad wolf.

4. The Volland version could be called "clean-cut" or "bare
bones" in that the narrative includes few details; the Disney
version, however, is full of details. For example, before the
weather in their Edenlike valley prompts them to build
houses, the pigs, who are described as plump, fat, and curly-
tailed, spend their days swimming in a pond, running in a
meadow, and taking afternoon naps under tall sunflowers.[37]

5. The Volland edition is a hard-edged story, that is, a story
with a clear beginning (mother pig sends three little pigs off
to seek their fortunes), middle (each pig attempts to make a
place for himself in the world, with the first two pigs failing
and disappearing from the face of the story and the third
little pig succeeding and remaining in the story), and end
(whereas the straw and stick houses are too flimsy to keep
out the wolf, the brick house keeps the third little pig safe
and he lives happily ever after with his mother). The Disney
record works against a sense of conclusion or finality, however, by having the wolf continue to plot against the pigs
even after he has climbed down the chimney of the brick
house and landed in the kettle of hot water. After the episode
of the hot water in the Volland edition, the story says, "So
he [the big bad wolf] went away, and that was the *end* [my
emphasis] of him" (*Great Children's Stories* 1972, 65),
whereas the Disney version says that the third little pig
knew the wolf would come back to catch them.

6. In the Volland version there is no reference to death (the
two pigs who build the houses of stick and straw are
"chased away" by a wolf who does not even threaten to eat
them, and they are never heard of in the story again [*Great*

Children's Stories 1972, 62]); in the Disney version the prospect of being captured and eaten (roasted in a pan with
carrots and potatoes cut up by the two bad little wolves) is
a recurring threat.

7. The Volland version does not moralize; the Disney version
    is replete with moral judgments. For example, the record
    presents play as bad, as the source of vulnerability to pre-
    mature death (though the brick house is presented as nearly
    impervious to the wolf, even it cannot save little pigs who
    "sing and dance all day," as do little pigs 1 and 2) and
    presents a life of all work and no play as good, as the
    source of security and survival in a dangerous, wolf-in-
    fested world.

Although I am not assuming that Mark necessarily attended to
or registered all of these discrepancies or that he was not free to
attend to discrepancies other than the ones I have noted, or even
that he was able to keep track of and conjure up for inspection
(verbalized inspection, visualized, etc.) the discrepancies he did notice, it is true that everything I have mentioned, as well as much
more, became part of Mark's perceivable landscape when he was
exposed to the Volland and Disney versions of "The Three Little
Pigs." In addition, it seems to me that, with the appearance of the
Disney record, Mark's tasks proliferated and that the greater number of tasks, which in itself would have added to the difficulty of
executing them, was complicated by the fact that they were interde-
pendent. Though I cannot know how Mark's consciousness ordered
or prioritized them, I do think that grasping each story as a story
remained the basic or ground task that made the other tasks possible. In other words, though he was faced with one title, he had
two substantially different stories, one in a book and one on a record,
so that he not only would have had to grasp the Volland version as
a story and the Disney record as a story but also would have had to
grasp the Disney version in light of the Volland and the Volland in
light of the Disney.

For instance, his effort to grasp the Volland version in its own
right could have involved an attempt to grasp the story as a sequence
in which the mother pig is "poor." And his attempt to grasp the
Walt Disney version in its own right could have involved an attempt
to grasp that a change in the weather transforms sunflowers from a

satisfactory to an unsatisfactory place to nap. On the other hand, his attempt to grasp the stories in light of each other could have involved an attempt to grasp "The Three Little Pigs" as a story that has a poor mother pig when it is read from a book but no mother pig at all when it is played on a phonograph. One tangent point I am trying to make here is that, in addition to being faced with the task of coming to terms with discrepancies in content, Mark was also faced with discrepant or different vehicles for that content. Or, to consider an example involving plausibility of character motivation instead of the facts of the story or its vehicle, Mark's effort to understand "The Three Little Pigs" could have involved an attempt to grasp that in one version (the book) a wolf blows houses in so that he can chase little pigs away, whereas in another version (the record), a wolf blows houses in so that he can capture and roast little pigs for his dinner. And though Mark or any child might deal, through time, with the two discrepant versions in any number of ways,[38] I think that until he had chosen a way to deal with the versions, the discrepancies would have thoroughly tried him, intellectually, emotionally, imaginatively, spiritually, psychologically, physically, or any other way we might want to divide his being for purposes of discussion. I also think that however he chose to deal with the two versions of the one title, his choice would remain forever open to revision.[39]

In addition to a child laboring to grasp as story a narrative that would not "stand still," I also see Mark as a child whose particular situation was enough like the situation in "The Three Little Pigs" to invite him to experience the story as his own, that is, as a story about a boy named Mark, the oldest of three sons, who lived with his mother and father in a house built of cement block. I think, furthermore, that he was a child who at some point in his listening did take the little pigs' situation to be a reflection of his own and also that he took it to be a revelation in that certain life possibilities— the possibility of being turned out of one's house, of napping under a sunflower, of dying prematurely through the hunger or malevolence of a wolf, of singing and dancing all day, of living a life of all work and no play—presented themselves to him for the first time. In other words, Mark was not sustaining the role of listener as detached observer by listening to the story as an *irrelevant* story about others, about animal characters who lived a curious, amusing, and dangerous life, but in a foreign place and time unconnected to his own. Nor was he listening to it as a *relevant* story about others, as a

story about humanlike animal characters who, despite their geographical and chronological distance from him, could teach him
some widely applicable lessons about physical survival. On the
contrary, Mark seems to me to have perceived his own situation as,
in essence, the same as that of the three little pigs, and both situations
as ones confronting him with existential questions for which he was
both ready and not ready.[40] He was ready in the sense that, unlike
some readers, he was susceptible to the questions or able to "see"
them. And he was not ready in the sense that he did not have ready
answers for them and was thrown into the chaos of trying to work
them out through time. In this not-ready readiness, it seems to me
that Mark could be any one of us at one time or another in our
lives, but, to make a couple of specific and widely accessible comparisons from the world of adult literature, he reminds me of
Shakespeare's Hamlet encountering the ghost of his dead father (a
ghost that Hamlet can see but whose appearance creates conflict)
and of Madame de La Fayette's Princess of Clèves encountering her
love for the Duc de Nemours (a love she is eventually able to name
but that she does not know whether to accept or reject). One significance of being thus thrown into chaos is that it could have prompted
Mark to turn to the story of the three little pigs and its moral for
guidance in much the same way as he would normally have turned
to adults, a turning that would have had the potential to create
tremendous conflict whenever the point of view of the story and of
the adults in his life were at odds.

    In addition, insofar as Mark's perception came in a flash, its
potential to disconcert him might be compared to Mark's looking at
the illustrations in the book his parents read to him and discovering
that the little pigs, or at least one of them (perhaps always the same
pig, perhaps a different pig—which pig am I?—at different times),
had his face, or perhaps compared to his answering a knock at the
door only to open it and face himself. To elaborate a little, his perception of the story as essentially his own could have occurred in a
moment of connectedness, a moment in which he connected such
previously mentioned and fairly obvious things as that he lived in a
cement-block or bricklike house and that there were houses of brick
(or brick and stone) in the story, and that there were three little boys
in his family and three little male pigs in the story. There could also
have been much more context-specific connections, connections
therefore less apparent to a general viewer. For example, one context-
specific connection Mark might have made and that would have

depended on his degree of sophistication in relation to the ambiguities of language, as well as on his exercising his sophistication, concerns the word *poor*.[41] On the one hand, the mother pig in the Volland edition was described as having to send her three little pigs away from home because she was "very poor" (59); on the other hand, Mark's mother was sometimes addressed or referred to as "poor" (usually by her elders among family and friends) in the sense of "You *poor* girl, three little boys to take care of and the oldest not even three years old when the third was born—I don't see how you do it." Thus, Mark's experience with the word *poor* outside the context of the story could have left room for him to equate his mother's poorness with the mother pig's poorness (or the reverse), a connection that takes on another dimension if we recall that the demands of caring for the three little boys figured in the decision to send Mark to preschool. And even if connections such as these were not made all in a moment but separately, one or more at a time, there still could have been a moment in which he felt their combined impact as a sudden dawning that the three little pigs' situation was his own.

That a small child could see his or her own reflection in a story does not seem particularly problematic. Though I suspect that the tone or flavor of Mark's recognition of himself would have been different than what I am about to describe, I think that many of us have had the experience, either as adults or as children, of playing an informal game I remember playing with my children when they were small. It is the game of telling the child a story that is "made up" but that is actually a very thinly veiled event from the child's own past that had been deeply felt by the child and that the adult tells expressly so that the child will experience an invitation to see him- or herself through the veiling. When these stories work, there is a moment of recognition: often the child becomes wide-eyed, grins, tugs at the adult's sleeve, or perhaps pats the adult's hand impatiently or signals in some other way the need to speak, and announces, "But Mama (or Daddy, etc.), the story you're telling is not about somebody named Chris. It's about me! About the time we went shoe shopping and . . . ." As the ellipses indicate, the child often follows the announcement of recognition with his or her own narration of the past event. For those who may not be familiar with this game, it might be worth recalling the television show from the fifties titled "This Is Your Life," in which public figures from various fields would have their life story sprung on them on camera and which public television's "Sesame Street" uses as a model for one of its segments.

If we accept that small children can recognize themselves in such "made-up" stories, stories told specifically to trigger such recognition, I see no reason that we cannot also accept that such recognition could occur incidentally, in the absence of adult intent, and that Mark may have recognized his own life situation in the life story of the three little pigs.[42] Furthermore, I think it is possible that Mark's recognition may have elicited a companion perception of seeing his own life as a story, not only in terms of its having found its way mysteriously into a book, but also in the sense that a life, like a story, comprehends any number of objects in any number of relationships that "unfold in a definite sequence of events" (Schachtel [1959] 1984, 260). And it is this double comprehension of "The Three Little Pigs" as a veiled story of his own life and of his own life as "storylike" that seems to me to present Mark with another of the tasks I want to separate out from his labyrinth of tasks, which is the very difficult one of trying to make sense of his own life as it has appeared to him as object from the horizon of the story. That the difficulty could be complicated by his exposure to two versions of the story is an understatement. In fact, I see Mark as a child who ultimately must strive to make sense of three versions of the story or, depending on his and our perspectives, three stories—first, the Volland edition, second, the Disney version, and, third, the three-dimensional flesh-and-blood version that is his own life—all three of which are stories in their own right but all three of which are also partially woven together, the weaver being Mark, the integrative threads being the shared title that links the first two versions and the shared content that links all three versions, and the disintegrative threads or "loose ends" being the discrepancies between the versions and the questions that the story could raise about his place in the world as a place that unfolds and shifts through time.

Something that might have further complicated his task of making sense of the three stories is that, whereas a child who is told a veiled story about him- or herself listens in the presence of the adult who has done the veiling and who is watching for and preparing to receive and affirm the recognition as well as explore any thoughts or feelings it might arouse, Mark listened to the Volland edition in the presence of adults who had not made up the story. Instead, they had turned to it as one story in a volume of stories introduced as classics that belong to a child's heritage and that have great power to delight (*Great Children's Stories* 1972, 5).[43] In addition, Mark listened to the Disney record in the "presence" of narrator Sterling Holloway. As for the question of Mark's ability to distinguish fantasy from reality, which some readers may want to raise, I should clarify that I am not here suggesting that Mark did not know that his own life was real in a sense that the lives of the three little pigs were not or that he was having trouble distinguishing reality from fantasy. Although the task of distinguishing the two almost certainly at times would have engaged him, and although he doubtless at times would have failed to keep the distinction clear, it is not the task I am at present trying to separate out from his labyrinth of tasks. Instead, I am speaking about the task of making sense of his own life, a life that I think had been revealed to him as *object* through his listening to the two versions of "The Three Little Pigs."[44]

However, even if I am right in seeing Mark as a child who perceived his situation as that of the three little pigs and also as storylike, I still have no way of knowing when the perception occurred and whether his initial experiencing of it was positive or negative or both. Nor do I know how subsequent listenings and other life events might have modulated his understanding and the quality of his experiencing. For example, on first hearing the Volland edition, did Mark immediately make the connection between the three little pigs in the story and the three little boys in his family? And if so, did he also immediately become caught up in the question "Which pig am I"? Or did he simply assume himself to be in the position of the third little pig? As I said above, I cannot answer such questions in any conclusive sense. I can, however, explore these and other such questions and in so doing at least provide a fairly concrete and specific sense of an experiencing within the range of the possibilities suggested by his particular situation.

Taking the question "Which pig am I?" if Mark did become caught up in it, then he may well also have had to make sense of the words *first, second,* and *third* as used in the book and on the record to differentiate among or "name" the three little pigs,[45] a task that brings up a point that feels like a quibble and is somewhat digressive but that needs mentioning to keep the record straight. Although I myself had always assumed (as had several others I have checked with to make sure my assumption was not eccentric) that the pig who builds the house of bricks (the third little pig) is the oldest pig and, on the basis of my assumption, had further taken for granted that Mark, as oldest son, would identify with the third little pig, neither the Volland nor the Disney version says anything about which pig is the oldest, middle, or youngest. If I add to this silence on the question of age our habit of referring to the first-born child as the first child, the second-born child as the second child, and so on, then according to the story's phrasing and the logic of usage, the third little pig would be the youngest, an interpretation that strikes me as all wrong and that raises the question of why I, and others, had assumed the third pig to be the oldest and of how Mark, as oldest son, might have made sense of his relationship to the three little pigs.

Actually, my assumption that the third little pig was the oldest could easily be explained if I had been exposed to a version that characterized him as the oldest. And it could also be explained, in the absence of such a version, by saying that in our culture the oldest son has historically been the son of privilege and has also been typed as the responsible son, or, at least, as the son in whose responsibility our culture has a vested interest. As a child of my culture, this history could have taken precedence over the connection between the phrases *third child* (or *third pig*) and *third-born child*. Another factor that could have influenced my assumption and that would separate the story's use of the word *third* from our common use of it to mean "third-born" is that, to create a simple and direct plot, one that moves in a straight line towards the conclusion, the brick house must be the third house built. In a story whose characters do not have true names, the pig who will build the third house is understandably referred to as the third little pig. As for how three-year-old Mark might have dealt with the question "Which pig am I?" and the potentially confusing use of *first*, *second*, and *third*, my feeling is that he would have been prone, initially, at least, to see himself as the third little pig. One reason is that Mark had been born into a culture traditionally regarding the oldest as the son of privilege. As an oldest son himself, particularly as one involved with a story in which the privilege of immunity from premature death (that is, the privilege of physical survival) is linked to the building of a brick house by a third little pig, Mark could hardly have helped being drawn into an identification with the third pig.[46]

I also think, however, that Mark's identification with the third little pig, though strong, would not have been absolutely secure from doubt. And I think this, first, because an intimate involvement with the story could have sensitized Mark to the ambiguous chronological relation among the little pigs. In addition, I think that because as a human being Mark would have experienced different moods and a shifting perspective, he would also have had mixed feelings about being in the position of the third little pig. For example, if it was while hearing the Volland edition that he first perceived his position as parallel to the third little pig's, was he disconcerted by the absence of a father pig? Or did he perhaps assume that the father pig was at work or on a trip? Or did he simply not think about a father pig at all? And how about the fact that the Volland edition does not include the first and second little pigs in the "happily ever after" ending? Would their exclusion have saddened him? Been a relief? Would he perhaps have failed to note their fate? Or might his experiencing of it have shifted according to how he was getting along with his mother and his brothers? And how might the appearance of the Disney version have affected his perception of being in the position of third pig? Would he have become preoccupied with the absence of the mother pig? Would any anxiousness have been unqualified or mixed with relief? Would he have felt guilty? Would he have noted the development of the third pig as a character who establishes and maintains his claim to the brick house through rigid adherence to a life of physical labor? Would he have focused on the enlarged role of the two little brother pigs? On their characterization as frivolous and irresponsible pigs who "dance and sing all day" and require constant looking out for and repeated rescuing from the wolf? And how might Mark have felt about the prospect of the third little pig being his brothers' keeper instead of his mother's?[47] And what about a life of all work and no play? Would the security of brick have been enough to make so dichotomized a life appear worthwhile?

It seems to me that the above string of questions (which, though perhaps appearing overlong, does not even begin to suggest the number and range of questions that could be asked) makes clear that there is plenty of room within the boundaries of the story for Mark to have experienced mixed feelings in relation to an identification with the third little pig. But it also seems to me that the presence of the wolf in both stories and his transformation from a character who in the Volland edition merely chases little pigs away from the houses he destroys to a character who in the Disney version plots to capture the pigs with the intention of eating them for his dinner has two likely consequences. One would be to increase immeasurably the significance of a brick house as a place that could keep a pig safe from premature death. Another would be to tempt Mark, especially when he was feeling insecure, to hold tight, first, to the idea that to live in a brick house means to be elite, to have a better chance of immunity from premature death than those who live in more fragile houses, and, second, to the fact that he, Mark, had been born the oldest son in a family that lived in a bricklike house.

As for the adults in Mark's home life, although I earlier described them—including myself—as responding to his resistance to preschool with a patent diagnosis of separation anxiety or anxiety in the face of a strange situation, I have yet to describe their response to Mark's involvement with the Disney record, and I mean their response before his mother made a connection between the cement block of Mark's home and the unpainted redwood of his preschool. Interestingly enough, though the adults were aware of the involvement and even commented on the seriousness with which Mark took the record and the transformation it wrought in him, no one attempted even a patent analysis of it. That Mark's involvement might be something they could make sense of, and not simply the arbitrary or unfathomable antics of a child, did not seem to occur to anyone. On the one hand, some of the adults exhibited an attitude that could be characterized by the following comment: "Yes, Mark, I do see you over there with that record of yours, and I suppose if I stopped to attend to it, I would have to say that something is going on with you, but I've simply got too much going on right now to stop and take a closer look." For these adults, the awareness of Mark's involvement with the record was similar, for example, to the White Rabbit's awareness of Alice's presence in Wonderland—they perceived the involvement, but always on the run. Consequently, whether by design or unintended side effect, or perhaps an interplay between the two, their busy-ness diminished the likelihood that they would ever truly encounter Mark's involvement.[48]

On the other hand, some of the adults exhibited a passive awe or amazement in the face of Mark's behavior, an awe evidenced in comments like the following: "Have you seen Mark with that record of his? The way 'The Three Little Pigs' gets him going is really something," or "How strange that a story like 'The Three Little Pigs' should get a child so worked up. Oh well, that's just Mark, I guess." And none of the comments ever approximated anything so active as "What's the matter with everybody around here? Can't anybody see that Mark's record is eating him alive?" For these adults, it was almost as if they were tourists and Mark's involvement was one of the wonders of their itinerary, a curiosity placed squarely in their path that might elicit oohs and ahs, but a curiosity about which they were not curious, at least not in any overt way that is visible to me as I look back.

Furthermore, several of the adults shifted back and forth between the two attitudes, depending on whether they were "working" or "on vacation," but the shifting never jostled them enough to move them towards a third perspective, and perhaps from there on to others. In fact, the only adult who could be characterized as having taken action in relation to Mark's involvement was one with whom Mark spent a lot of time, both at his own house and at the adult's. The adult's action was to encourage or dote on Mark's involvement. Fascinated by Mark's behavior as we are sometimes fascinated by a novelty (say, a windup toy whose performance startles us on cue, a toy that "behaves" other than our experience with inanimate toys has led us to expect and that does so with perfect predictability each time we wind it up and let it go) and also interpreting Mark's involvement as a clear sign that the record was his favorite, the adult bought himself a copy of the record to keep at his own home. That way, as the adult saw it, Mark would have the pleasure of playing the record even when visiting at the adult's house. I would guess, however, that the adult's pleasure in observing a "windup" Mark also figured in the purchase.[49]

In considering the adult response to Mark's involvement with the record from my present vantage point, I am struck by the capacity for playing the role of audience and for categorizing Mark's involvement as an aesthetic object beyond understanding or, in the case of the doting adult, as a novel performance by a celebrity whose "talent" could be tapped, managed, or cultivated, instead of viewing it as the involvement of a child who deserved to be understood in his own right. I am further struck by how devoid the adults seemed to be of any sense of their own power to question the situation they shared with Mark and, if deemed appropriate, to transform it. As for why the adults were not curious and did not seek to understand, this seems to me an important question and one that would certainly have implications for Mark's experiencing. One way to begin to understand their passivity might be to relate it to a perception or categorizing of "The Three Little Pigs" as a classic, one that they themselves had loved as children (here the point is the categorization of the story as loved and not whether the adults had really loved it as children) and that could be depended on in turn to delight their children or, to reverse the burden of responsibility, that their children could be depended on to experience as delightful.

According to this perspective, when Mark's experiencing of the record did not coincide with the adult expectation, with anything remotely classifiable as "delight," the adults at some point perceived, perhaps only as a bare glimpsing, the discrepancy. But the power of what had been expected, of the traditional scenario—perhaps one that had "danced in their heads" in advance of their presenting Mark with the record (there is no denying how satisfying it can be to share something from one's own childhood with children of the next generation)—was so great that the discrepancy, although it had not wholly escaped their attention, was overwhelmed and absorbed into the background as some sort of negligible fluke. No doubt there were other factors. That Mark was a male child, that he was perceived as overprotected, that his mother was concerned about being overprotective, that intervention is not always easily distinguishable from interference, and that our culture perceives children as beings who "go through" stages and "grow out of" things, for example, could all have figured in the adult passivity. And so could the fact that Mark's involvement with the record was exhibited for the most part within the privacy of family, friends, and home, whereas his resistance to preschool was much more open to public scrutiny.

Less obviously related factors that could have figured in the passivity include such things as our culture's general valuing of "trial by fire" and our strong commitment to free speech and opposition to censorship.[50] These factors, however, also involve inherited perspectives that we tend to invoke without taking the time to reaffirm their pertinence to a specific case as it presents itself. They also lend themselves, therefore, to the argument that the situation in which the adults found themselves was one in which tradition, that which we are born into and take for granted, the "is," was powerful enough to obscure existence: Mark's struggle to navigate through a labyrinth of tasks that ranged from grasping a story as story to encountering the possibility of premature death as well as the possibility of immunity from such death.

Having depicted Mark as an overwrought child isolated by tradition from adult guidance, I now want to move back in time to orientation day and the question of how Mark's involvement with his record could have colored his initial experiencing of preschool, and I want to begin by considering Mark's attitude towards his world. In light of all that I have said about his being overprotected from physical mishap by his mother, about his being given very free rein in respect to his involvement with the record, and about his intense resistance to preschool, it may seem to follow that Mark would as a rule encounter his world with the question "How can I protect myself from you?" As I suggested earlier, however, in my discussion of Mark's initial response to the prospect of preschool, I do think the prospect interested as well as alarmed him and that, between the moment he was told he would be attending preschool and the moment he stepped out of the car on orientation day to face the school for the first time, he did at times address the prospect with the question "Who or what are you who are part of this same world of which I am a part?" (Schachtel [1959] 1984, 222).

Because the above assertion about Mark assumes a certain attitude towards Schachtel's question, let me spell it out. In the sense that even a stereotypic labeling or the vaguest, most cluttered, or idiosyncratic filing system presupposes the question "Who or what are you?" this question is the ground for much perception. It is also a question that can be asked for its own sake—out of a disinterested curiosity about the identity or essence of what is being perceived— or with a predefined and practical goal in mind (practical in the sense of a goal other than the goal of discovering for its own sake the identity of the object being perceived). For example, predefined, practical goals might be expressed through such questions as "How can I use you? How can I protect myself from you? How can I both use you *and* protect myself from you? How can I protect myself from you *by* using you?" In other words, we do not have simply one "who or what" question that is by definition always the ground for a disinterested openness to the identity of the world, but two such questions, one interested and one disinterested. The quality of the question, furthermore, can fluctuate through time with immeasurable speed, and, depending on the answer we receive, what began as a disinterested inquiry can become an interested one or vice versa.[51]

In Mark's case, I think fluctuation would have been characteristic and extremely undisciplined and that at times he would have experienced the shift of his own perceptual attitude (say, from disinterested to interested) as disintegration or infirmity so that the ground or base question would hardly have seemed a base at all but more of a disappearing floor or quicksand that alarmed him. I also imagine that as Mark, Laura, and I drove to the preschool, he experienced a great tumult of images or perceptions, and also thoughts and feelings, and that this tumult was influenced by his fluctuating perspective just as his fluctuating perspective was influenced by the tumult of images.

As for the specific images, I think they would have been drawn from a variety of landscapes. Some would doubtless have been drawn from the landscape of his home, which we drove away from— for example, the feel of his bare feet on shag carpet as he stepped out of bed the morning of orientation day, the smell of baby powder and soaking diapers from the bathroom, the sound of his dog Elmo scratching at the door, the taste of pancakes with butter and warm syrup at the kitchen table, the sight of the outgoing mail fastened by a clothespin to the box outside the front door. Other images would probably have been drawn from the landscape of the stories and records and television programs that Mark encountered—for example, the Volland mother pig spurting tears from inside the fence as her three little pigs, also spurting tears, left home, the cartoon character Speed Racer defeating yet another villain and entering the winner's circle yet another time, Mr. Rogers changing from his business jacket into a more casual sweater to begin his visit, the evening news reporting events from around the world to his mother and father, and Walt Disney's big bad wolf chasing the first little pig away from the blown-in house of straw and shouting for the pig to stop and that he would be caught regardless. Still other images would no doubt have been drawn from the landscape of our drive—for example, Mark's mother fastening Mark securely into the back seat and giving him a good-bye kiss, Laura being already fastened snugly in across from him, the marigolds and pansies blooming in the church flower bed at the outskirts of his neighborhood, the river below us as we crossed the bridge leading out of town, the street signs and the traffic signals that defined our route, our chatter and our silences as we drove.

In addition to these three categories of images, and who knows how many others, I think there would have been a category that encouraged connections between the several landscapes—his dog Elmo's scratching could have encouraged thoughts of the wolf and a connection between his house and the houses in "The Three Little Pigs," the marigolds in the church flower bed could have encouraged a connection between the home neighborhood and the Edenlike "happy little valley" where Disney's little pigs nap under sunflowers until the weather prompts them to build houses, the snug seat belt might have suggested the rope the Disney wolf uses to bind the first and second little pigs, Laura (even though a girl) might have suggested a fellow captive child-pig, and I, as driver, could have suggested the big bad wolf speeding off with my captives towards a den disguised by the label "preschool," or, at the opposite extreme, I could have suggested a rescuer who retrieved the captives and sped them towards the security of brick and stone.

I also imagine that all of Mark's various perceptions had the potential to traverse the boundaries of their categories, mingle every which way, and be gathered together and ordered by Mark to form a dramatization of his own life as the life of a child-"pig" and that any drama Mark might create could at any moment shift in favor of another. Although as not-Mark I cannot know, either in broad outline or elusive nuance, the specific drama or dramas he did create, I do think they would have been colored by his being in a state of suspension arising from his encountering, in the Disney version, the possibility of premature death and his encountering, in both versions, the possibility of his own immunity. And even if the story in both its versions and all its reverberations was not uppermost for Mark when he arrived at the school—that is, even if the ride, as a movement towards the actualization of his potential to become a preschool student, had rendered the story peripheral or, in the extreme, invisible—Mark's possessed experience of the story would certainly have remained within immediate reach and could readily have contributed to a tension between his capacity to question the school out of a desire to know it as itself and his capacity to question the school out of a desire to protect himself from a strange or unknown situation. In other words, I think that it was a tightly-strung, intense Mark who stepped out of the car, that Mark's very turning of his gaze towards the preschool encompassed a posing of the question "Who or what are you who are part of this same world of which I, Mark, an oldest son born into a house of cement block, am a part?" (Schachtel [1959] 1984), and that the preschool met his gaze with all its raw, unpainted redwoodness. I also think that this meeting brought the landscape of "The Three Little Pigs" crashing down around Mark and that the preschool answered his question with an awful equanimity, "I am no stranger to you, Mark, but the house of

sticks, whose meaning you know well, and today, though an oldest
son born into a house of cement block, you face my flimsy wooden
frame as your horizon."

Whatever sense Mark might eventually make of the preschool's
answer, however he might eventually come to live the sense he
made, and however the sensemaking might change with time and
place, he was in my opinion at the moment of encounter—a moment
whose temporal stretch is incalculable—uniquely primed or, to use
Erwin Straus's term, "subjectively ready" (1982, 78), to experience
the horizon of the preschool as quicksand and falling sky. And I
mean quicksand and falling sky in at least three senses. Most obviously, the horizon faced Mark with his own vulnerability to premature death, a vulnerability that could have been particularly shocking
to a child who had been insulated by or holding tight to a belief in
his own immunity. Second, Mark could have perceived an incongruity in the fact that the very same adults who had enrolled him in
"a house of sticks" had given him a record teaching the folly of
such houses, a perceiving that could have added to the dreadfulness
of the horizon by facing Mark with his own vulnerability at the
same time that it faced him with the fallibility or limitations of the
adults he would usually have counted on for guidance. Third, if
Mark had been "set" for strangeness of place, if he had ridden to
the school expecting to face a new or strange situation, then the
very familiarity of the school could have added to his shock.[52] Given
a horizon of multifaceted dreadfulness, Mark could hardly be expected to find the school inviting, no matter how much effort the
school had made to create a supportive setting designed to accommodate children, except, perhaps, if it had gone to the trouble of
building a preschool of brick.

In fact, the classroom's very design could conceivably have contributed to Mark's resistance. The low shelves of child-size toys or
jobs as well as the child-size tables and chairs could have suggested
fragility or weakness and therefore repelled a Mark who had learned
from his record to trust only imperviousness and strength. And the
circle time, which included songs, games, and informal talk, could
have made Mark wary because such activities were in direct conflict
with the philosophy of the record, a philosophy asserting that "work
and play don't mix," that pigs who "sing and dance all day" are
particularly vulnerable to the wolf, and that such frivolous behavior would make a pig sorry, whereas the third little pig's life of all
work would keep him safe. Even the preschool's kitchen area, with

its carrots and celery and paring knife, could have repelled Mark by reminding him of the episode on the record in which the little wolves cut up vegetables and apples to roast with the two captured little pigs.

The significance I see in what I have been saying, then, is that the exterior of the school itself would have been sufficient to provoke intense resistance in Mark, and even if he had gotten past the dreadful exterior, the interior could have been perceived by him, not as an unambiguously inviting place, but as an extension of the dreadfulness. In other words, Mark's intense resistance to preschool (not only his refusal to explore the school on orientation day but also his subsequent encapsulation of his objections in the pronouncement "I don't like that place!" his wary alertness when his mother took him for his second visit, his having to be carried kicking and screaming into the classroom on the first official day, and his refusal to sit in the circle or join in the circle-time activities) seems perfectly understandable, although in quite different terms than those the majority of adults offered in their first analysis.

As a child experiencing the immediate future of preschool as so much dreadfulness, Mark appears to be in need of nothing so much as the concernful guidance of an attentive and respectful adult. And yet what Mark received from the adults in his life was, in relation to his involvement with the record, a distancing of themselves through busy-ness and awe and, in relation to his intense resistance to preschool, a distancing of themselves through a "too facile" application of an overgeneralized abstraction. To clarify this last, let me add that by too facile I mean an application in which the adults assumed that because all the usual ingredients for separation anxiety or a strange situation were present, then this anxiety must as a matter of course have been what Mark was experiencing. I also mean an application in which separation anxiety, in all its generalized abstraction, was assumed sufficient to encompass Mark's anxiety, in all its individual specificity.

At least this distancing was what Mark received from the adults until his mother made the connection between the redwood preschool and the cement-block house. Once she made that connection, the entire history of Mark's involvement with the record was experienced by her as a history of need gone unperceived, a history that was not separate or compartmentalized from his resistance to preschool but that was intricately interwoven with it. Her labels for the history were *neglect* and *abandonment*, and though the words are harsh in that Mark's mother in no sense exhibited the carelessness these words typically bring to mind, I think she used them because they captured the dismay she felt at discovering that a child can feel neglected or lost even when adults are making the effort to guide.

Though she, furthermore, did not overgeneralize this history to rationalize her overprotection in other aspects of Mark's life, neither did she let any guilt feelings at membership in the category of overprotective mother prevent her from acting in this particular case.[53] Sitting down with Mark, she talked to him about his record. Though most of the content of the discussion has been lost to memory, it included asking Mark if he would like to keep the Disney record out in the open with his other records or whether he would like to keep it in the closet where she or his father could get it down for him when he asked for it. Mark chose to keep the record in the closet. Although he continued for many months to include the story in his play and conversation, Mark gradually, with interplay between home and school, came to participate fully and enthusiastically at preschool. The intervention also seemed to make an immediate difference in his life by invigorating him and transforming him from a child whose world held him a lone captive to a child who exercised a degree of control over his own life.

Although, when the subject comes up, Mark's mother still reproaches herself for not having intervened sooner, I think that Mark had at least three reasons to feel invigorated by the intervention and his mother to feel good about herself. To begin with, through the one act of sitting down beside her son and breaking the silence that existed between them on the subject of his involvement with the record, Mark's mother acknowledged him for the isolated child he was and in so doing juxtaposed his alienated aloneness with their concernful togetherness in a way that allowed for learning through dramatic contrast: that is, she made it possible for him to feel his alienation as something distinguishable from something else—in this case, concernful togetherness. Second, she presented him with a possibility that had very likely never occurred to him before, a possibility that may seem negligible to us in its obviousness but that to a young child may have been an epiphany: the possibility that a record, even one that had been treated as part of a collection, need not be kept out in the open within his easy reach, as had become customary, but could be separated out from the collection and stored away to create space, or, depending on our point of view, distance, between the record and himself. Third, she gave him an opportunity to choose whether or not to actualize this newly arisen possibility. Thus, the intervention of Mark's mother is for me a truly educative or nurturing act: it recognized a child for who he was, it encountered that child in his world, it vitalized his world as a place of potential and possibility, and it offered him an opportunity to take a step towards becoming himself through choice.

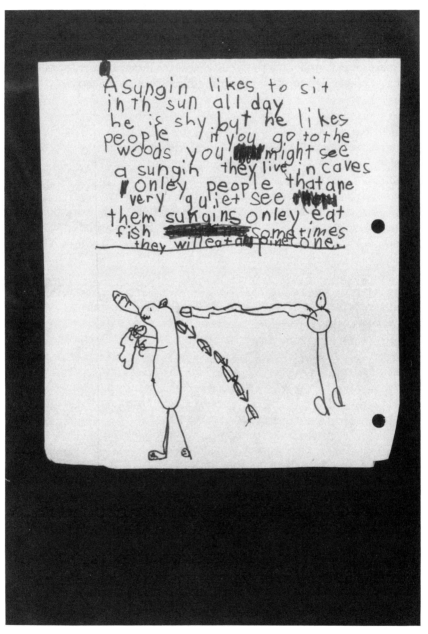

A sungin likes to sit in th sun all day he is shy but he likes people if you go to the woods you might see a sungin they live in caves Onley people that are very quiet see them sungins onley eat fish somdtimes they will eat a pine cone.

The child who wrote this story says that the drawing is of "a hunter shooting at a sungin."

3

David at Home

> There are caverns
> under our feet
> with rivers running deep in them.
>
> Shirley Kaufman, "Looking at
> Henry Moore's Elephant
> Skull Etchings in Jerusalem
> During the War"

When David, whose anger I explored in Chapter 1, was in fourth grade, just about the time he turned nine, his teacher assigned an autobiographical essay. Following her instructions, he and his fellow classmates wrote about their lives from birth through adulthood, and all of the essays were displayed on the classroom bulletin boards at open house, which was where his father and I first read the essay.[1] For his first paragraph, David had written the following:

> I was born in 1973 near midnight. That means I can see ghosts when they want to be invisible.[2] When I was an infant, I had to get a butch because the doctors needed to put medicine in my head. Almost as long as I [can] remember I have wanted to be a marine biologist.

David's description of himself as someone whose time of birth meant he could see ghosts when they wanted to be invisible and his mention of the butch haircut (David had been hospitalized briefly at age three months for a suspected case of meningitis and had had his head partially shaved so that antibiotics could be administered intravenously) introduced two themes—the theme of our human potential for discovering what hides or is hidden and the theme of our ever-present or congenital vulnerability to death—that are central to human existence.[3] Touching on these two themes again in his third paragraph, David wrote that his preschool teachers had once discovered a gopher snake on the school grounds and that he had had a friend from kindergarten to third grade "who had a heart problem" (a birth defect, as David knew, that would prevent the friend from reaching adulthood unless the defect could be corrected through a series of high-risk surgeries). It was to the narration of his future adult life as a marine biologist, however, that David devoted over two-thirds of his essay.[4] Employing past tense, which gave his narration the feel of accomplished fact, and sustaining the above two themes while introducing others, David looked back on his adult life mainly as a series of achievements, many of them quite spectacular.[5] This section of the essay begins as follows:

> I went to college and stayed until I was 25 to get a doctorate. I liked the notion of someone calling me "Dr." I started out as a marine biologist's helper. I loved that so much so much [sic] that I stayed there for 3 years. But when I was 28 I decided to try for being a marine biologist myself.

Among the spectacular achievements he goes on to mention is that he became rich and famous by age thirty. As David puts it, "By the time I was 30 I was a millionaire and one of the most famous men in the U.S., I was discovering new fish *even* [my emphasis]." Though there is room for more than one interpretation, the structuring and diction of this sentence suggest that David placed great value on the discovering of new fish. The placement of the final independent clause could mean that David perceived the wealth and fame as arising from his discovery of new fish, and the word *even* underscores the high value he placed on the act of discovery. For me, this valuing of discovery echoes his earlier reference to his capacity for seeing ghosts, an echoing I want to note here because I will be returning to it later in the chapter.

That David's autobiographical essay did not mark the birth or first putting into words of his desire to be a marine biologist and that he had not settled on marine biology solely to meet the requirements of the assignment could have been pointed out by many people in David's world, particularly by his father and me, who, as his parents, were the primary audience for David's long history of talkativeness on this subject. As his parents, we also could have pointed out that just as David had wanted to be a marine biologist for as long as he could remember, so David had tended to pursue involvements with water, particularly bodies of water and the life forms living in them, for as long as we could remember. In addition, as David's mother, that is, as his primary caregiver or the adult who spent more time with him than any other adult spent, I could have added that he had experienced a very intense but relatively short-lived fear of bathing when he was seven years old, which would have made it about a year and a half before he wrote the autobiographical essay quoted above and a few months or so after the picnic described in Chapter 1. Although I intend eventually to describe David's fear in some detail, I first want to describe his childhood involvement with water, mainly because I think a child's fear (or anyone's) emerges from a personal world and is best understood in that context.

The body of water David felt most drawn towards as a child was the northern Pacific Ocean. My impression of his relationship with the ocean was that he regarded it as an intimate and provocative friend whom he did not get to see nearly as often as he would have liked (we vacationed there, but not often enough to suit David) but with whom he could, no matter how long between visits, immediately take up the friendship as if there had been no separation. Probably his favorite activity was to wind his way along the beach at low tide and climb out over the large rocks covered with limpets, brown kelp, and colonies of blue mussels so that he could get close up to the tide pools, where he would discover orange and pink starfish, red-spotted crabs, spiny purple sea urchins, and tentacled squishy green anemones. He still remembers a third-grade field trip on which he observed several crabs stripping the meat from a dead eel in a tide pool close to the shoreline, something he had never seen before.

As a child David also traveled to the rivers, lakes, and streams of the Sierra Nevada and was especially keen on the American River, which ran from the Sierra Nevada down through the valley where he lived. Closer to home he gravitated to the pond at the nature area behind his elementary school. And in David's own backyard there were the wading pools he played in during summer, the networks of canals and the holes he dug in the dirt and sand and filled with water from the hose or a bucket, and the irrigation ditches his father dug the years we had a garden—all of which could hold David's attention for long stretches at a time. In the garden area there was also an old enamel washtub that sat beside a row of artichokes transplanted from David's grandfather's garden. For several springs, David and his sister and I stocked the washtub with polliwogs, mosquito fish, pond snails, and algae-thick, mucky water from the neighborhood pond. Sloshing out beyond its banks, David would net some of the larger polliwogs (bullfrog polliwogs that take two seasons to mature, we later learned) that could not always be found among the masses of smaller polliwogs and mosquito fish that inhabited the shallow water at the pond's edge. Once the tub was stocked, David would squat or kneel in the dirt and stare down into this tub-aquarium, where he could observe the mosquito fish gobbling up mosquito larvae or watch the polliwogs metamorphosing through their several stages into the small green tree frogs that would eventually leap from the floating wood chips onto the rim of the tub and into the garden proper. Later, David would find the frogs at the base of sugar-pea plants, on the sides of fence posts, and in the clumps of weeds that grew along the rotting railroad ties and rusting wire fencing that bounded the garden.

Inside the house there were the double sinks in the kitchen where he sometimes played and the sink and tub in the bathroom that he shared with his sister, Laura, and that he would disappear into for hours at a time, occupying it as if it were his personal laboratory. Outfitted from a wide range of sources, David's portion of the bathroom cupboards and counterspace was crammed with equipment that he used in his experiments and that included "real-life" equipment (measuring cups and spoons, flexible straws, vinegar, baking soda, water colors and paint brushes, liquid soap, tissue papers from home permanents, old perfume bottles, slide film containers, a plywood board cut to fit across the bathtub to create a work surface) as well as a large assortment of commercial toys (a houseboat with finger puppets, a sailboat, an assortment of action figures—G. I. Joe and *Star Wars* figures, scuba divers—and a toy model of the "Gilligan's Island" set that fit easily into the bathtub).

When David worked in the bathroom-laboratory (alone or with Laura or a friend), he often took the role of research scientist, conducting experiments at the sink or in the bathtub that made use of the real-life equipment mentioned above. But he also liked to move the toy action figures through narratives that centered around the exploration of water and especially liked to take them and his boats and other paraphernalia into the tub with him, letting it fill almost to overflowing around him and the toys, adding more water if the level dropped, and becoming so engrossed that it was often difficult to get him out of the tub.

Because the baths David took during the hours he spent in his
bathroom-lab were timed according to his urge to play in water
rather than the need to get clean or have a shampoo and because
any washing that took place was purely accidental, there were also
the baths that I, and on occasion David's father, instructed David to
take when evening found him still grimy. Even though he did not
initiate these baths, once they were under way David tended to
draw them out far beyond a shampoo and a scrub so that they
became all but indistinguishable from the playful baths described
above.

In addition to three-dimensional bodies of water (the bathtub,
the garden washtub, the American River, Pacific Ocean, and so on),
David also involved himself with the two-dimensional ones pictured
on television and illustrated in books and with the sounds and
words that accompanied them. For example, there were the television
documentaries about the ocean that David watched avidly as well
as such weekly fictional comedies and dramas as "Gilligan's Island"
and "Flipper" that he watched just as avidly.[6] And there were the
books he checked out from the school and the public library as well
as those that belonged to him or to his family and friends and to
which he had ready access. Both fiction and nonfiction books presenting images of water filled his shelves, three favorites being his
sister's *Life of Fishes* and his own *Treasure Island* and *Shark Lady*.

David also had a photograph album that included snapshots of
vacations to the Pacific Ocean as well as to the American River. On
the last page of the album he had mounted a photograph of his
great grandmother standing beside a large wooden scaffold from
which hung a 140 pound sailfish she'd caught on a trip to Mexico.
She'd given the photograph to David one day when he had been
visiting at her apartment and, spotting it in one of her albums, had
become enthralled with it. Finally, there were the bodies of water
that might be called "dimensionless"—those that occupied David's
waking imagination and that sometimes manifested themselves in
his fantasy play and those that he dreamed about while he slept
and that I heard about when he talked about his dreams, most often
over breakfast.

It was the David I have been describing, this child who played
for hours in a bathtub filled almost to overflowing, who sloshed
through mucky pond water to net polliwogs, who loved to explore
the tide pools of the northern Pacific coast, and who had wanted to
be a marine biologist for as long as he could remember, who, one

evening when he was seven years old, objected to taking the evening bath I had instructed him to take. His reason? He said he had let the bathtub get "too full." At the time it did not occur to me that David was afraid to take his bath and that his objection to the water's depth was a cover for his fear.

I remember the evening David made his objection as one that had fallen into a pattern that had prevailed an average of three nights or so a week and that I had come to make the most of and to value. Contrasting dramatically with another kind of evening (the kind in which the needs of family extend right up to and beyond bedtime so that there is no moment for the privacy of repose or self-nurturing), the pattern of the evenings I had learned to value went about like this: shortly after dinner David's father would go to his studio to work for several hours. Laura would become occupied with some project of her own, and I would start a bath for a grubby David, telling him as I did so that he would need to keep an eye on it and get in promptly if he wanted to have time to play as well as get clean before bedtime. With both children "taken care of," I would become absorbed at one of the tables or on the couch with some activity of my own, and in so doing I tended to inhabit the world of my activity almost as if it were my separate residence, as I suppose my husband probably inhabited the world of his studio, my daughter the world of her project, and my son the world of his bath. On the evening in question, however, after Laura and David were situated and I had settled into my work, I realized that the bathwater had stopped running but that there were no bath sounds. I did not hear David turning the water faucet on and off to maintain the water level and the temperature. Nor did I hear David's body squeaking against the sides and bottom of the tub as he moved about, or the thumping and splashing and slamming as he climbed in and out of the tub to rummage in the cupboards and drawers for some toy he had forgotten or that he had only just realized he wanted.

As I remember it, I either called out to David from where I sat, telling him to get on with his bath, or I went down the hallway partway, told him the same thing, and returned to my work. But then, a little while later, I realized that there were still no bath sounds. Irritated at this second interruption, and probably grumbling to myself about never having enough private time, I set aside my work and went down the hallway to the bathroom, where I found David sitting on the floor beside a bathtub full of water, his toys spread out around him. Our conversation went very much as follows:

Jane: David, you're still not in the tub. What's going on?

David: [Silence.]

Jane: What's the matter David? Have you lost something? Is there a toy you can't find? One of your figures? Your goggles?

David: No.

Jane: Well, then, hurry up and get in the tub. Otherwise the water will get cold and you're going to have to start all over. Besides, you won't have any time left to play.

David: I don't want to play tonight, and I'm not really very dirty. So I don't think I'll take a bath after all.

Jane: Not dirty? But David, you've got mud caked on your neck. And your arms are streaked with it. I can see it from here. The bottoms of your feet are all dirty, too. So if you don't want to play you can just put all that stuff back in the cupboards. But you've got to get in the tub and at least get the mud off.

David: I let the bathtub get too full.

Jane: Too full? You're telling me the bathtub is too full? David, you've got to be kidding. There's not another person in the world who likes the bathtub full the way you do. So quit fooling around and get in.

David: But if I get in when it's so full, it will run over the sides and all over the floor and under the cupboards.

Jane: But David, this is crazy. The water always runs over the sides of the tub and all over the floor and under the cupboards when you take a bath. And it never bothered you before.

David: But you don't like it when the water goes all over the floor. You get all crabby and say the linoleum is peeling up and that the boards will get all rotten.

Jane: No, David, I don't like it. And maybe I do get crabby. But it doesn't seem to me that's what we're talking about here. To tell you the truth, I don't know what we are talking about. I mean, how come tonight, after all those other nights, you're all of a sudden concerned about flooding the bathroom floor?

David: [Silence.]

Jane: Oh, all right. I agree with you. The bathtub is too full. So let's stop arguing about it and let some water out. . . . There, that should do it. Now get in and take your bath.

David: It's still pretty full.

Jane: Still pretty full? Okay, David, I'll let some more water out. No, better yet, I'll keep letting water out until you say when. Okay? . . . Okay?

David: Okay.

Jane: David—the water's almost gone. Don't you want me to stop?

David: I guess so.

Jane: Great. Now hop in and get clean. I'll be in the other room.

David: Mommie? . . .

Jane: What is it, David?

David: You could bring your stuff in here. You could sit on the toilet seat and work while I take my bath.

Jane: Not tonight, David. I've got my stuff all arranged in the other room. And anyway, you said you're not going to play, so you won't really be in here long enough to need any company. When you're through with your bath get pajama'd and put away your toys and we'll get Laura and find a book and read for a few minutes on the couch before bed.

David: Mommie? . . .

Jane: What is it now, David?

David: Since I'm not going to have toys or play or anything like that, couldn't I just sit on the counter and wash off in the sink?

Jane: You want to wash off in the sink? But David, we just spent half the evening getting the bathtub to a level that satisfies you. And now you want to forget about the bath and wash off in the sink. What is it with you tonight, anyway?

David: [Silence.]

Jane: All right, David. Wash off in the sink. I don't know why I'm arguing with you about it. Besides, the water in the tub is probably cold by now. But don't forget to get your feet clean. And wash that mud off your neck and arms. I'll be in the other room working. And I don't expect to have to come in here and remind you to get going again. Do you understand?

David: Yes, Mommie.

As I said earlier, it did not occur to me at first that David's behavior was motivated by fear. In fact, at first I did not consider his motivation at all, and I think this was because my experiencing of our conversation tended to minimize or peripheralize all thought of motivation. Although I certainly did not say to myself, "Now let's see—how did I experience the conversation I just had with David?" I do think, in looking back, that I experienced it on the following five levels:

1. As baffling in that David's objection to his bath, especially his saying it was too full, seemed wholly unlike him

2. As an ill-timed interruption that made me feel impatient, and then angry, with David

3. As a personal failure that frustrated me because I had not been able to handle the interruption efficiently enough to get the evening "back on track" more quickly and so ensure myself the private time I had been counting on; and also as a personal failure in that David had not only "won" the power struggle but in winning had managed to talk me out of making sure he did something that all good mothers are

supposed to make sure all dirty children do, which is to take a bath *in the bathtub*

4.   As an example of David's ability to use language to his own ends, in other words, of his ability to manipulate me with language, a manipulation that also suggested his cleverness and intelligence and so prompted me to experience frustration in the face of manipulation and pleasure in the face of intelligence

5.   As emotionally draining

In addition to these five levels, I think there also was a sixth, which was the experiencing of the conversation as "story material." By "story material" I mean that I experienced my conversation with David as an event to tell about rather than as an event to keep silent about, which would have made it "confidential material"; as an event to question or reflect on, which would have made it "research material"; or simply as an event that was not worth any further attention, which would have made it "inconsequential material." In other words, I experienced the conversation as the sort of event that stays vividly with us and that we feel an urge or need to render to another human being. And by this I do not mean to imply that story material and other kinds of material, say, research material, cannot overlap. Nor do I mean that we cannot question the action in a story as we tell it or tell the stories that have given rise to our questions even as we proceed with our questioning. What I do want to suggest is that the voicing or rendering of these events can become the sole focus of a moment. When it does, we can become so intent on conveying the event, and eventually so habituated to it, that we forget we have additional capabilities, capabilities that are especially important if the event has diminished us or others. One such capability is to question the sources and implications of the event. The other is to explore changes aimed at preventing diminishment in the future.

In the case of my conversation with David, I could have chosen to tell the story, but not question it, to any number of people in any number of settings. However, for purposes of illustration I want to limit myself to just one person in just one setting and assume that when David's father returned home from the studio and we were alone, we asked each other about our respective evenings and that my response took the form of a narrative that expressed, without my being consciously aware of it, the five levels (baffling, interruptive, emotionally draining, etc.) I listed above:

> My evening? Well, when you left for the studio it looked like everything was going to be fine. I was sure I was going to have some time to myself. But then everything went wrong. I didn't get any privacy to work at all and it was really frustrating. After the dishes were done, David and Laura wanted me to watch them do some cartwheels and somersaults and stuff in the backyard. But when we got out there we discovered that the people behind us had left their sprinklers on and flooded most of our yard. David and Laura had to play in that strip of grass by the roses and there wasn't enough room. They kept bumping into each other and getting all mad, so we came in the house. Laura had a bath and that seemed to make her feel better because she curled up on the couch with a Nancy Drew. David chattered away at me for a while and then I started his bath and told him to keep an eye on it and get in before it overflowed, that I would be working in the living room. He said okay and headed down the hallway, and I thought the evening was all set. But then, just as I was getting involved with my work, I realized David wasn't taking his bath. He'd turned off the water, but there weren't any bath sounds. I told him to get on with it and he said okay again, so I thought we were back on track and went back to my work. But after a little while I still didn't hear any sounds, which really irritated me. So I went into the bathroom and there he was, sitting on the bathroom floor with his toys all spread out around him. I thought he might have lost something and that if we could just find it, things would get moving. So I asked him. But he said no. So then I asked him why he wasn't in the tub. And do you know what he said? He said he had let the tub get too full. That's right, *too full*. It was strange. Not like David at all. I mean, I've never known anyone to love a full tub the way he does. The linoleum is even peeling up where it meets the tub because of the way he fills it right up to the top and then thrashes all around so that the water spills over. And then, after he said the bath was too full and I said I'd never expected *him* to say that, he said I always complain when he gets water on the floor. Which is true, but not something I'd ever expect to hear David remind me of. I guess it just goes to show how bright he is—turning my own argument against me like that. Anyway, I let a little of the water out and told him to get in. But he just sat there and said it still looked pretty full to him, which only frustrated me all the more. I started to say something really nasty but bit my tongue and simply suggested that I let the water out until he said "when." But he never did. The water level just kept dropping and he just kept sitting there silently. Finally, when there was only an inch or so of water left, I asked him if he

didn't want me to stop. And he said okay. So I thought we were finally all set. But we weren't. Because after all the time we'd spent adjusting the water level, he decided he didn't want to play with his toys after all and asked me if he could just wash off in the sink instead. I know it wasn't the same thing as making him take a real bath, but I had just simply had it by that time and the whole thing had really gotten under my skin. It was like I'd lost all this time I'd been looking forward to having to myself. And all because of some whim of David's. God, but there are times when that child mystifies me. And it was all so exhausting.

Although, as already suggested, the category of storytelling represented by the above monologue can help relieve some of the pressure of an emotionally charged and disconcerting experience by allowing us to put it into words and share it with another human being, there is a danger that the relief can become so satisfying in itself that it prevents us from seeking an understanding of our experience that we have the power to achieve. Tautness relieved by lamentation with a subsequent building towards more tautness can become the rhythm of our lives, and we can get into the habit of saying, once we have relieved the pressure by telling our story, "There, that feels much better; I'll be able to get back to work now," instead of saying, "There, that feels much better; now I will be able to sort out the event that has so upset me and make changes to improve the situation."

Of course, even when we do turn our attention to sorting, understanding does not always come easily. In the case of my conversation with David, I think that even if I had tried to make sense of David's remark about the "too full" bathtub instead of merely labeling it uncharacteristic, I still would not, initially, have zeroed in on fear. For one thing, David's life history, insofar as I knew and understood it at the moment he voiced his objection to the full tub, did lend itself to my viewing his behavior as "mystifying." For another, I was in the grip of a vocabulary that assumed, through such words as *characteristic* and *uncharacteristic*, that behavior is essentially, and at a fairly discernible level, predictable and consistent. Most obviously, David's history of taking play-filled baths would have directed me to look for a motivation other than fear. And there would have been no shortage of alternatives. Because at age seven David tended to daydream and also to become deeply absorbed in his activities, I might have theorized that he had begun daydreaming as he entered the bathroom to keep an eye on the bathwater, that he had turned the water off and sat down on the floor to get his toys out, and that he had simply gotten lost in his own thoughts until I prompted him to get on with it. At that point he could have "gotten on with it" by getting his toys out of the cupboards and then becoming absorbed with them right there on the floor until I had come into the bathroom and we had had our conversation. He then could have decided that he'd "played" long enough and, never one to be particularly interested in baths as a way to get clean, set about turning my own past complaints against me until I capitulated. Another motive I probably would have considered, even though David had denied it in our conversation, was that he had lost some object he regarded as crucial to his play and that he had been moping about it to the point of not wanting to communicate it. A third possibility would have been that I or someone else had done something to make David feel small and powerless in the recent past and that his resistance to his bath was his way of trying to regain some sense of control over his own life. Each of these theories would have been plausible, and, as it turned out, they were not entirely irrelevant; none of them was even close, however, when it came to the central source of David's resistance.

Besides David's life history, several other factors minimized the chance that I would have considered fear as his motivation. Although I didn't realize it until I discovered his fear, I thought of David as too old to be afraid of his bath. Certainly when he was a toddler he had often objected to having a bath when it also meant a shampoo, and he had hated to have the suds rinsed out of his hair, but that had been a long time before he was seven. Another obstacle to my considering fear was that David's father and I saw ourselves as understanding when it came to our children's fears. We had both had fears as children that we had kept secret, and we had wanted things to be different for our children—not different in that they would not have any fears but different in that they would feel free to talk about them. Because I thought we had communicated our feelings to David and Laura, and because in the past they had talked about various fears, I was pretty much closed to this possibility.

David's smokescreening also helped prevent my discovery of his fear, and so did some specifics of the setting. It was not as if David had been objecting to a bath in some strange place or situation, say, at a friend's house where he had never been before, or in his own home but while in the care of a relative stranger, such as a new

babysitter. And, of course, the range of emotions I experienced during our conversation also stood between me and the discovery of
the clues that did exist. The most obvious clue I overlooked was
David's request, about three-quarters of the way through our conversation, that I keep him company during his bath. The request
really belonged to his earlier childhood, when he had been too
small to bathe without some supervision, and if I had considered it
in light of all the rest that he had said, that is, if I had considered
each part of the conversation in itself as well as its relationship to
the whole, I think I would have had the best chance of discovering
the fear he was hiding. I say this because when his fear finally did
emerge, his request that I stay and work in the bathroom was one
of the first things that came to mind.

One final obstacle that I think was significant, though it does
not please me, is that our conversation took place in the privacy of
our home and that the absence of any observing eye or audience
made it less likely, at least in this particular case, that I would
puzzle over David's behavior, which is not to say that I do not
value privacy in the context of nurturing but rather that I want to
acknowledge the potential of privacy to support neglect and complacency or a preoccupied inattention as well as to support care.
And so, even if I had experienced my conversation with David as
something to research as well as something to tell about, I do not
think my research would have led me very directly to his fear. Nor
do I think it would readily have occurred to me that his fear had a
concrete source in his life history, ironically a source as concrete as
the source I argued (in Chapter 2) that Mark's fear of preschool had.
However, when David told me about a recent incident in his life,
one that I had not known about and that I would have had little
chance of discovering except from David himself, my initial experiencing of the conversation with him as story material was transformed into an experiencing of it as material that called for research
and action.

The incident, which was not at all remarkable on its face, occurred when he visited a sports club with his friend Samuel. Precisely when and under what circumstances David told me about
the incident, I can't remember. I do know that he told me at home
and that at most it was within three or four days after we had had
the conflict over his bath. It also seems to me that in addition to that
first sink bath, he had substituted at least one more and maybe
several for his usual tub bath. But whether he told me about the

incident at the club during a discussion about the change in his bathing routine and whether he initiated the telling "out of the blue" or whether I prompted it with some question or remark, I don't remember.

Something I do remember is that his style of narration was very different from the style I depicted above in my hypothetical monologue delivered to David's father. Whereas in that monologue I spontaneously intertwined the narration of the content of David's and my conversation with my emotional response to it, David, in his narration of the incident at the club, said nothing about being afraid, nor did he mention by name any other emotions he may have felt.

Instead, he narrated the several actions that constituted the incident as if he were reporting what we might classify as "straight news." And then, at the end of his narration, he made one very abstract, ambiguous comment, or "editorial" remark. Actually, *incident* is, in one sense, a misnomer because, even though the actions David narrated had, as I eventually realized, come to form a unit for him, he narrated the incident as a string or series of actions that might have been a casual answer to the casually asked question "What kinds of things did you and Samuel do at the club, David?" In contrast to his listlike organization, however, his voice became so emotionally charged that it would have been hard to mistake his narration for casual chatter about the current events of his life. Although the monologue I am going to offer below does not attempt to approximate David's diction—I can't remember it well enough to do that—it does include the content of David's report and also suggests the generally noneditorial style:

> At Samuel's club we went swimming. We did that for quite a while. Then we went in the TV room they have there. A Tarzan movie was on. It was in the middle and some bad guys were in the jungle. They tied Tarzan down to stakes on the river bank. One of his arms was in the water and a bunch of piranhas kept splashing around his arm. Then the bad guys went back to the jungle and Tarzan got his knife from somewhere and cut the ropes. He cut the ropes of the lady tied next to him too, and he ran across the river with her. After that we went back to the pool. I didn't want to go swimming anymore. But Samuel did and he got back in the water. So I did too.

If the intensity of David's voice had not caught my attention, his mention of piranhas juxtaposed to his one statement about how he felt (he had *not* wanted to go swimming again) would have. By the time he had completed the above "report" and become a silent presence before me, I had flashed back to the conversation in the bathroom,[7] run through it in my mind, and concluded that he had objected to his bath for the same reason he had not wanted to get back into the pool, which was that he had been afraid, and still was afraid, of being attacked by piranhas. I also concluded that his listlike style was purposeful in that it allowed him to test my sensitivities without explicitly stating his fear. Another way of looking at his style would be to say that David had experienced the incident at the club both as "story material" and as "confidential material" and that the tension between the urge to share it and the urge to keep it secret had led to a compromise. Although I don't remember who said what immediately after David's narration, I do remember that at some point David himself confirmed that he had not wanted to get back in the pool or take baths in the bathtub because he was afraid of piranhas.

Having spoken about his fear, David seemed tremendously relieved and was eager to talk about piranhas. Despite his interest in water and water creatures, his knowledge of these fish seemed limited to what he had learned in the Tarzan movie, and he seemed to have fully embraced the movie's image of them as a monster-fish.[8] The main thrust of his talk was to say that piranhas were meat eaters who were always hungry, that they traveled in schools, and that they would instantly and automatically attack any creature they found in their waters, including a human being, and strip it to the bone. For obvious reasons, avoiding all possible contact with this monster-fish had become a top priority of David's.

I mainly tried to follow David's conversational lead, but I did have several priorities of my own. These included wanting to understand his fear, to accept it as real, and to ease it enough to allow him to bathe and play in water without being terrified that piranhas were going to "get" him. I also wanted to restore an evening routine in which three or so nights a week I was able to have some time to myself. Though my knowledge of piranhas consisted of unverified fragments of information picked up here and there, I found myself spontaneously offering David details that would establish a boundary between him and the monster-fish that seemed to have taken on mythical proportions. Agreeing with him that piranhas were meat eaters and so potentially dangerous to human beings, I added that I did not think anyone had ever documented these fish actually having eaten a human being. I also said that because of the very traits he had described to me and because so few people had very much firsthand or documented knowledge about them, piranhas would naturally be the choice of moviemakers who wanted to keep an audience on the edge of its seat by placing Tarzan, or some other hero, at the mercy of such a fish. I went on to say that piranhas were native to tropical climates and rivers in certain parts of South America and that our climate and rivers were very different from those in their native habitat. I further commented that even if piranhas could survive in our rivers, I did not see how they could survive in the swimming pool at Samuel's club or in our bathtub at home and added that the water that filled sinks, bathtubs, and wading pools had been chemically treated at a water plant, that swimming pools had additional chlorine added at the pool site, and that such treatments discouraged the growth of plant and animal organisms found in natural bodies of water. To illustrate my meaning, I reminded David that any polliwogs we had caught and kept in tap water had died after a short time and that to survive they needed pond water. Finally, I told him that even if piranhas had been able to live in tap water in our bathtub, they would have needed it deep enough to swim in, and I suggested that if he continued to feel afraid to bathe in the tub, he might want to try taking baths in very shallow water.

David chose to follow this suggestion, for a while filling the bathtub with only an inch or two of water. At first he took these baths only when he needed to get clean, giving up altogether the baths he had initiated from an urge to play, and he stayed in just long enough to wash off. But gradually (I don't remember exactly how long it took, two weeks, or three at most) he began to let the water level rise almost to overflowing and once again became so absorbed in play that he sometimes had to be practically dragged out of the tub so that his sister could have a turn or so that he would get to bed on time. He also began to initiate the play-filled baths that he had taken, before his visit to Samuel's club, pretty much when he felt like it.[9]

Although it was reassuring, and seemed fitting, to discover that David's behavior had roots in his life history and to see him reclaim the bathtub in his bathroom-lab, and although I felt that once he had communicated his fear we had worked it through fairly well, my feelings about the way his fear had emerged were mixed. I was disappointed in myself for at first dismissing his behavior as arbitrary, and it made me feel vaguely sad to think that David had found it necessary to conceal his fear with talk of an overly full tub and water on the floor. I wondered what the concealment might have cost him in personal dignity and self-esteem and what it might have taken to have made him feel sufficiently at ease in the world, and at ease with me, his mother, to have spoken up about his fear right from the start. And although I did not think about it at the time, I have since wondered what it might have been like for David, after he had seen the Tarzan movie, to live in a home environment so expressive of his involvement with water and so full of people who regarded him as a child who wanted to grow up to be a marine biologist. It seemed to me that his fear of piranhas, especially during the time he kept it secret, could have transformed his setting into something like a taunt.[10] And what might it have been like, I wonder now, if he had kept silent about his fear indefinitely, perhaps turning his back, for no apparent reason, on his involvement with water, or perhaps participating according to the expectations of those around him, as he had participated at the club by getting back into the pool with Samuel?[11]

After David's fear had passed, I would sometimes find myself thinking about it, observing to myself such things as that it was quite a leap from the jungle setting of the river in a Tarzan movie to the concrete and fiberglass setting of the swimming pool at the club and to the private sanctuary of David's bathroom-laboratory. Though I would point out to myself that the unfamiliarity of the pool setting (David had been there, at most, only once before) could have contributed to his fear, it bothered me that his fear had alienated him from a place in his own home that he regarded as his ownmost sphere. And by this I do not mean that I thought it was unfortunate that he had been alienated from his bath (although I did think this as well) or that it was unfair, or something we might describe as "quite a shame," but that his alienation seemed disproportionate to the provocation of the movie. There it was, however, a bit of behavior that made infinitely more sense than it had before I had known about the Tarzan movie, but that did not make as much sense as I would have liked. And so I proceeded to think about David's behavior from time to time, reviewing it to myself and then losing it again in the tumult of daily life, sometimes dismissing my sense of extremity as a wrong impression.

One day some time after David gave me permission to write the story of his fear and I was well into an initial draft, I asked him if he would be willing to talk with me about any memories he might have. He not only said he would but also began relating his memories on the spot, some of which I had never heard before and that went a long way towards clarifying the sources of his fear as well as his initial concealment and experiencing of it. Instead of having to make sense of David's fear solely on the basis of my own memories, I realized that I was going to be able to offer his memories as well. During the course of writing, I approached him with specific questions on several occasions, and we taped a few of our exchanges. But almost without exception his memories were more detailed and fluent when the subject of his fear came up while we were talking about something else or when he sought me out on his own because he had remembered something or felt in the mood to talk.

At some point in the course of our discussions, I asked David why he had gotten back into the swimming pool at the club if he had been afraid and why he had kept quiet about his fear the evening I had asked him to take a bath. David said he had been afraid people would think his fear of piranhas was silly. When I asked if he thought his fear of piranhas had really been *that* silly, he said his fear of piranhas getting into the bathtub had been *ridiculous*. In emphasizing the word *ridiculous*, he seemed to be using his standards as a fifteen-year-old to judge the fear he had had as a seven-year-old. However, though the word *ridiculous* was softened by his half-humorous tone, I don't think the tone entirely negated the judgment he made. Nor do I think his view of the fear as ridiculous was exclusively his fifteen-year-old one. Instead, my impression as we talked was that, in addition to having felt, at age seven, self-conscious in front of Samuel at the club and in front of me at home, David had himself perceived the fear as ridiculous or fantastical. Rather than alleviating his fear, however, the perception had made him feel self-consciously ashamed and his shame had become intertwined with his fear so that he had had to live them both.[12]

The first thing David emphasized about the incident at the club that may have made him feel self-consciously ashamed was that Samuel, so far as David could tell, had shown no signs of being frightened by the movie and had suggested returning to the pool as if nothing had happened. Given that David and Samuel had watched the same movie but had had different emotional responses, David seemed to have assumed two things: first, that one of the responses must be unmerited or "wrong" and, second, that it was his fearfulness that was wrong. Such assumptions suggest that David had tacitly accepted and lived—at least for a moment in the context of the sports club—the idea that there is such a thing as a standard, normal, or appropriate response to a given situation (a response the situation calls for) and that if, in a party of two (or more), one person responds fearfully and another does not, fear is the non-standard, abnormal, inappropriate, and thus shameful response.

Perhaps significantly, David had had some previous experience perceiving himself as the child who is afraid as opposed to the child or children who are not. One of these experiences involved such science fiction and horror movies as *The Alien* (1979), *When a Stranger Calls* (1980), and *The Silent Scream* (1980), movies with television ad campaigns that frightened him enough to make him switch the channel or turn off the set when they came on. He would also come home from school some days (between kindergarten and second grade) and talk about horror or science fiction movies that friends at school had seen. Usually the friends had told the scary parts of a movie and David would tell them to me (sometimes all he would say was that the scary parts were too awful to tell about),[13] commenting on how much his friends had liked the movie, on how much the other children had loved hearing about it, and on how he never wanted to see the movie and wished his friends had never mentioned it to him. Although at home we did not treat David as if his fears were ridiculous or try to sell these movies to him so that he would fit in, but instead attempted to listen to him and discuss the way such movies are made and acknowledge his personal taste in films and books, I suppose he may have experienced his response to these movies as the minority response (probably it never occurred to him that, even among the children who appeared to love telling and hearing about the movies, some may have been frightened and others playing a role) and as one that set him apart from the norm established by the majority of children.

Despite his fear of scary movies, however, David was not one of those children we sometimes characterize as "afraid of every-thing," and in fact was quite interested in and hospitable towards such widely feared creatures as spiders and snakes. I can remember his amazement when one of his sister's friends who was a horror movie buff had been afraid to use our bathroom until I removed a spider from the wall (he could not fathom how anyone who watched horror movies could be frightened by a house spider), and I can also remember that when we would recreate outdoors or visit zoos or museums, he was always intrigued with snakes and eager to

DAVID AT HOME 75

handle and familiarize himself with nonpoisonous ones. Although he was probably more aware of a fear of snakes as common in our culture than a fear of spiders and so was not surprised when other children did not want to handle snakes, he did view a fear of both snakes and spiders as silly, and so it could be argued that in these contexts he judged the fears of others according to the same assumptions I have been arguing he made in judging his own fear of piranhas.

A second aspect of the incident at Samuel's club that had disconcerted David was the incongruity he perceived between his own fear and Samuel's lack of it in light of the fact that Samuel as a rule had always been more apprehensive about water, and particularly about swimming, than David had. In discussing this incongruity, David recalled that as a child Samuel would rarely leave the shallow end of a swimming pool, that he seemed always to be edging towards the sides of the pool, that he had not liked to put his face in the water or his head under water, and that when he got frightened he would pretend he was cold and get out of the pool to warm himself on his beach towel in the sun. On the other hand, David observed that he, though no daredevil in the pool, had liked to frogswim with his whole body under water and had not been one to flee the pool on the pretense of getting warm, at least not before he had seen the Tarzan movie.

David went on to say that it hadn't made any sense to him that the Tarzan movie should so radically have altered his own attitude towards the club pool without also increasing, or at least provoking, Samuel's characteristic reserve. Although this second point I am making is so closely related to the one made above that it may seem the same, the difference I see is that point 1 above is about David's attitude towards *normality* or the desirability of certain emotions or behaviors (in this case the normalness of being afraid versus not being afraid) and point 2 is about his attitude towards the *consistency* or predictability of behavior in light of individual personalities or life histories.[14] In addition, implicit in David's observation about Samuel's inconsistency is the further assumption that people are supposed to be consistent rather than inconsistent. But if we compare his assumption about fear as not normal or standard and inconsistency as not normal, inconsistency seems the lesser of the two "abnormalities." If the choice is between the two, inconsistency is preferable to fear (less an error or deviation). Furthermore, if inconsistent behavior involves a movement away from fear, such movement, though often seen as not normal (inconsistent) in terms of life history, is a movement towards the standard in terms of emotion and so is an inconsistency that signals a shift toward normal or desirable behavior. According to the assumptions David seems to have made, then, his fear was less acceptable, more an "error," than Samuel's inconsistency, and it is these assumptions that seem to have been a major source of David's self-consciousness and shame and of his decision not to tell Samuel or me about his fear.[15]

That these assumptions pervade our society and are arguably rooted largely in a desire for stability and a fear of abandonment and the unknown probably does not require comment, but I do want to recall that the assumption about consistent behavior was central to my own frustration the evening David objected to taking his bath (I found his behavior "not like him," or inconsistent). I also want to mention in passing that though we may not be able to get along without norms, we also seem to have a real propensity for generating and instituting norms that mutilate the human spirit, perhaps because, in failing to deal directly with our fears of rejection, abandonment, and death, we lay the way open for these fears to dictate our concept of normality.

A final point I want to make here is that David's assessment of both his own fear and Samuel's casualness as inconsistent does not have to be accurate for my argument about David's hierarchy of assumptions to be valid. For example, both David's and Samuel's experiencing of water and the Tarzan movie could have involved subtleties that David did not perceive, subtleties that would reveal apparently inconsistent behavior to be consistent—in the sense of comprehensible—after all. In short, David's perception of inconsistency could have been superficial. However, a revelation of consistency at a deeper or less visible level would not alter David's valuation of fear and consistency; he would still have been a child who perceived his own behavior (including his own emotions) and the behavior of others in terms of normal and not normal.[16]

In addition to talking with me about his fear as one that alienated him from the norm that he saw as the basis for acceptance or rejection by others (as well as by himself) David also talked about the main sources of his fear of piranhas. As far as he can remember, there were at least two. One was the episode in the Tarzan movie he had told me about when he was seven but that fifteen-year-old David talked about in much more detail and with an eager seriousness that seemed determined to pinpoint the specific aspects of the movie that had so frightened him.[17] The first disturbing aspect was that the villains in the movie had tied Tarzan's arms and legs (and also the arms and legs of a female companion) to stakes on the riverbank so that one of Tarzan's arms was immersed in the water, which was inhabited by piranhas. The second disturbing aspect involved the movie's method of emphasizing the presence of piranhas. Using underwater photography, the movie focused in on the turbulence surrounding Tarzan's arm. David said that though in retrospect he recalls the special effects as very poor, at the time he saw the movie the impression of Tarzan's arm being overwhelmed (*overwhelmed* was David's word) by piranhas was unmistakable and convincing, even though the fish themselves were never shown. David also said, repeatedly, that it was this image of the water in commotion, of its white frothing turbulence, that had most affected him and that he could not shake. Given the turbulence, David said he simply could not understand how Tarzan's arm could have remained undamaged. As David put it, Tarzan "cut the rope that was holding his hand and pulled it out. . . . the thing was, it was like undamaged—that was the thing I could never understand, even back then—was his arm was completely undamaged." Later, in further discussing the effectiveness of the turbulence, David said that if the movie had shown Tarzan's arm actually being attacked by the piranhas, it would have been bad, but that what can be imagined is worse.[18]

In talking about Tarzan's escape from his captors, David made clear that he had experienced the episode with the piranhas as having implications for his own life rather than as an episode to which he was merely a passive audience. He said he had really been bothered when Tarzan, after cutting the rope that held the immersed arm, had had to voluntarily put the arm back in the river because his captors had reappeared on the scene and he had needed to fool them into thinking he was tied just as they had left him. David also said he hadn't known if he would have been able to follow Tarzan's example, by which he meant risk his arm voluntarily. And David added that the movie had made him wonder if even his own survival would have been enough to make him do something that truly frightened him. In the second of several conversations we had on this topic, and the only one I was able to tape, David expressed his doubt as follows:

[Tarzan] heard them [his captors returning] and the only way he would be able to escape without them tying him up again was to make

it look like he was still tied up, so he had to put his arm voluntarily
back in the water and that was one of the things that kind of scared me
. . . you wouldn't be able—I don't know if I would be able to voluntarily put myself . . . letting your body be harmed so you can escape with
your life—I probably wouldn't have been able to do that—I don't
know if I would have, and, and, intense pain, taking intense pain so
that you can keep your life, and, that's what he had to do—so he put
his hand back in the water.

A related observation David made was that when Tarzan's captors had disappeared back into the jungle and Tarzan had taken his
arm out of the river for the second time, finished cutting his ropes,
and also the ropes of the woman tied next to him, he had had to
cross the piranha-infested river to escape. David described the
crossing by saying that Tarzan's feet had seemed barely to touch
the water as he ran. At the time, David had thought how crucial it
would be to run just as Tarzan had run in order to escape having
one's feet and legs attacked by the piranhas.

Although the Tarzan movie is the only source that I recall David
mentioning when he was a child, during the discussions we had
while I was writing about his fear, he told me that around the same
time he visited Samuel's club he had read a Franklin Dixon Hardy
boys mystery, *The Masked Monkey* (1972), that also included a frightening episode with piranhas. Borrowing David's copy of the mystery,
I skimmed through it. In the chapter "Fish Bait," hero-detectives
Frank and Joe Hardy, while on a case in Brazil, are fooled by their
host, Joachim San Marten (who turns out to be the villain), into
taking a swim in his backyard pool, which San Marten has instructed
his subordinates to booby-trap with piranhas. Given the swimming
pool at Samuel's club, the significance of the pool in the mystery
seemed immediately obvious. As I skimmed through the mystery,
however, it seemed that the lead-in to the scene with the swimming
pool, the development of the scene itself, and several other parts of
the mystery were also worth considering in relation to David's fear.

Immediately preceding the scene with the piranhas, the Hardy
boys have their motel room burglarized by a trained monkey.
Catching the monkey in the act, Joe says that a human being is
behind the burglary, and the narrator tells us that the boys felt
themselves held by an evil power and targeted by a "malevolent
force . . . bent on their destruction" (Dixon 1972, 67). Thus sensitized
to the presence of evil, Frank and Joe are on the alert when their

host-villain leaves them to swim in his pool. Just as Joe is about to dive into the pool, they are saved when Frank recalls their Aunt Gertrude's advice—"Look before you leap!" (70).[19] Cued by Aunt Gertrude's maxim, Frank warns Joe not to dive, and the two boys, looking into the pool, see a whole school of fish. On a hunch, Joe throws a piece of ham from his breakfast into the pool. Before it can sink, a school of small fish attack. Becoming "a swirling horde of ferocious predators" (71), the fish gobble up the ham. Shaken, Frank and Joe identify the fish. "Piranhas!" they exclaim. To confuse their host and give themselves time to escape, they raid his refrigerator and throw a roast beef, two hams, and a pork and a lamb roast into the pool, the result being that "the piranhas were on them in a flash. The water boiled with the assault" (71). When the assault is over, only bones remain. Although David had told me that the turbulence of water in the Tarzan movie had been very disturbing and that what he had been able to imagine was worse than a graphic depiction of an actual attack on Tarzan's arm would have been, I wondered, as I read *The Masked Monkey*, if the "swirling horde of ferocious predators," "the water that boiled with the assault," and the bones left at the bottom of the swimming pool had not played a part in provoking David's imagination and intensifying his response to the attack on Tarzan's arm.

I also want to note that in both the movie and the mystery the villains exploited a creature from nature to further a scheme for amassing personal wealth and that in the mystery (and perhaps also the Tarzan movie, although, not having seen it, I can't say for sure) the heroes had the capacity to "see through" the villain's scheme. Frank and Joe were able to see beyond the monkey who had robbed their hotel room to the human being who had masterminded the burglary, they were able to sense the presence of "some evil power" or intangible force, and they were able to discover the identity of the school of fish in their host's swimming pool.

In their ability to "see through," the Hardy boys recall the David who, as a fourth grader, wrote in his autobiographical essay that he was born at a time (midnight) that gave him the power to see ghosts when they wanted to be invisible and who wrote in the same essay that one of his accomplishments in his projected adulthood had been to discover "new fish even." Within the context of David's experiencing of the Tarzan movie and the Hardy boys mystery, there were numerous "ghosts" or "new fish" for David to discover, ghosts that had the potential to contribute to his experiencing of piranhas as fearful creatures and to his avoidance of his bath. And here I am thinking of the terms *ghosts* and *new fish* not only narrowly or literally (*ghost*: the spirit of a dead person; *new fish*: an aquatic animal recently experienced or become known) but also broadly or figuratively (*ghost*: any existence or presence that is invisible or undiscovered or unknown; *new fish*: any existence or presence that was once invisible, undiscovered, or unknown but that has recently been seen, discovered, or understood) so that a ghost that is seen would be synonymous, or nearly so, with the discovery of a new fish and a fish that has not been seen would be synonymous with a ghost.

One ghost David could have discovered in the Tarzan movie was the literal ghost of Tarzan. Although Tarzan did not actually die, his vulnerability to life-threatening situations was dramatized when he was captured, and the idea of ghostliness as the absence of flesh was suggested by the image of the flesh-and-blood arm that the piranhas could have reduced to a mere skeleton. Similarly, the Hardy boys did not actually die, but they were placed in a life-threatening situation, one in which the bones of the meat raided from their villainous host's refrigerator suggested all that would have remained of Frank and Joe's bodiliness if they had dived into the pool. Another discovery David could have made in the movie and mystery was of a new fish, a fish that he had been vaguely aware of before but whose full monstrousness, as dramatized by the movie and the mystery, may not have been brought home to him before.[20] The fish, obviously, was the piranha, a creature that could make ghosts of human beings, who are nothing if they are not their bodies, and a fish that therefore lent itself to exploitation by villains.[21] Stated more generally, the movie and the mystery gave David an opportunity to discover the vulnerability of any adventuresome or heroic person, that is, of any person that David would have referred to as a "good guy," through the efforts of malevolent human beings or "bad guys."

Of course, some might argue that because fictional heroes such as Tarzan and the Hardy boys always escape "in the nick of time," a child identifying with them would learn to believe in his or her own physical invulnerability rather than, as David seemed to have learned, in his or her vulnerability. Though I do think this happens, I also think that it is only one of many possible impacts such material can have. Another equally plausible impact, one that I see at work in David's case, is that a child will identify with the hero's capacity for finding him- or herself in life-threatening situations but not with the capacity for escaping from such situations. One explanation I would offer for a partial identification is that though children may become caught up in an adventure story to the point of experiencing it as real, or, at least, as possessing enough verisimilitude to encourage a willing and thorough suspension of disbelief, children are also capable of making subtle distinctions between reality and fantasy and of separating themselves from the fictional hero at any one of a number of points in the adventure. Though David may have experienced himself as occupying almost literally the position of the Tarzan who was staked to the riverbank and of the Hardy boys who nearly took a swim in the piranha-inhabited pool, it does not necessarily follow that he experienced himself as escaping as they escaped. In fact, any identification David experienced with Tarzan or the Hardy boys could have been broken at the moment of escape.

Possible explanations for a broken identification are many and would depend on the specifics of a child's situation and life history, but four possible explanations I want to offer are these: first, identification could be broken if the child questioned the movie's believability. In the case of the Tarzan movie, David did question that Tarzan's arm could have remained unharmed given the vigorous attack by piranhas. Second, a child's identification could be broken if the child were generally aware, as David was, that Tarzan and the Hardy boys were heroes in a continuing series of stories and that the people who write the stories must arrange for them to escape even the most apparently inescapable situations so that the heroes can appear in subsequent narratives. An implication of this explanation is that a child would grasp that the chance of a serial hero's survival is controlled by very different factors than those that control the life of a real-life adventurer. Third, identification could be broken if the child pinpointed the specific qualities that account for the hero's escape (as David pinpointed Tarzan's skill in running across the river and also his willingness to voluntarily risk physical harm to save his life) and judged him- or herself as lacking in those particular qualities. Fourth, the identification could be broken if the child had, in real life, experienced being caught but not escaping unscathed, or if the child had been nurtured by an adult whose own life had been fraught with such experiences and who had imparted, intentionally or unintentionally, a strong sense of human vulnerability to the child. It seems to me, moreover, that these explanations for a partial identification with a fictional character, in this case a serial hero, have important implications for education; instead of abstracting a pattern of identification that we adults have happened to perceive and then assuming that this perceived pattern is *the* pattern (the pattern that holds for children in general), we need to acknowledge that the reality is potentially much more complex and that a child's pattern of identification will be as expressive of the child's own life history as it will be of the hero's.[22]

In addition to discovering the physical vulnerability of good guys to piranhas, David also had an opportunity, in the movie and mystery, to discover several other abstract and general principles, principles that could have contributed to his fear or that, if he had already discovered the principles elsewhere, could have been reaffirmed or modified by the mystery and movie. The first, which is particularly apparent in *The Masked Monkey*, is that reality, or what we experience, is multidimensional. Probably the most obvious way the mystery demonstrates this is through the multiple identities of some of the characters. For example, Joachim San Marten presents himself as a good samaritan and upstanding citizen who earns an honest living as a professional trader in wild animals. Actually, however, he has a second identity as a gang leader who runs a "Change-Your-Identity operation" that provides criminals with "new faces, personalities, and passports" (Dixon 1972, 171), an operation that makes use of San Marten's considerable animal-training skills, which, for example, he uses to train a monkey to steal identification papers for his gang. And this trained monkey, when it burglarizes the Hardy boys' hotel room, wears a mask, a mask that confuses Frank and Joe. The narrator describes the masked monkey-burglar as "a hideous-looking simian" (65). And Joe, in describing the monkey as "the ugliest brute [he's] ever seen" comments that he would have thought the monkey was a nightmare if his brother hadn't been present to verify his perception (66). But at the end of the book a very different monkey is unveiled. Joe removes the monkey's mask to reveal "a pleasant, gentle simian face" that responds with bright friendliness (175).[23] The explanation for the transformation is that the mask has been wired with earphones and that San Marten has been instructing the monkey, through a radio, to commit criminal acts. By dramatizing the world's great potential for ambiguity and dissimulation, *The Masked Monkey* could have played a part in prompting David to begin (or in encouraging him to continue or resume) a radical questioning of the constancy and trustworthiness of his personal landscape, including the landscape of his bathroom-laboratory. Furthermore, when Joe questions and affirms the reality of the monkey during the burglary, he does so with the full involvement and support of his brother Frank, whereas David, in his questioning of the trustworthiness of the water at the club swimming pool and of his bathtub at home, had no such "sidekick" or alter ego with whom he was willing to share his perceptions.

A related principle that David could have discovered in the movie and the mystery is that the instructions, rules, or advice we encounter day in and day out, instructions that we often take for granted as commonsensical and label as maxims, are sometimes ambiguous to the point of appearing inconsistent or contradictory, particularly when abstracted from a specific context. The example I want to offer concerns one rule implied in the movie and one rule stated overtly in the mystery, an example that would have required David to experience the movie and mystery in relation to each other rather than as rigidly bounded experiences. The rule the movie implies is "He or she who hesitates is lost," and it is embedded in Tarzan's on-the-spot decision to put his arm into the piranha-inhabited river a second time. The rule the mystery overtly states is "Look before you leap," and it is recalled by Frank just as Joe is about to dive into the swimming pool full of piranhas. Another way to express these two rules would be to say that the movie advises its audience (through the action of the hero) to risk—to "dive"—and that the mystery advises the audience (through a maxim associated with the Hardy boys' Aunt Gertrude and through the action of heroes Frank and Joe) to be cautious—not to dive.

In relation to his avoidance of tub baths, David may have felt (in addition to being terrified by the piranhas) pressured by two conflicting models, the model of Tarzan putting his arm back into the piranha-inhabited river and the model of the Hardy boys drawing back from the similarly inhabited swimming pool. Furthermore, if David had abstracted the images from the context of the movie and the mystery, he could have experienced them as contradictory orders even though in context they are compatible: in the movie the villains are already on the scene, which means that Tarzan has little time to consider alternative action, whereas in the mystery the villain is still out of sight, which allows the Hardy boys some time to identify the fish and stage a cover that does not require them to risk their bodies. Additional specifics suggesting compatibility are that in the movie Tarzan is called on to risk only one arm and later his feet, whereas in the mystery a dive into the pool would have risked the whole body.

That seemingly inconsistent rules such as the two discussed above have the potential to confuse not only a child's sense of how to survive but also a sense of how to live up to the standards of a given culture, and so retain standing, or place, as a valued member of the culture, does not always occur to those of us in charge of children. Given this initial oversight, it is unlikely that many of us would think to teach a child to recognize the anxiety that can arise from trying to adhere to rules that appear to contradict each other and also to distinguish between real and apparent contradiction. For example, specifically in relation to distinguishing an apparent contradiction from an actual one, it is unlikely that we would think to teach a child that such sayings as "Look before you leap" and "He or she who hesitates is lost" need not be experienced as abstract and absolute rules that are contradictory but instead can be experienced as choices to be grounded in, among other things, the specifics of various situations that may share similarities but that also may be quite distinct.

As for why we sometimes fail to perceive our children's potential for becoming confused in the face of contradiction, apparent or otherwise, the reasons are no doubt various and complex. One possibility is that we do not conceive of children as subject to anxiety, which it seems to me is much the same thing as saying that we do not conceive of them as perceivers. Another possibility is that we have only the most limited knowledge of our children's worlds and so have little exposure to the rules or instructions they may be discovering. And even if we did have knowledge of their worlds, we might not focus on the content, except perhaps to make such passing comments as "I read that book, too, when I was about your age" or "What is that movie you've got on there? Oh, I guess I missed that one."[24]

A third possibility is that we ourselves choose between options so effortlessly that we are too distanced from the child's difficulty, which is the difficulty of the beginner, to perceive it. And here it should be noted that such adult effortlessness could arise, at one extreme, from an intuition subtle enough to make fine distinctions without conscious reflection or, at the other extreme, from a follow-the-leader mimicry that is oblivious not only to the contextual compatibility of some rules that may sound contradictory in the abstract but also to the potential for such rules to sound contradictory in the first place. A fourth, less obvious possibility is that we ourselves are still such beginners that we sense disparity only vaguely, as an inarticulated stress that nags at us but that we cannot accurately label or sort out. Or, even if we have gotten as far as articulating the perceived disparity, we may find ourselves in the "child's" quandary about how to choose in the face of it, that is, about how to choose so that we have the best chance of surviving physically but at the same time the best chance of avoiding a choice that might jeopardize our standing in our own eyes or in the eyes of others.

Among those of us who feel no vague stress and who are not in a quandary over choosing, it is also possible that some are so busy searching for the ultimate book of abstractable rules (or so busy enforcing or trying to live up to a book already written) that even if we did perceive disparity or contradiction among abstractions, we would immediately set about debating which half of the contradiction was in error and needed excising rather than first considering the possibility either that the contradiction was an illusion arising out of a false equation having been drawn between situations that are similar but also distinct or that it was an ambiguity implicit in the human condition.[25] For adults such as these last to have authority over children seems to me especially unfortunate; even if the children manage to articulate inconsistencies and, further, to discover that some are merely apparent and others implicit, they will still have to cope with the superficial perception of the adults in power.

In addition to discovering that the world is ambiguous and multifaceted and that ambiguity can involve tension and contradiction (or the appearance of it), David could have discovered, in both the movie and the mystery, the penetrability of boundaries. The very presence of Tarzan and his captors in Africa (David says the captors were Nazi soldiers or sympathizers) attests to the penetrability of the boundary that divides the Western world from what Westerners often term "the jungle," black human beings from white, ethical behavior from unethical, and so on. Similarly, in *The Masked Monkey*, the Hardy boys travel to foreign Brazil, San Marten travels to the foreign United States, and the gang's activities suggest the crossing of the boundary that separates ethical and unethical as well as legal and illegal behavior. David also had an opportunity, in the mystery, to discover that established boundaries can shift through time—for example, that civilization can encroach on nature through, say, the building of a city, just as nature can encroach on civilization by reclaiming the land on which we build. At one point in the mystery, Frank and Joe fly over a large expanse of jungle until they reach a relatively small and unimpressive city that their pilot says Americans would label "a ghost town of the Amazon" (Dixon 1972, 78–79). The pilot's remark concludes his explanation about how an opulent pink and white marble building came to stand in the midst of the ghost town, the building being the opera house of a major city all but obliterated through time by a shifting economy.

To a mother who had felt uneasy about her son's fear that piranhas would attack him in the bathtub, *The Masked Monkey* seemed the perfect counterpart to the Tarzan movie. The mystery reiterated the movie's presentation of the hero as vulnerable to premature death as well as the image of the piranha as a dangerous fish that lends itself to exploitation by villains. The mystery and movie also complemented each other, each obliterating one of the two main boundaries that as a rule separate piranhas from human beings. The boundary separating land from water and terrestrial from aquatic life is crossed, in the movie, when Tarzan's arm is submerged in the river. In the mystery the traditional line between nature and civilization is crossed when the villain, San Marten, arranges for piranhas to be released in his swimming pool. Whereas in the movie piranhas never leave their wild habitat, in the mystery they do; whereas in the mystery Frank and Joe never come in contact with piranha-inhabited water, in the movie Tarzan does.

An implication is that if David had seen only the movie, he could have reassured himself that he would be safe from the monster-fish as long as he did not venture into the jungle, and if he had read only the mystery, he could have reassured himself that he would be safe from piranhas as long as he did not share any body of water they inhabited.[26] Having been exposed to both, however, he may have felt that he had no safety zone. Furthermore, though Frank, Joe, and Tarzan, as already mentioned, all escape their encounters unhurt, in the mystery the bones of the meat Frank and Joe throw into the pool suggest graphically what would happen if the boundary between the human body and the world outside the body were penetrated by piranhas. And since David himself stated in our discussions that he could not understand, even at seven, how Tarzan's arm could have escaped undamaged, it seems plausible that David would have assumed that if he were to share water with piranhas, his own fate would not be to escape unhurt but to be reduced to cleanly picked bones.

Finally, leaving little undone that would contribute to the image of the world as a place where the boundary between civilization and nature is routinely penetrated, the mystery presents a villain, San Marten, whose legal or "cover" profession as a trader in wild animals depends on penetrating the jungle and procuring wild creatures to fill the zoos of civilization. Though zoos admittedly are traditionally themselves rigidly bounded places, the transporting of wild creatures from one place to another always carries with it the risk that they will escape and terrorize us within the boundaries— within the "privacy"—of the worlds we define as ours, a risk that the mystery dramatizes when a king cobra escapes from its cage in a warehouse at Kennedy Airport and corners Joe, who has volunteered to help capture it. In the narrator's description, nature loosed within civilization poses a decided threat to the physical survival of the civilized, as represented by Joe. After the twelve-foot cobra assumes a strike pose and locks its eyes onto Joe's "with a malevolent stare," Joe stands as "immobile as a statue," feeling sure that if he moves, "the fangs would pierce his leg, pumping venom into his blood stream that would cause him to die in agony" (Dixon 1972, 106–107). Though Frank rescues Joe at the crucial moment, the scene nonetheless dramatizes the risk of importing wild creatures into civilization.

If my conversation with fifteen-year-old David made clear that at seven he had had ample exposure to fictional material that could have provoked his fear of piranhas invading the privacy of his bath, our conversations also made clear that in his childhood fantasy play he had been exploring the flexibility of boundaries long before he saw the Tarzan movie or read the Hardy boys mystery and that he had found water a particularly stimulating medium for this play. In other words, even granting that my selecting out of pertinent details favors my perspective and may obscure more powerful patterns to which I am not sensitive, it was a little as if David's life prior to his exposure to the mystery and the movie had been designed especially to prepare him to experience them as he did.

One topic we focused on in our conversations was water as a substance. David said that when he was small it had intrigued him because of its uniquely fluid tangibility. His view can be seen in the following excerpt from one of our discussions, an excerpt in which he contrasts the fluidity of water to the solidity of the objects that make up so much of our landscape, and the tangibility of water to the ethereality of air:

88

I always liked water. It's just like, for the same reason . . . I was going to become a marine biologist, I just liked water. I mean, it was like built in—I don't know how, exactly. It's just that water is so totally different from anything else . . . . I mean, everything around us that you see is solid and I mean, you can pick it up and hold it. Or air . . . you . . . air is . . . everything is, around us is either totally tangible or completely intangible—like air—you can't see, you can't taste (really), you can't smell, hear [it] or anything . . . but water is kind of between the two [solid objects and air] and it's different, it's kind of unique . . . because you can taste water, you can . . . sense it with all your senses but somehow it's not the same, because you can't actually get hold of it, it just like drips through and stuff. It has a totally different texture . . . it has a totally different like whole way of being existent than anything else because it doesn't stay put, like it doesn't stay . . . like this [the couch he was sitting on] stays and water doesn't . . . so water is fascinating because it's so different.

And later, in an untaped discussion, he made an effort to communicate his childhood enthusiasm for the tangible by reminding me of how uninteresting he had found numbers and arithmetic during grammar school. Saying he had not wanted to take the time to focus on arithmetic because he was always so fully taken up with what he could touch, hear, see, taste, and smell, he added that, for the most part, he had considered pursuit of the abstract, as represented by arithmetic, a waste of his valuable time.

As well as finding its tangibility attractive, David said he was also drawn to water by its alienness, by the fact that it is not the natural medium of human beings and that we can't breathe in it. In connection with both its alienness and its fluidity, we talked about water's receptivity, that is, about the way it receives objects and creatures that find their way into it and also about its receptivity in the sense of being what David termed the "do-all chemical" or "universal solvent." He mentioned that one of his most memorable dreams from early childhood was of being chased by an ominous figure and hiding in deep water until help arrived and that one of his most memorable childhood fears was of being attacked by a shark while exploring the ocean. He also discussed how much he had liked to mix things with water; for example, he said that water had been a basic ingredient in the various "potions" he recalled concocting in the bathroom-laboratory, and he also recalled that he had liked to let brushfulls of the colors from a tin of water paints dissolve into his bathwater.

Based on my conversations with David, the primary generalization I would make about his experiencing of water as a substance is that his child's curiosity and urge to explore had been provoked by the combination of alienness and uniqueness, by water's being a substance that lies midway between the solidity of ground and the airiness of space, and by water's being a substance in which we cannot naturally exist. The secondary generalization I would make is that his attraction to water for its own sake was complicated by a tension arising from his perception of it as both dangerous and protective. At the same time that he was addressing his watery landscape with the question "Who or what are you who are part of this same world of which I am a part?" (Schachtel [1959] 1984, 222), he was also addressing it with the questions "How can I protect myself from you (or your inhabitants)?" and "How can I use you, either to delight me or to protect me from danger?" At the same time that he benefited from the receptivity of water, from being able to cross the boundary between land and water and explore the alien substance that so attracted him, he was also endangered by it. Given this double-edged experiencing of water, his exposure to the Tarzan movie and the Hardy boys mystery could have fixed his attention entirely on the need to protect himself. Instead of finding himself fully engaged in an act of exploring water-the-unknown, an act that was intertwined with an along-the-way discovery of water's various usefulnesses and perils, David could have found himself fully engaged with his fear of piranhas and of water as their ownmost sphere. Deciding that the surest protection was to avoid immersing himself in water, David could then have found himself faced with the problem of how to live in a world that had come to identify him as a child who loved water, for example, as a child whose mother had characterized him, the evening he objected to the fullness of his bath, as loving to bathe in an overflowing tub more than any other child she knew.

David's discussion of *bodies* of water (rather than water as a substance) also suggested an interest in the flexibility of boundaries that predated his exposure to the Tarzan movie and the Hardy boys mystery. David began this discussion by saying that the ocean had always been and still was his favorite body of water, even though he was no longer interested in a career in marine biology. I responded by saying that, in addition to the ocean, it seemed to me that he had been involved with all sorts of other bodies of water. David in turn responded with a series of clarifying remarks. My impression was that he felt that I had an inadequate grasp of his childhood relation-ship to bodies of water and that it was up to him to make certain I did not misconstrue it. He seemed particularly intent on making me understand that, though as a child he had indeed been interested in bodies of water other than the ocean, his interest had always been in wild outdoor bodies of water and never, as he put it, in "domestic" ones. When I mentioned all the hours he had spent playing at the kitchen and bathroom sinks and particularly in the bathtub and asked if these did not qualify as "domestic," he said that he had never thought of them as sinks or bathtubs but had always imagined them to be wild places—oceans, rivers, lakes, ponds, streams.

In our discussion, David focused specifically on his childhood experiencing of his bath. He said the bathtub had been a particularly good place for imaginative play, not only because it was almost always available to him and because it did not require a trip to the coast or the mountains but also because of its great privacy and because of its controllability. Contrasting the bathtub and a public swimming pool, David said that public pools were generally terrible settings for imaginative play because it was so hard to get his imagination going when so many different strangers in so many different groups were involved in so many different activities all at the same time. He also said that even if he had been able to get his imagination going, a public pool did not readily allow for a private place or space that would be all his to play in and that others at the pool would necessarily respect and keep clear of. In contrast, the bathtub allowed him to imagine as freely as he liked. What I heard David saying, in essence, was that the secure boundaries we associ-ate with a private niche fostered his imaginative exploration across boundaries and that the bathtub was just such a private niche.[27]

When I commented to David that his fear of piranhas had emerged at the club pool, which was public enough to have the same drawbacks as a public pool, he pointed out that the TV room at the club, which was small—about the size of two bathrooms, he said—had been right next to the pool. He also said that he and Samuel had been the only two people in the room while the movie was on, which meant he had had plenty of privacy in which to get imaginatively involved and also that when he had stepped out of the TV room, he had immediately faced the water. David also said that though he had not been particularly frightened by the movie while watching it, he had no sooner stepped out of the TV room and set eyes on the pool full of water than he had felt overwhelmed by fear and that he had felt the same way when he faced his bathtub full of water at home.

Besides talking about the freedom to imagine that the bathtub afforded, David also talked about the control he could exercise in the bath. He said that in the bathtub he could use the faucet to control the water level and to create such natural phenomena as waterfalls, and he described how he had liked to tether his houseboat to the faucet, turn the water on high, and pretend that the boat was navigating a rough sea. He also said he could use his supply of liquid soap to make mountains of bubbles that he experienced as icebergs and that he could control the turbulence of the bathwater with his body, creating whirlpools or waves by twirling his finger or hand in the water in a certain way he had learned through trial and error or by moving his body back and forth in the tub. Within these landscapes he created, he said he could move his toy plastic figures through all sorts of story lines, sometimes having them explore the waterfalls, icebergs, or waves and whirlpools, sometimes having them confront them, and frequently borrowing story ideas from episodes of "Gilligan's Island" or "Flipper" or from other sources he had come across. What really mattered in these bathtub narratives, David said, was that they involved conflict and exploration of the unknown. He added that as a rule the conflict was between good and evil, or "good guys" and "bad guys," and that the bad guys could be human beings or creatures such as sharks.

David's comments about his bathtub play suggested that one reason the Tarzan movie and the Hardy boys mystery had so captured his attention was that they dramatized the questions of exploration of the unknown and of the flexibility of boundaries that had already engaged his imagination. His comments also made it pretty obvious that though his bathroom-laboratory had indeed been his private niche, a place he could turn to when he sought privacy with water, it was for that very reason also a place for his fear of piranhas to flourish. Alone with himself in the bathroom, he had very little to distract him from becoming entirely absorbed in whatever was on his mind. Though very obvious and though something I probably would not have missed if the child involved had been some child other than my child and the home involved some home other than the one I lived in and "presided" over, this potential of David's bathroom-lab to be a place where any emotion could thrive, including fear, had eluded me for some time. When I finally did grasp it, however, I also understood the reason David had answered my question (early in our discussions) about how he could have been so afraid in his very own bathroom-lab by saying, "My imagination just took over." As for his comments about why the swimming pool at the club had proved an exception to his usual experiencing of public pools, I found them convincing and was struck by the similarity between the TV room's nearness to the pool at the club and the nearness of David's books and toys, and our own television, to his bathroom at home. Both at the club and at home, he had had a provocative landscape and the privacy in which to become imaginatively involved with it.

During his description of his bathtub play, David had taken a few minutes to talk about his childhood fear of sharks. Although his view of sharks had undergone several changes in his childhood, he had initially viewed them as involuntary or mechanistic killers that attacked any human beings who so much as crossed the boundary between water inhabited by sharks and land. He said that even when he had read a biography of marine biologist Eugenie Clark—*Shark Lady* (McGovern 1978)—and begun to understand that whereas the great white shark, though not a mechanistic killer, might be quite dangerous, some other species were relatively harmless, he still had not come to terms with the issue of size. Instead, he had simply thought of sharks as fish and of fish as creatures that lived in water. One consequence of this blending of general and specific had been that he had not experienced the size of a shark in relation to the size of a bathtub. Consequently, when playing in the tub, he had sometimes been frightened that one of the dangerous sharks, particularly the great white, would literally turn up in the tub and "get" him.

David further explained how he finally did come to terms with the size of sharks. He said that he had read somewhere that great white sharks were about forty feet long but that he had never visualized how long forty feet was until he had been sitting at the family room table one day and happened to focus on the length of the wall opposite the table. It occurred to David that the wall must be eighteen or more feet because he could see that at least three of his father, who he knew was just six feet tall, could fit end to end along the wall. Recalling the forty-foot figure he'd seen or heard quoted for great white sharks, David realized that forty feet was much longer than even the wall and that such a large fish could never fit in a bathtub. According to David, this visual grasping of

size had been a tremendous relief to him because it meant he no
longer needed to worry about a great white shark getting him while
he played in the tub. At one point in our discussion he did qualify,
however, saying that sometimes his imagination could so thoroughly
create a sense of wild landscape that he would feel as if he were
actually in the ocean and that a shark or sharks were nearby. He
added that when this happened he was able to control his fear and
avoid panic by reminding himself that though the ocean he imagined
the bathtub to be could contain all species of sharks, the bathtub
was literally too small, and too shallow, to contain a shark large
enough to be dangerous to a human being. In other words, before
grasping size, his fear of sharks had been outside his control, but
after grasping size, he had been able to shift back and forth between
a literal and a metaphorical experiencing of the bathtub in order to
prevent his fear of sharks from interfering with his play; and it was
the small size of the tub (or the large size of the shark) that he had
fixed on as the obstacle that would protect him from the threat of
invading sharks.

Although during David's and my discussions I am not sure
who made the transition from the subject of sharks to piranhas,
David was the one to observe that piranhas, unlike sharks, were
small enough to fit into the bathtub (the piranhas in *The Masked
Monkey* are described as "not more than eight inches long" [Dixon
1972, 70]) and that because they are carnivorous and travel and
attack in schools, they were the perfect fish to alienate him from his
bath. As David talked more about his fear, I got the impression that
without the bathtub's depth and breadth functioning as a protective
barrier against invasion, David had, as a child, ascribed unreservedly
to the dictum "Where there's a will, there's a way," as well as to this
dictum in reverse. He seemed to have distinguished the sort of
boundary that was most likely to protect him from sharks from
those boundaries that were less secure, and then felt safe so long as
the boundaries he experienced as insurmountable remained intact.
For example, after he had commented that piranhas were small
enough to fit into the bathtub, I asked him if, as a child, he had
thought at all about how piranhas could have gotten into his bath.
He said he could not remember actually thinking about it as a child
but that he had simply assumed "they would somehow come up
through the drain."[28] Here he was quick to acknowledge the im-
plausibility of this method of entry and to say that many details
would have had to be worked out, but it was apparent that he had

not viewed sharks and piranhas as in the same category when it came to the likelihood of their turning up in his bath; the boundary between bathtub and shark seemed to fit into the category of uncrossable boundaries, and the boundary between bathtub and piranhas into the category of crossable boundaries. To illustrate that piranhas entering the tub through the drain was not an altogether eccentric idea, David cited a horror movie he had heard about in which alligators find their way into the sewer system of a city and then break out of the system into the city at ground level.[29]

Although David's childhood fear of piranhas and his assumption that they might enter the tub through the drain could suggest an inability to distinguish adequately between reality and fantasy or, at least, an inability to fully control a very active imagination, I do not see either as the *ground* for David's fear. I would agree that both played a role, particularly an inability to control his imagination. I think, however, that a more basic source for his fear was a keen sense of his own vulnerability, and though this sense may arguably have been too keen for his own good, I think it was nevertheless grounded in a fairly sophisticated sense of the imperfectability of systems. What I mean by this is that I think David had begun to grasp, or had grasped in a flash, and perhaps only for a moment, the way in which a boundary that provides maximum protection against one threat can be useless against another. I also think he had begun to grasp that there is no way to protect oneself from all threats at once and forever, not even in one's ownmost sphere and not even with the benefit of the human imagination. In addition, I think he had comprehended the way boundaries fluctuate through time, the part the human will to explore and to control plays in these fluctuations, and the multiedged nature of these changes; for instance, I think he had begun to see that a shift in boundary can impoverish our understanding of the world, enlarge it, protect the lives of human beings, or endanger them, and that these conse-quences of change can take place one at a time, all at once, or in any combination.

As for David's fear that piranhas would literally find their way into his bath, I find the chance of their turning up improbable but not ridiculous, and I also think his distinction between piranhas and sharks as to the relative likelihood of their turning up in the tub is a valuable one. Although I am not saying that piranhas have actually ever found their way into anyone's bath and although I certainly do not think that David, or any child, need live in fear that they will, I do know that piranhas, though their possession is legislated against in many areas, are an aquarial fish, one that human beings have found fascinating enough to transport from the fish's native habitat into the public and private aquariums of cultures where the fish is not indigenous. In addition, I know, quite by chance, as I picked up the following bit of information or trivia one day on the car radio, that a strange-looking fish spotted in California's San Joaquin River (a river about an hour's drive from David's home, but not a river with which he was familiar) was identified as a piranha and that those making the identification speculated that the fish had been released into the river from someone's private aquarium.

Though an aquarium (private or public) and the San Joaquin River (or any river) admittedly cannot be equated with David's bathtub, these bodies of water nevertheless are linked in that all three are large enough to contain piranhas. If we add to this fact such day-in-and-day-out practices as the use of a sink or bathtub or old mason jar as a holding tank for the family's pet tropical fish while the official aquarium is cleaned, the adaption of fishbowls and tanks for planters that we rename terrariums, and the simulation of pond conditions in anything from an old enamel washtub in the garden to a fiberglass pond complete with fountain, filter, and lily pads installed by a professional landscaper, then I think it becomes clear that in addition to being separate and distinct, aquariums, rivers, and bathtubs are also part of an overlapping continuum created by our human capacity for metaphor. Further, I see no reason to assume that children cannot experience such "containers" in their overlapping continuity as well as in their distinct separateness. And so I think that even on a literal level, and even if its immediate antecedents were a pair of fantastical fictional works, David's fear was not hopelessly ridiculous but grounded in an intuitive sense that interconnectedness and change are two of the constants of reality, constants that fascinated him in themselves but that also had implications for his physical survival.

Though David's own comments make clear, moreover, that his specific fear of piranhas and his avoidance of his bath were immediately provoked by the fictional adventures of Tarzan and the Hardy boys, evidence for the penetrability of the world's boundaries was also fully present in his flesh-and-blood landscape, a presence that I think helped prepare him to respond to the movie and mystery as he did and a presence that, for the very reason it is real, neither can nor should be hidden from children, whatever the method, however good the intention. Even limiting myself to the contents of this essay and David's and my discussions about his fear, I find so much evidence of his exposure to the flux of the world that I must be selective. One example I want to draw from his fourth-grade autobiographical essay (which I quoted from earlier) concerns two boundaries, the boundary between the adult and the child (in the sense of a being who defers to the greater wisdom or experience of adults) and the boundary between nature and civilization. "When I went to preschool once," says David in his essay, "the teachers found a gopher snake. They wouldn't let us near it because they said it might be dangerous. I think that they were dumb."

Notable in this passage is David's judgment of his teachers' response to the gopher snake as "dumb." I take the judgment to be David's way of saying that the response was excessive to the provocation of the gopher snake, that gopher snakes are not dangerous to human beings, and that, at least in the context of his fourth-grade essay, David was not going to respect the traditional boundary between the adult as wise and the child as ignorant but instead was going to speak up on the basis of his child's knowledge in a way that recalls the child-hero in Anderson's "The Emperor's New Clothes." In addition to David's judgment itself exemplifying his potential for penetrating boundaries, the judgment also implies his understanding that human beings in our culture traditionally maintain a boundary between themselves and snakes and that the preschool grounds are a place that human beings have claimed for civilization. In other words, unless we are putting together a lesson plan for a unit on reptiles and the snake is in a cage or perhaps preserved in a jar of formaldehyde, the gopher snake belongs *off* the school grounds, that is, in nature or the wilds, and as often as not, teachers will not welcome a snake, even one as harmless to human beings as David knew a gopher snake to be, onto the school grounds. At the same time that David was judging his teachers, then, and revealing his own interest in, knowledge of, and tolerance for a creature that frightens many, he was also revealing his substantial knowledge of the system of boundaries typically ascribed to by our culture.

A second example I want to consider illustrates David's movement back and forth across the boundaries separating nature and civilization and also land and water, adults and children, and, in a metaphorical sense, reality and fantasy. The example is his stocking of the backyard tub-aquarium with polliwogs, mosquito fish, pond snails, algae, and pond water, which required him to leave the civilization of home and penetrate the natural world of the pond, which was also the world of water. In his observation of and engagement with life in the alien medium of water, David's activity overlapped with the activities of such real-life adults as marine biologists Jacques Cousteau, whose book on whales David had on his bookshelf, and Eugenie Clark, whose biography was instrumental in transforming David's blind and panicky fear of all sharks into a respect for and understanding of sharks as a great and varied category of fishes. In his penetration of the natural world of the pond and his importing of the pond creatures into his tub-aquarium, David's activities overlapped with the activities of the fictional adult gangster Joachim San Marten, who in *The Masked Monkey* transports wild animals from the jungles of Brazil to zoos all over the world and who has his subordinates import piranhas from the Amazon River to the swimming pool in the backyard of his private residence.

Another example of David's exposure to the vulnerability of boundaries, in this instance the boundaries between nature and civilization, land and water, and reality and fantasy, concerns the photograph of his great grandmother standing beside the sailfish she had caught while vacationing in Mexico. When David and I discussed the photograph, I mentioned that his enthusiasm for it had raised a question in my mind in that he had never been particularly interested in water as a medium for sports, including fishing. He responded by saying that though he himself did not like to fish very much or to kill fish for sport, the photograph had still attracted him, for two main reasons. First, he said that seeing a human being standing side by side with the sailfish had impressed upon him in a very special way the literal size, the *largeness*, of creatures that swim in the ocean. Second, he said he had responded to the fact that it was his grandmother in the photograph and that having someone in his own family catch such a grand fish was a revelation to him because it made him realize that the world of his imagination and the world he read about and saw at the movies and on television, on the one hand, and the world of *his* real life, on the other hand, were not so distinct and separate as he had thought, and that what we imagine in our play or what we read about and see other people doing not only could *really* happen but could really happen to *him*. And so, rather than experiencing his great grandmother's achievement narrowly or within the rigid boundary of his and her personal specificity, that is, rather than experiencing it as the achievement of a sportswoman whom he could emulate only by himself becoming a sportsman, David had experienced her achievement on a much more general and expansive (or fluid) level—as the achievement of a woman with whom he was connected by blood and who in her life had ventured far beyond the boundaries of the apartment with which he tended to associate her, into the Gulf of Mexico, as a woman who, through the gift of a photograph of a memorable event in her life history, had helped him to perceive the world as a place that was full of possibilities, not only for other people, people like Tarzan, the Hardy boys, Jacques Cousteau, and Eugenie Clark, but also for him, that is as a place in which David's imagination could body forth.[30]

Of course, a world that is experienced as open-ended faces us not only with the possibility of triumph but also with the possibilities of suffering and death. In addition to exposing David to the vulnerability of the boundaries discussed above, his life in the real world had also exposed him to the vulnerability of a creature's body to the world outside the body. For example, in the tub-aquarium in his garden, David had had a chance to observe (in addition to the polliwogs metamorphosing into frogs and leaping from the sides of the tub into the garden proper) the mosquito fish he had imported from the pond gobbling up the mosquito larvae that wriggled in the water. And, as I mentioned earlier in a different context, David had observed, while on a third-grade field trip to the ocean, some rock crabs stripping meat from a dead eel that floated in a tide pool close to shore.

The real world had also offered David plenty of opportunities to grasp the vulnerability of the human body. In his autobiographical essay he wrote about the friend he had made in kindergarten who had been born with a heart defect. In the essay he said only that his friend had "a heart problem," but in playing with his friend and in hearing his friend's mother and me talk, David had learned a lot about his friend's condition. He knew, for instance, that his friend's supply of oxygen was inadequate to sustain vigorous physical play and that he had to take breaks when his breathing became labored or when his complexion took on a bluish tint. He also knew that over a number of years his friend would undergo a series of corrective surgeries and that the surgeries as well as the defect were life threatening. In other words, David knew that his friend would die unless the boundary between the outside world and his body was penetrated by the surgeon's scalpel, or, to look at it another way, unless his friend and his friend's parents behaved similarly to the Tarzan who had risked his body voluntarily in order to have the best chance of saving it.

In David's autobiographical essay, he also refers to the illness that had hospitalized him during infancy. Whereas his reference to his friend's heart defect does not explicitly mention penetration or invasion of the body, David's reference to his own illness does. "When I was an infant, I had to get a butch because the doctors needed to put medicine in my head," David says about the experience he had undergone when he was three months old. Though obviously he would not have been able to remember the experience to talk about it and had doubtless written about it on the basis of his father's and my telling of the story ("butch" was his father's phrasing), the experience had been marked by a number of instances in which his body was penetrated by the outside world. Before being admitted to the hospital, David had run a fever that suggested that a bacteria or virus had entered his body. It was eventually determined to be a virus, and one that, ironically, had very likely entered his body through breast milk. When David went to the doctor's office, the doctor penetrated his spine with a needle in order to extract a sample of fluid to check for the cloudiness that would indicate an infection and also to try to determine through tests if the cloudiness was caused by the meningitis bacteria. Once David had been admitted to the hospital, he had had a strip of hair shaved from his head and a needle inserted into a vein under his scalp so that a precautionary antibiotic could be administered intravenously. In the hospital he also had had his arms placed in cloth restraints to keep him from dislodging the IV. After being released from the hospital, he had returned to the doctor's office for a follow-up spinal tap to make certain the fluid was clear.

From where I stand, the image of David's small infant body lying prone in the hospital crib, his arms restrained—doctors and nurses within "striking" distance—is reminiscent of the image of Tarzan's muscular adult body staked prone on the riverbank with one arm tied by his captors so that it was immersed in water inhabited by piranhas. In fact, when I consider David's hospital stay, or when I look at the quick pencil sketch of Tarzan staked to the riverbank that David drew to help me visualize the image he remembered from the movie, I find myself thinking that an attack by piranhas is an apt metaphor for what his infant-being must have experienced. I also find myself wondering if his experiencing of his illness might have been one of the who knows how many events in his life history that contributed to the intensity with which he experienced Tarzan's predicament. Though I cannot verify the degree or quality of the impact David's illness and hospital stay may have had on him, though my attention to it is doubtless entwined with a mother's residual guilt at her child's hospitalization, and though I know there are those among us who would argue that infants simply forget such experiences and that no lasting impressions are made, I am of the opinion that they do not forget and that lasting impressions are made.

Infants may not possess a vast array of cognitive categories with which to order their experiences, and they may not have the benefit of words with which to order and communicate their experiences, and so obviously have no way to demonstrate their memories to us, or to themselves, in the ways we are accustomed to having memories demonstrated, but I nevertheless think infants do comprehend such experiences with all of their five senses, and with their emotions.[31] I also think that they are capable of remembering such experiences in their distinctiveness from other experiences and that they probably categorize, cross-categorize, and recategorize these early experiences in light of later ones as well as later ones in light of earlier. In David's case, I suspect that, in addition to the pain (though I have never had one, the pain of a spinal tap is said to be intense), he experienced a profound sense of violation, abandonment, disorientation, and meaninglessness—meaninglessness in the sense that, though he was not too young to suffer or to die, he was too young to grasp the nature of illness or medical treatment and so would not have had what psychiatrist Viktor Frankl (1971, 164), in quoting Nietzsche, has called a "why" to help him bear his infant suffering.

And even if David's illness was not one of the experiences that colored his response to Tarzan's ordeal, it was still an example of one of the countless opportunities children have day in and day out to experience the penetrability of boundaries and the flux that pervade our world, a penetrability and flux that I think we could take up more explicitly in our children's education, especially in its disturbing or negative manifestations. I suppose our inattention to or avoidance of this facet of reality could arise from our own fears of pain, abandonment, and death.[32] And I suppose it could be encouraged inadvertently by our conviction that the first priority of nur-

turing children is to provide a secure base from which they can
grow and explore the world, although I must add, despite my own
commitment to providing secure bases for children, that I suspect
this conviction is at times itself intertwined with our personal fears
of change. On the other hand, I suppose that for some of us our
inattention could have arisen in large part out of habit and the
ignorance that habit can create, in other words, out of being born
into a world in which this particular pattern of oversight has been
operating for so long that any connection between the oversight
and our own fears has been all but destroyed. One consequence is
that the inattention becomes mechanical rather than purposeful.
Those of us who would be all for talking with our children about
these issues if our oversight were brought to our attention keep
silent because the pattern is invisible to us, a fish we have not
discovered, a ghost we have not seen.

Though I have not meant for David's world to appear as one in
which flux and penetrability were consistently negative or positive
but rather as a complex reality in which the two were intricately
interwoven and in which value derives from vantage point, David
was nevertheless, on the evening he avoided taking his bath, clearly
experiencing the prospect of his bath as a threat to his survival. On
that evening, rather than identifying with his great grandmother's
triumph or with Tarzan's or the Hardy boys' escapes, David was in
a position parallel to Mark's as described in Chapter 2 and was
identifying with those creatures in our world who get caught and
eaten—for example, with the two little pigs who were regarded as
succulent by the hungry wolf, with the bones that floated at the
bottom of the pool in *The Masked Monkey*, and with the sailfish his
great grandmother had caught that hung dead by its tail fin from
the scaffolding in the photograph on the last page of his album.
And, though when David was seven it was an event lying still five
years into the future, David was also in a sense identifying with the
child I wrote about in Chapter 1, the girl of four who was "eaten"
by the heat of the kitchen oven in her own "home," an oven, a
niche, into which it appeared she had been placed, and secured, by
her mother's boyfriend. In addition, then, to experiencing what we
commonly refer to as a *childhood* fear and often attribute to an over-
active imagination or to an inability to distinguish reality from fantasy, David was in my opinion also encountering his personal vulnerability to death and attempting to navigate through the world in
light of his encounter.

If my interpretation is accurate, if he was indeed engaged with the question of how to live his vulnerability, then what he needed in the way of guidance was far more than I gave him. First of all, I do think it was right to acknowledge his fear instead of trying to deny it or talk him out of it with such presumptuous and insulting remarks as "You say you're afraid of piranhas? But David, that's the silliest thing I've ever heard. Piranhas live in tropical jungles, not in bathtubs, so you just get that nonsense right out of your head," or, at least as bad, "Afraid of piranhas? But David, you're much too brave to be afraid." Second, I think that in general it was appropriate for me to share—but not to force-feed—my own view of piranhas and to cite the reasons I felt it would be unlikely for them to find their way into his bath. I think it would have been better, however, if I had researched the information about piranhas that I gave him; we might even have researched the subject together. Or I could have helped him get started, and he could have been the one to inform me about whatever information he found. If research had figured in my response, I could have minimized the chance that I was passing along misinformation, and if he had participated in the research, he could have enlarged his sense of his own capacity for gathering and weighing available evidence on subjects important to him. I also think it was a good thing to allow him to back off from tub baths for a while and to let him reclaim his bathtub gradually and according to his own rhythm.

In addition, however, to making an effort to help restore David's confidence in his bath and expand his knowledge of the creature that had so frightened him, I think I should have made an effort to talk with him about the broader, more general issues I have argued were embedded in his very specific fear, particularly the issue of our vulnerability to physical and emotional, or spiritual, assault and death. And here I am not talking about forcing a discussion of these issues on him or about frantically trying to make up all at once for the time in which these issues had not been an integral part of our being together. Nor am I talking about exploiting his fear of piranhas as an opportunity to burden him with all of my own insecurities so that he became my child-hostage, my captive audience. Instead, I am talking about gradually integrating my efforts to make him feel secure and confident enough to explore the world at large with an effort to openly acknowledge and talk about the threats to physical and spiritual well-being that are ever-present in our children's as well as our own lives. In doing so, I do not think I would have been speaking to David about anything he had not in some sense already discovered for himself. But I do think I would have been taking a beginning step towards alleviating any pressure he may have felt at experiencing himself as an isolated knower, that is, as a child who had been born near midnight and who could see ghosts when they wanted to be invisible. I also think I would have been taking a beginning step towards providing the only truly secure base it is possible to offer a child, which is the base of an open and honest acknowledgment of the complex and ambiguous nature of the world, a base from which David could have chosen to live his personal vulnerability in any number of ways, and a base from which I think he would have had the best chance of living it with dignity, courage, and self-understanding.

A girl of eight sits in her backyard, aware that
she is being photographed.

4

But What of Laura?

> I am troubled
> for more than a week now
> On a bare island
> without grass or shelter.
>
> Máiri MacLeod, "A Complaint
> About Exile" (translated from
> Gaelic by Joan Keefe)

Laura has remained a relative stranger thus far. Though her name and her relationship to David and Mark distinguished her from the others who figured to varying degrees in the preceding stories about the two boys, she has been relegated to the fringe or periphery of the action, a child about whom I have communicated only a few details, and then only as the details pertained to the lives of others. I have treated her, in other words, much like a minor or supporting character in a fictional story who has no life outside the boundary of what is written and whose life within the boundary matters only insofar as it touches the lives of the main, or more important, characters.[1] Or, to offer two alternative comparisons, I have given her as little of the spotlight as the girl-child has historically received in real life or as those "model" children of both sexes sometimes receive in our public schools and in our homes.

If we consider the previous three chapters and ask what has been said of Laura, we would discover the following few bits of information: at the picnic in Chapter 1, David mentioned his sister as someone who liked hot dogs on french rolls and thought hamburgers were "sickening," and in my role as narrator, I mentioned, as support for a point about the more central Mark, that Laura had influenced my purchases in the direction of her own tastes while helping me shop for the picnic groceries. In Chapter 2, her role was larger but still a minor or supporting one. She was the four-year-old

105

friend who had started preschool a session or so before three-year-old Mark and had loved her school so much that I had recommended it to Mark's mother. Hoping Laura's friendship with Mark and her familiarity with the school would help him gain a positive first impression, we had arranged for Laura to accompany him on his orientation visit to the school. She also carpooled with Mark when he became an official student and, according to my speculation (and though she was a girl), she may have played the part of one of the three little pigs in Mark's fantasy life.

She was, in Chapter 2, the child who witnessed and was shocked by Mark's refusal to enter the classroom on his first day and whose body served as the screen that protected him from having to participate in circle time until he was ready to join in voluntarily. In Chapter 3, Laura's role was reduced to pretty much its size in Chapter 1. About the only references to her were that she shared a bathroom with David, that she sometimes took part in the experiments in the bathroom-laboratory, and that she frequently got involved with some personal project in the evenings, the one "project" mentioned being to curl up with a Nancy Drew mystery. Laura was also the subject of several endnotes, some of which I wrote in a conscious effort to work against her subordinacy, a subordinacy my chosen focus in the text not only depicted but also, through the depiction, literally prolonged.[2] A text can radiate life, however, because writing it all down can help us see what we might otherwise overlook, and my growing sense has been that if Laura, as daughter, is to receive her due, I must acknowledge the part I have played, as her mother, in prolonging her subordination. And so I here acknowledge it. Having taken this first step, my sense is that I must begin the work of following through, the work of focusing fully on Laura and her world. It is to this work that I now turn.

Despite her peripheral role in previous chapters and unlike the minor or supporting figures in a work of fiction, Laura had a life history marked by a wide range of experiences, including experiences as intensely agitating and generally painful as the experiences of David and Mark already described. Among these experiences (and here I am obviously limited to those I know about), some are recalled by Laura, who is now sixteen, with a vividness and enthusiasm that belie their originally painful nature. In my experience, such enthusiasm often means one of two things. The first is that the rememberer has abstracted a truth from the experience that increases the ability to navigate by increasing understanding and establishing a relationship between rememberer and experience that is akin to that between traveler and landmark. The second is that the rememberer's attention has been captured by the experience but without revealing an abstractable truth; it is as if the experience has said, "Hold on to me. Though I may not make perfect sense to you now, I have captured your imagination and may at some point in the future help you find your way."

One experience of Laura's that illustrates the first category (experiences that reveal abstractable truths) is her memory of Mark's being forcibly carried into the preschool classroom on his first day, a memory I have mentioned previously; the truth Laura abstracted from it was that a place one person approaches with joy, another can approach with dread. Also illustrating this category is Laura's memory, not yet mentioned, of being engulfed, when she was about four, by a wave as she was being introduced to the Pacific Ocean by her father and me, who each held one of her hands while walking with her towards the tide line. The wave had not been big enough to engulf us or her brother, who was riding on his father's shoulders, but only Laura.

Taken by surprise (I doubt she had ever thought that a wave could engulf her, and this was not something that her father and I had thought to mention in our pretrip rhapsodies about the ocean) and too frightened by the strength of the wave to feel anything like wonder or exhilaration, she had been very indignant, at us and at the ocean. And she had become more so when her father and I, thinking it would comfort her and not understanding that she would experience it as a second engulfment, had wrapped my oversized flannel-lined jacket around her soaking body, all the while exchanging tall, adult smiles at her short, child's plight. The truth Laura associates with this experience is that parents can be much less competent and understanding than they are generally made out to be.

To illustrate the second category of experience (those that command attention without revealing an abstractable truth), I would point to Laura's memory of a dream she had when she was four or so and that she will as a rule relate with great precision and animation at a moment's notice. In bed with a bad case of flu and fever, Laura had called out in the night, telling her father, who went to check on her, "I can't sleep, there's a wolf in my ear." As she later told us, and as she would tell us now and again over the years, she had dreamed that she was riding to the mountains in the back seat of a station wagon with some other children. Two women (the driver and a friend) rode in the front seat and everyone was facing forward when for some reason Laura turned and looked into the back of the station wagon, where she discovered a wolf. Laura says that when the wolf knew that she knew it was there, it thrust its head forward and growled ferociously in her ear. However, no one else in the station wagon heard or saw the wolf. When Laura tells her dream, she does so with great care, as if she is sharing something dear, but she has never disengaged herself from the telling and abstracted a truth.

Also among the intense experiences of Laura's childhood are those that I witnessed and remember but that Laura has no more been able to recall than Mark has his introduction to preschool or his fear of the big bad wolf. Laura has no memory, for instance, of how frightened she would become, between three and four, at the sound of air force jets breaking the sound barrier as she played in the backyard of our house or of how she would leave her play and run to her father or me or some other familiar adult when the noise began and hold tight to a hand or leg or waist until the noise subsided and she felt free to return to her play.

A third group of painful experiences that fall somewhere between the vividly remembered and the unrecallable are those that Laura will acknowledge as having occurred when someone else brings them up and that she does herself remember, although disjointedly, but that she talks about with a reserve and an emotional flatness that contrast sharply with her animation when recalling such experiences as Mark's introduction to preschool, her wolf dream, or her engulfment by the wave. My own feeling is that we all have had experiences of this third sort and that we never quite succeed in forgetting them altogether or escaping the hold they have over us so long as we turn away from them. I also think that for us, as well as for Laura, these are often experiences in which we have been accused, often unfairly, of committing the very "sin" we ourselves most dread (the sin that would compromise or negate the identity we believe assures us our place in the world) and that the accusation has come at a moment when we lacked the sophistication to sort out what was happening to us and assert a position. Though several of Laura's experiences mentioned above tempt me as subject matter and would allow me to focus on her every bit as fully as I have focused on David and Mark, it is to an experience Laura does not like to talk about that I want to turn my attention.

So far as I can recall, Laura herself has brought up the experience only twice in her life. Though I think many adults would dismiss it as so much kid's stuff, particularly in comparison to their own grown-up problems, in my opinion it was the single most damaging experience of Laura's school life, one that she described, when I asked permission to write about it, as so thoroughly traumatic that she had "blocked it out." Laura did give me permission, however, and she eventually had more to say about the experience than I originally expected she would have.[3] As Laura's mother and as the person who had chosen to tell her story, I found myself wondering, as she began to open up, if the time had come when she would begin to take a look at this experience from her past, perhaps even find some meaning in it that would enlarge her understanding of herself and of the world. On the other hand, from the time I first thought of telling this particular story, I have been concerned that my telling could turn out to be an error in judgment and that Laura will feel, once the story is told, as if I have invaded her privacy, stolen a bit of her past, and wrapped it awkwardly, as in a jacket that is not hers but mine.

The experience itself, which was spread over about three months, was of Laura's term as student council treasurer of her school, an office she was elected to during the first semester of fourth grade, when she was just turning nine. Because the physical layout of the school, the structure of the student council, and Laura's school identity as she entered fourth grade will all figure in my exploration, I want to begin by describing them. In addition, to avoid possible confusion later, I should point out that I am going to offer more introductory information than I myself had at the time Laura ran for treasurer.

According to Laura's principal, schools can be divided into those whose physical layout gives a good initial feeling to people entering the grounds and those whose layout does not. In our district, he regarded Laura's school as one that gave a good initial feeling. Although the designs of the public elementary schools I have encountered often strike me as revealing the insensitivity of adults to the needs of children, I agreed with the principal to the extent that Laura's school gave a better initial feeling than most other schools I was familiar with.

Set comfortably back from the street on a large parcel in the midst of a suburban neighborhood that had lots of mature shade trees, plenty of shrubs and flowers, and relatively little traffic, especially during school hours, the school spanned kindergarten through sixth grade. There were three permanent buildings—one central building housing the administrative complex, the library, and most of the classrooms, and, at either end of this building, two others. One of these others was set in front and to the west of the main building and housed a cafeteria-multipurpose room, a kitchen, and a small anteroom. The building to the east was set flush with the main building and housed the kindergarten, which had its own enclosed playground. Both of these buildings were connected to the main one (but not to each other) by covered, paved breezeways.

The front door of the main building opened onto a wide entrance hall. Bounding a classroom, the wall to the right was solid, but the one to the left had a door leading into the reception area of the administrative complex, which in turn led through to the teacher's lounge and on into the school library. Included in the administrative complex were the secretary's office (separated from the reception area by a counter), a small supply room, the staff restroom, the nurse's room, and the principal's office, which had a door onto the outside. At the end of and perpendicular to the entrance hall ran a long hallway in both directions. The first- through third- and the fifth- and sixth-grade classrooms (in other words, all but the kindergarten and fourth grades) and the library were all situated along this hallway and had doors opening onto the hall as well as the outside. More often than not, the walls of the hallway were covered with individual student work and group projects—everything from science to English to art—that gave the hall a perennially celebratory air.

Directly behind the main building was a large blacktop divided into the primary-grade playground (grades 1 through 3) and the upper-grade playground (grades 4 through 6), and behind the blacktop was a wooded area that was out of bounds during regular school hours unless the children were accompanied there by an adult for some specific project. West of the main building was a large grassy area where the children were sometimes permitted to eat lunch and play games or simply sit with friends and talk. Also to the west and catty-corner to the upper-grade playground were two temporary classrooms that were entirely separate from the three permanent buildings: that is, these temporary buildings, or "portables," as they were generally called, were not connected to the permanent buildings or to each other even by a breezeway, though I suppose there would have been footpaths worn through the grass.

Installed by the district to ease overcrowding, for several years these portables were used as fourth-grade classrooms, one of which became Laura's.

Although Laura says the children thought of the portables as special and viewed being assigned to class there as a treat, many parents felt that the portables isolated fourth graders from the goings on in the main building and worked against a sense of integration and community. A few parents contended that the teachers assigned to these rooms became professionally "sloppy," the reasoning being not only that the main building promoted interaction that was vitalizing to teachers as well as students but also that the greater visibility of the teachers in the main building encouraged them to keep on their toes. I do not recall any specific opinions the staff may have voiced about the portables, but I would guess that the principal had not been thinking of them as part of the whole that formed the school when he classified it as one that gave a good initial feeling to those entering the grounds. In general I would say that adults involved with the school regarded the portables as an "evil" made necessary by the district budget, an evil they were willing to put up with because it was equitable in that every child became a fourth grader.

My personal view, which evolved through time, was that the portables, despite their ugliness and incongruity, had potential advantages and disadvantages that would vary from teacher to teacher and child to child (for that matter, probably from day to day, hour to hour, and moment to moment).[4] I also thought that for better or worse the portables did limit the interaction between the fourth-grade students and teachers and the students and staff housed in the main building and that given the school's concept of fourth grade, the logic of the decision to house fourth graders there (I do not know how the decision was made) was questionable, although it is also true that whatever grade had been housed there, questions could have been raised.

Fourth grade was conceived of as a pivotal or transitional year in which students moved out of the relatively protected or confined world of the primary grades, where most of every school day was spent with the same teacher in the home classroom, into the more open and less protected world of the upper grades, where children were expected to become increasingly independent of adult support and responsible for themselves, and where any given school day could take a child away from the home classroom and teacher to lessons and activities in other parts of the school.[5] In addition, in fourth grade, children who lived a certain distance from the school and had previously had bus privileges were expected to walk to school or find their own transportation. Fourth graders also began to spend their recesses on the upper-grade half of the blacktop instead of on the primary-grade half, and they began to eat lunch during the second, or upper-grade, lunch period. In other words, fourth graders began to mix, day in and day out, with that group of children—the upper graders or "big kids"—that many fourth graders had previously held in awe.

A shortcoming I saw in housing fourth graders in the portables was that during the very year they should have been shedding some of their awe for the big kids, and also for the teachers of the big kids, the fourth graders were not housed next door to the fifth and sixth graders so that proximity could work to diminish awe but instead were moved out of the main building altogether. Though many fourth graders may have experienced being housed in the portables as a treat and though much good may have come to them as a result, it was not an experiencing with any clear relationship to the expectation the school had of them, which was that they make the transition to the upper grades.

One additional way the school evidenced its concept of fourth grade as a year of increased independence and responsibility was to make it the first year students could run for one of the four schoolwide council offices. Officers were elected twice a year, and the election process, especially in the fall, was fairly elaborate and lengthy, including a formal campaign period of about a week that was marked by the display of posters and campaign buttons and the promotion of slogans. The campaign culminated in a convention in the multipurpose room. Third- through sixth-grade classes presented initiative measures aimed at influencing school policy (the right to eat lunch on the lawn, for example) and listened to the candidates' campaign speeches and watched supporting skits. After the convention (I think it was the next day), the four officers who would lead the student council were elected.

The council, which drew its members from the third through sixth grades, was made up of commissioners selected by teachers to manage various school volunteer programs (for instance, the volunteer tutoring program), senators and representatives elected by a popular vote in each classroom, and the four schoolwide officers (treasurer, secretary, vice president, and president) elected by a popular vote of the third through sixth graders. Only sixth graders could run for president and only fifth graders for vice president, but both sixth and fifth graders could run for secretary and treasurer. Fourth graders, newcomers to the process of running for a schoolwide office, could run only for treasurer. Third graders could not run for any schoolwide office but could vote for these offices and could send a class senator to student council.

A typical outcome of student council elections was that fourth graders running for treasurer usually lost. I suppose this could have been because the presence of fifth and sixth graders in the race meant that the competition was usually too stiff for fourth graders, and, though I do not recall any of the staff saying so, I suppose the competition could have been built into the system intentionally. That way, fourth graders could have gotten some experience campaigning for a schoolwide office while having little chance of actually winning a place on the council that may have been viewed as too demanding for some of them. Such a control would have been in keeping with the philosophy of gradually integrating students into extracurricular activities. And if the staff had wanted to make sure a fourth grader won a schoolwide office, they would only have had to restrict candidates for one of the offices to fourth graders, as they had done with fifth and sixth graders. But even if the typical loss by fourth graders running for treasurer was merely an unintended side effect that everyone had come to accept, the fact remained that over the years only a few fourth graders had won the office and that Laura became one of those few.

Laura emerged from third grade and moved towards fourth grade, and the treasury, having in my opinion been identified by the school as a competent, conscientious, and cooperative student who could work with a minimum of direction from teachers and who did above-average work in all her subjects. In other words, although it is true that she could be aloof or reserved and that, particularly in the early grades of public school, she liked to get her bearings before she would open up to new people and places, she emerged from third grade as what is often referred to as a "self-motivated child," an "independent worker," or a "model student."

An early sign that the school had identified Laura as competent and conscientious was that when she was two weeks or so into first grade, she had been transferred, along with some other students, into a first- and second-grade combination class formed because of fluctuating enrollment, a transfer that the school explained was based on the intellectual and emotional maturity of the students as reflected by standardized test results and teacher evaluations. Other signs were her good citizenship grades and the almost exclusively positive comments Laura's kindergarten and primary-grade teachers made on report cards. Laura's classmates also seemed to have defined her as competent and conscientious and often called her after school to check the details of homework assignments. In addition, her third-grade classmates elected her class senator, and though not everyone will view peer endorsement as carrying much weight, in my experience elementary school children elect officers they perceive as both capable and dependable.

My response to Laura's school identity was to feel pleased as well as concerned. It seemed only fair that her teachers and peers should recognize her competence, conscientiousness, and ability to work independently, traits I myself valued. And it was great to see how good she felt when she was elected third-grade senator. But I also felt that an identity centered around conscientiousness and competence could easily become limiting or constrictive and subtly but acutely stressful. For one thing, my general opinion is that we adults who share the world with a competent and conscientious child can become so dependent on him or her to bear the standard, to be at one and the same time our salvation and our showpiece, that we forget to help the child learn how to relax and simply live, how to gain some respite from the competence and conscientiousness through simply being. For another thing, it seems to me that once we so define a child, we are often intolerant of any efforts the child makes to gain some respite and that we sometimes turn on or abandon the child when performance begins to shift or slip, all the while justifying our abandonment on the grounds that the child has betrayed us or let us, or others, down. In addition, I think such children quickly learn to overmonitor themselves and to fear that any deviation from the "rules" will jeopardize their public standing. I also think such children are perceptive enough to see that others value us, despite a lot of adult verbiage to the contrary, to a great extent for the persons we have become (for our presence), and that to change in certain ways can mean to lose this aspect of the others' interest.

For all of the above reasons, I felt that Laura's school identity entailed a certain risk, a great risk, actually. But because Laura was competent and conscientious, and a girl, I also felt that she would be a prime candidate for the role of mother or teacher's helper (a role she played to some degree in relation to Mark in Chapter 2), and I was concerned that she might, like so many girls before her, let this role stand in the way of making a true effort to become herself. I was afraid, in other words, that the combined force of her school identity and her femaleness might convince her to think of herself as a person who existed solely to help or serve or please others and not as a person who herself deserved and had a right to please herself and to ask for and receive help. Furthermore, I was afraid this self-image might encourage a rhythm or pattern of doing the work of others for her whole life instead of taking the time to discover what her own work was to be. And here I would like to emphasize that I am not assuming that to become oneself means to pursue a self-interested individualism that cares nothing for the needs of the group. Instead, I am assuming that a human being who is not in the process of becoming him- or herself is not in a position to contribute to the well-being of the group—to its immediate physical survival, perhaps, but not to its well-being.

Another way of expressing my concern would be to say that I was afraid Laura's school identity would lead to an emotional and spiritual malnourishment that no one would notice. The more general perception reflected in my concern was that children who are defined as helpers do not always themselves get properly fed. Focusing on the joy that can come from feeding others, we forget to teach these children the potential for such feeding to be emotionally, intellectually, and spiritually draining work. In addition, we fail to make the distinction that the joy of feeding others is not equivalent to and is no substitute for the joy of being fed by another or of learning to feed oneself, but instead is one of the three experiences of nurture, each one valuable in and for itself. And so, given my way of looking at the world, I felt concern for Laura. Even given my concern, however, I did not, when she was a young child, have the know-how to express my concern so that it would be heard (by her or anyone else), nor had I the insight to realize that one of the best ways to teach Laura to relax her competence and conscientiousness would have been for me, and also for her father, to have relaxed ours. In short, I felt concern but did not live it in a way that could have made a difference.

Though Laura has not spoken directly to the question of her school identity, she did make several comments, in my recent conversations with her, that relate to her self-image in the primary grades. Concerning her independent style of working, Laura said,

"I never needed that much help, except for like, maybe a question on an assignment or the normal interaction that you have—I mean, everyone has *some* interaction [with teachers]." Later, specifically in relation to how she would have felt if someone had offered help when she did not need it, she said, "For me, if it was like a math problem and someone was trying to help me, and I didn't need help—I'd be like, 'Could you please leave me alone?'" And concerning her desire for interaction with her teachers and her recognition that such interaction, because she was an independent worker, would not likely arise out of a need for her help, she said:

> Most of my teachers I liked well enough to get the interaction. . . . because I liked my teachers, even though I didn't need the interaction, I got some of it anyway. I would go talk to them, about something, this or that or whatever. . . . they didn't need [to help me with school work] and they knew they didn't need to. So they were able to use that time for people who did need it. And there were people who did need it.

Not necessarily transparent or one-dimensional, Laura's comments raise questions about her experiencing of her independence. Did she prefer to be left alone when she understood a problem because she liked her own company and the experience of coming to terms with a problem on her own? Or was her preference influenced by her sense that when she worked alone she was being a help to her teachers by freeing them to spend more time with needy children? Or was she perhaps influenced by both these considerations? Was her statement "I mean, everyone has *some* interaction" a simple acknowledgment of reality? Or did it contain a note of apology or self-justification that suggested she was being influenced by our culture's conception of independence as the almighty virtue and of dependence as something feminine or weak? Although these questions do not have clear answers, I do think Laura's comments suggest a child who had grasped a central truth about the way a public school classroom works. The truth is that a public school teacher never has enough time to help everyone who needs it, one consequence being that independent workers are a decided advantage—or help—to the teacher because they take up so little of the teacher's time.

My impression of Laura's attitude towards the school's identification of her as competent and conscientious was that she took it very seriously, was proud of it, and worked hard to maintain it but also (and here I am hard pressed to find the right words) that she delighted in it or was "tickled" by it and felt a warm affection and regard for herself as student and, generally speaking, for her teachers as well. Even acknowledging her self-sufficiency, it seemed to me that she experienced her relationship with her teachers as a collaboration of great appeal.

As part of Laura's working hard, however, she exhibited what I felt was a too stringent conscientiousness about classroom rules, rarely allowing herself any latitude or exercising any discretion on her own behalf. She took great care, for example, to observe playground boundaries and stay out of the main hall during recess and lunchtime, she did not ask to get a drink or use the restroom during class time if the teacher's rules were that these needs should be taken care of during recess time, and, when doing written homework, she made every effort to fit her work on the kind of paper the teachers had instructed students to use and did not like to settle for a substitute even if the school had not provided enough paper for an assignment and the stores around our house did not carry the same kind.

Although I think the stringency had its main source in her affection for her teachers and her conviction that the rules had meaning and if followed would as a matter of course lead to a child's fulfilling his or her own promise and becoming someone, it was my impression that the stringency also gradually took root in a worry about making mistakes and jeopardizing the good opinion others had of her and that she had of herself. Even considering, however, that Laura took great care, as she emerged from third grade, to follow the rules and avoid mistakes, I do not think that at eight and a half years old she had the least understanding, in any reflective sense, of the intricacy with which our sense of self-worth and loveableness can become interwoven with our sense of success or failure in the public eye or of the anxiety that can result when anything remotely interpretable as failure is experienced by someone in which the two have become intimately entwined.

The day Laura burst in the front door after school and announced that she was going to run for treasurer, she had that animated quality I associated with a deep, spontaneous, and confident sense of involvement. All in a rush she announced that she was going to run, that her good grades and her third-grade experience with student council were important, and that she was going to have to get busy and write a speech, make posters, and organize a skit. She said that some classmates had agreed to help her, and she added that even though fourth graders could run for treasurer, they almost never won, but that she didn't care about that.

Mainly, I was surprised by her announcement. Even though I had worked as a volunteer at the school since Laura entered kindergarten, I hadn't taken any particular notice of the structure or workings of student council and knew little about the upper-grade teachers who acted as advisors. It simply had not occurred to me that becoming a fourth grader meant that Laura would have an opportunity to run for a schoolwide office or that her third-grade experience as senator and her good grades might make the opportunity seem like the natural choice for her. Until it dawned on me that running for treasurer was not classed with going on a school field trip or signing up for, say, the school band program, I kept trying to figure out how Laura could be running for treasurer when she had never brought home a permission slip or a sign-up form.

As well as feeling surprised, I felt a lot of reserve about Laura's announcement. Although at the time I couldn't have said why, I did not think she would like being treasurer and thought that a semester would be a long time to be committed to an extracurricular activity she didn't like. It also seemed to me that because she was a child who took a little time to orient herself to change, she would have plenty to do making the transition to fourth grade and the portables, getting accustomed to a teacher whose style of teaching was reputed among parents to be much less structured than the style of the teachers she'd had before, participating in a gifted program she'd begun in first grade, and integrating into her schedule the clarinet lessons and school band practice she had signed up for and that would, like the gifted program, take her out of the home classroom.[6] If she wanted to run for treasurer, I thought the spring semester would be a better choice.

In addition to thoughts supporting my reserve, however, I also had thoughts that challenged it. Chief among them was my concern that to question her decision would be to interfere in Laura's school life and possibly undermine her efforts to explore the world independently, a concern that was very much on my mind at the time because of an exchange I had witnessed between a parent and Laura's fourth-grade teacher at Back-to-School Night. The parent, a mother I knew casually, had begun the exchange by observing to the fourth-grade teacher that a lot of parents, herself included, had disapproved of the large quantity of difficult homework their children had been assigned by a third-grade teacher and of the way the teacher had accepted work from some students that had obviously been done by their parents. The mother then asked the fourth-grade teacher about her own homework policy and her opinion of parents doing their children's homework for them.

As the mother spoke, several parents around her began to nod their heads in agreement, and one or two made disparaging asides about the third-grade teacher. It seemed to me that the mother felt animosity towards the third-grade teacher, that the mother had no doubt that her assessment of the teacher was accurate and that parents had indeed been doing their children's work for them, and that the mother had a core of support among some of the parents whose children had had the third-grade teacher under discussion. In addition to conveying disapproval of the third-grade teacher's methods, the mother's comments also seemed to patronize the fourth-grade teacher; that is, the mother seemed to be letting the fourth-grade teacher know, without directly saying so, that if she were to win approval and support from parents, she had better not follow in the footsteps of her colleague.

The fourth-grade teacher answered that she did not believe in a lot of homework, that she felt it was best when children completed their work at school and homework was kept to a minimum, and that she thought it was a mistake for parents to have too much to do with their children's schoolwork. She also assured parents that she had been teaching a long time and that she knew the difference between student work and adult work and would not easily be fooled by the latter. Included in her comments was a general statement about what it meant to be in fourth grade. The point she stressed was that fourth grade was not a primary grade but an upper grade and that she would be expecting upper-grade behavior from the class, which meant, among other things, that they would be expected to do their work themselves.

For a moment after the exchange, an atmosphere of victory seemed to prevail among the mother and her supporters. At the time, my main or foreground response was to feel distaste for the exchange, indignation at the mother and her supporters for their criticism of the third-grade teacher, and embarrassment for the fourth-grade teacher at having behaved so deferentially towards the parents. On the other hand, my minor or background response had been to try to take in the teacher's comments about the meaning of fourth grade and to wonder if Laura's father and I were overly involved in her school life

I later told myself that the kind of exchange I had witnessed felt a lot different to the participants than to the observers and that, based on my acquaintance with the mother, the after-school pressure from homework would have had to be great before she would have protested. I also decided that though I would probably have found the exchange distasteful in most circumstances, I had been particularly upset because the third-grade teacher had been Laura's teacher, and I thought she had done a great job. I had been impressed not only with the quality of her teaching and her assignments but also with the amount of time she spent interacting with each child's work. In addition, I had liked her way of encouraging parents to give their children lots of support with assignments, and, in general, I had felt good about the help with homework my husband and I had offered Laura. Although we had not done Laura's work for her, we had approached some of the larger assignments as opportunities to give her the one-on-one attention in relation to research, writing, and drawing skills that it would have been impossible for a public school teacher with a class size of thirty or more students to give. My general philosophy was that though children sometimes need to work all on their own and get a feel for what they themselves can accomplish at some given point in time, they also benefit from moving hand in hand through a complex assignment with an adult who knows some of the subtleties of the route.

It was also true, however, that when it came to practicing this hand-in-hand philosophy, Laura's father and I could become quite intense and also tended to set very exacting standards, and so, in focusing further on the comments Laura's fourth-grade teacher made at Back-to-School Night, I began to think it might be a good year to step back and allow Laura more room to work on her own. In discussing Back-to-School Night at home, Laura's father and I decided that stepping back would be a good idea, and we also talked with Laura about her teacher's emphasis on parents placing themselves in the background so that students would have a chance to become more independent and responsible and about the possibility that in the past our help with homework had at times been stifling. Consequently, the day Laura burst in the front door and announced she was going to run for school treasurer, I recalled the decision to give Laura more space and worried that to voice my reserve or intervene would contradict my decision.

To gain some thinking time, I simply acknowledged Laura's enthusiasm and said that I didn't know much about the workings of student council and the election but would like to hear all about it. It was from Laura's talk that I gained some of the information I included in my earlier description of her school's student council program. After listening to what she had to say and talking briefly with her father, I decided it would be overprotective to intervene. And though I feel I would have made the same decision even if fourth graders had had a history of winning, I think their history of losing made my decision easier: that is, I think that I did not sort out my thoughts as carefully as I might have if Laura's chance of winning had been greater. Instead, I told myself that the typical workings of the system would pretty certainly protect her, that it would be silly to get all excited about an eventuality that had little chance of coming to pass and that might turn out to be a valuable experience for her even if it did come to pass.

During the campaign, Laura's father and I offered her all the support Laura judged allowable within the campaign guidelines, and her brother also helped her out, especially at school. We brainstormed campaign slogans and talked about the design of posters and buttons with her. We also played audience so that she could practice her campaign speech, which her classroom teacher helped her edit. One comment Laura made about campaign speeches, a comment someone at school had made and that she repeated at home, was that such speeches were comparable to promises that candidates make to voters. In her speech, Laura stressed her qualifications (her tenure as third-grade senator and her good grades, particularly in math). Although there is no copy of Laura's speech among her school papers, my recollection is that she saw her past achievements at school as having prepared her to take on just such a job as the treasurer's, and my recollection of the campaign is that she thoroughly enjoyed it, despite some anxious moments (giving her speech at convention, for example), and that it had met and probably surpassed her expectations.

On election day, David got home first (his dismissal time was earlier), and he announced excitedly that Laura had won. Then he said that maybe he should have waited to let Laura tell the news, and we decided that when she got home we would give her a chance to announce her win. When Laura did come home she entered quietly, didn't say anything about the election for a while, and then announced, quietly, that she had won. Listening to her, I couldn't tell whether she was containing a wild glee at her triumph—perhaps in keeping with her image of the proper demeanor of a newly elected officer—whether she had been surprised and a little subdued by her win, or whether she was simply tired out by the campaign and had had a full dose of noisy congratulations at school.

Instead of speaking openly about my confusion, which I have since learned is a very good thing to do, I followed her lead, congratulating her on her victory without any shouting or jumping up and down. So far as I could tell, she found the congratulations satisfactory, and when her father came home from work, the same calm prevailed. As I would discover much later, however, Laura had been disappointed by our calm response. In one of the only two voluntary comments I can recall her ever making about her experience as treasurer, she told me—it was one day when we happened to become intimately involved in a chat about all manner of odds and ends from the past—that she had been really shocked, and subdued, by the low-key response to her win. She explained that on election day she had assumed David would tell me she had won and that when she arrived home, we would immediately sweep her up in our wildly enthusiastic congratulations.

Although I have no way of knowing what impact, if any, her disappointment may have had on the distress she eventually experienced as treasurer, I mention it for two reasons. As one of the only two spontaneous comments she has ever made about her experience as treasurer, it hardly seems something I could ignore, even if its place in the story were not clear to me. And I have also included it because I think the discrepancy she experienced between her expectation and our actual response to her win may have been one of several discrepancies she experienced that fall semester of fourth grade. Taken together, I think the discrepancies eroded her confidence in her ability to understand reality, that is, in her sense of the present as a time and place in which the people around her could be depended on to realize the expectations raised by past behavior. I further think this erosion discouraged her from asking for help when she did begin to experience difficulty with the treasurer's job.

In the weeks following the election Laura did not volunteer information about her work on the council, but I did not interpret this as a sign of distress or even separate it out and consider specifically her lack of talkativeness on this one subject. For one thing, though practically from the beginning I have let readers in on the "secret" that the treasurer's job distressed Laura, I myself was not, from the beginning, in on the secret but had to discover it from the jumble of daily life. For another thing, Laura, from time to time, did refer to her student council duties, perhaps mentioning that she needed to remember to write a note to the principal so he wouldn't forget to buy juice bars for the Popsicle sales the council sponsored on Fridays during the school's two lunch hours. On Friday mornings she might also ask her brother if he had remembered his Popsicle money and if he had reminded his friends to bring theirs. And she might call a friend or two of her own to remind them that it was Popsicle day. In addition, Laura had plenty to say about a variety of other school-related subjects—for instance, she talked about not liking her clarinet lessons, about her teacher's forgetting to finish teaching the class the words to a new song, about a new friend at school who didn't speak English, about a dog that frightened her on the way home from school, and so on—so that it was not as if, following election day, she had fallen into a long and awkward silence about the job of treasurer in particular or about school in general. Instead, it seemed to me that the beginning of the fall semester, with its emphasis on introduction and transition, had become the middle, with its emphasis on settling into a rhythm that would support a gradual realization of all that had been initiated during the vigorous carving out of the early weeks. However, that something connected with school was troubling Laura and that she was making no progress contending with it on her own did, in time, become clear.

The first unmistakable evidence that Laura needed help was that she began to have trouble falling asleep at night, which was rare for her. When the difficulty became too pronounced to be explained by some temporary influence such as the approach of a holiday or a wild game or provocative story or conversation before bed, I noticed that her restlessness was restricted to school nights. I also noticed, as the restlessness increased, that she became even more tense at the suggestion that something could be bothering her. Even though she was usually the one to call me into her room, announce that she *could not* get to sleep, and say yes when I asked her if she wanted me to stay and talk with her for a few minutes, she wanted my company only as long as I did not touch on the subject of what might be bothering her. Once I did that, and even though she and her brother often took advantage of such bedside chats to air a worry or confusion, she would dismiss me with an "I'm going to go to sleep now," or an "I'm all right—you can leave now." And so I would leave. But she would not be all right. As often as not, later the same night, perhaps while I was reading on the couch or after her father and I had gone to bed and turned out the light, she would call out from her room, "Mother, are you still awake? Dad?" And when one of us would answer, "Yes, do you need something?" she would say, "No, I just wondered if you were still awake. Goodnight." And then we would say, "Goodnight, Laura," and that would be the end of it, until the next time.

After noticing that her restlessness was limited to school nights, I began to attend more closely to her behavior before and after school, and it was the after-school behavior that seemed to have shifted from what I thought of as typical or normal for her. Although her after-school activities remained generally the same, it seemed to me that her arrival home was more high-spirited than usual and that she did her homework, had her snack, played with her brother and friends, read her books, ate her dinner, took her bath, and talked to the people around her with a nonstop quality that was unusually intense. One activity she was particularly intent on was a small neighborhood club she and her brother had formed with a few friends. Instead of the fairly informal clubs that they had organized from time to time in the past, this club, with much supervision from Laura, spent lots of time scheduling meetings, trying to decide what officers to have, and discussing who would fill each job; in the end, Laura chose to be secretary and kept careful minutes of each meeting on three-ring binder paper. Considering that she was treasurer at school, I thought her choice was interesting but did not think about it beyond that. In trying to sort out what might be going on, it occurred to me that her after-school activities could always have been intense and that I simply had never looked closely enough to see it before. At the opposite extreme, I thought that in my eagerness to get to the bottom of her trouble, I was projecting an intensity that wasn't there. Even acknowledging this, however, my opinion was, and still is, that her spirits were unusually high on arriving home, that this was due to relief at leaving school behind, and that she was distancing herself from worry with wall-to-wall activity until bedtime, when she would be flooded by all that she had spent the afternoon trying to ward off.

Laura's before-school behavior seemed usual until the morning she told me in a very roundabout way that she felt sick and didn't want to go to school. Because she had never, since preschool, been one to avoid school, I did not immediately connect her illness to whatever was troubling her. Instead, I assumed she was "really" sick, told her to try to get back to sleep, and that I would check on her in a little while.

I had not checked back on her when the phone rang. The caller, who sounded about Laura's age, asked to speak to Laura, which surprised me because school had already begun. Though it would not have been unusual for a friend of Laura's to call before school to arrange to walk together or play after school, a call after school had started was very unusual. Explaining that Laura was sick, I offered to take a message. I don't remember the caller's phrasing, but she made clear that she would rather speak to Laura herself. This also struck me as unusual because I had rarely encountered a child who would repeat a request to speak to Laura (or David) after I—the adult—had offered to take a message, particularly if illness were the reason for not calling her to the phone. When I said I thought Laura was asleep, again offered to take a message, and added that I would try to lend her a hand if there were some problem (the only explanation I had been able to come up with for the call and apparent urgency to speak to Laura was that the caller was a neighborhood child who was getting a late start for school and hoped Laura was also late and would walk with her), the caller identified herself and stated her reason for calling.

It seemed she was on student council with Laura and that Mrs. Matthews, her classroom teacher, who was also one of the student-council advisors, had asked her to call because a council meeting was scheduled and they needed some information (as I recall, it was Laura's weekly treasurer's report or her account book) but couldn't find the information at school. It dawned on me at this point that Laura's illness could be related to her restless bedtimes and her intense after-school play and that all three could have a common source in the treasurer's job. I began to have all kinds of conflicting thoughts and emotions that I knew I would have to sort through later. My immediate impulse was to tell the caller that she would have to wait until Laura felt better to speak to her, and then to call the school back myself and leave a message for Mrs. Matthews to call me. What I did, however, was to ask the caller to hold while I checked to see if Laura was asleep.

Laura, who was in bed but awake, looked startled and, I thought, appalled, when I explained about the phone call (the way I imagine we all have the capacity to look when some dread enormity catches us in a place we had assumed was safe), and I must admit that I felt a rush of squeamishness at having abetted the enormity and also at having witnessed Laura's agitation. When I asked her if she had a message for the caller or if she wanted to call her back later or wait until she returned to school, she said no, that she would talk to the student then. She was on the phone only a minute or so, and I made a point not to listen.

Afterwards, in what I intended to be a friendly and interested tone, I asked Laura about the phone call—whether or not the confusion over the desired information had been cleared up and if everything was okay or if she would like a hand with something. She said everything was okay and that she didn't need any help, but she seemed so uncomfortable at my inquiry that I was left feeling concerned. I told her that I didn't know much about the workings of student council and that I supposed having the missing information could have been important but that even so I had been a little surprised by the phone call and had found it, on the surface, a little pushy or presumptuous. Although this was indeed how I felt, I also wanted to ease her apparent sense of being the plagued or guilty party and thought it might help if she could see that the school— despite the great authority it exercised over children—was not infallible or beyond criticism. Laura responded curtly, defending the caller as a really nice person who was only following directions. I said I hadn't meant to imply that the caller was necessarily pushy or presumptuous herself and that it was what appeared to be a policy of calling student council officers when they were at home sick that had struck me as invasive. I added that I thought calling a student at home, especially on the first morning of her absence and especially when she had such a good attendance record as Laura's, suggested a sense of urgency about the business of student council in relation to the other demands of life that I did not think was necessarily called for. And at some point I also said that even though I knew little about student council and so could easily have it all wrong, I would have thought that any information she might have was a fairly routine matter—unless, of course, it held some eagerly awaited news or some facts and figures necessary for other business to proceed—and that it could have waited until she felt better. Laura said I did not understand how things were at school. I said she was probably right, but that I would like to understand and that when she was feeling better I would like to get together and have her fill me in on how the council worked. Then she went back to bed, and I picked up wherever it was I had left off before the phone call.

As already mentioned, it had dawned on me during my conversation with the caller that Laura's illness and restlessness were tied in with the treasury. I also said that during the conversation I had experienced a lot of conflicting thoughts and emotions. Primary among the emotions had been a surge of anger at Mrs. Matthews, the teacher-advisor who had directed Laura's fellow student to call, and a surge of protectiveness towards Laura. Almost at the same time, I had realized that my anger and protectiveness were not free-floating but were grounded in an elaborate script or hypothesis about Laura's performance as treasurer and about Mrs. Matthews' perspective on it, both of which I had generated even as the caller and I talked.

My hypothesis was that Mrs. Matthews viewed Laura's perfor-mance as inadequate and felt that the inadequacy reflected a lack of responsibility that it was her duty, as teacher-advisor, to correct. The way I saw it, the confusion over the whereabouts of the missing information could have meant that a rule or guideline existed as to where the information was to be kept (perhaps in a particular place at school so that it would be accessible even when an officer was absent) and that Laura had not left the information in the proper place. In addition, I speculated that this failure to make the informa-tion available was not an isolated incident (if it had been, I doubted it would have prompted the phone call) but one among a number, or growing number, of "small" oversights that Mrs. Matthews took, when adding them up, to be evidence of a general carelessness or lack of conscientiousness. The confusion over the whereabouts of the information could have meant, it seemed to me, that Laura had fallen behind in her record keeping or that she was keeping the records chaotically. Although such behavior would not have been at all typical of Laura, it nonetheless seemed to me the kind of behavior that would best explain the phone call. On the basis of this projection, I further projected that Mrs. Matthews viewed Laura's absence from school as "suspicious"—as one that was not due to illness at all but to Laura's reluctance to show up at the student council meeting without her "homework" in good order and have to live, in public, before her teacher-advisors and her peers, the evidence of her own irresponsibility.

Because on the one hand I could accept that Laura might be having difficulties with the treasurer's job and that her illness could be connected to the difficulties but, on the other hand, could not accept that irresponsibility was the explanation for the illness or for her possibly substandard performance, I felt angry at Mrs. Matthews, protective of Laura, and resentful of the phone call.[7] In fact, as I said above, I had found the phone call a little pushy or presumptuous.

More specifically, my gut-level reaction to the call was to view it as the high-handed maneuvering of a too zealous teacher-advisor, one who had a passion for molding children into model citizens and who took for granted that the worthiness of the goal brought with it the right to occasionally behave imperiously. I also thought that the aim of the phone call had been to let Laura know that if she thought she had "pulled a fast one" by staying home, she was wrong and that, instead of succeeding, her ploy had been perceived as on a par with "having one's hand caught in the cookie jar": that is, her ploy had been regarded as a dishonest act of feigning illness and as the very sort of behavior Mrs. Matthews had needed to confirm her suspicion, which was that Laura was an irresponsible treasurer, one who shirked her duties and then hid from the shirking. Though my response was very negative as well as highly speculative, and may seem strikingly excessive to readers (especially since at the time I was not personally acquainted with Mrs. Matthews and had only the barest knowledge of Laura's responsibilities as treasurer), my response did, if nothing else, suggest how deep a distrust I—as parent or mother—was capable of feeling towards my daughter's school—as represented by Mrs. Matthews—and towards the ability of the school and its staff—particularly its teachers—to understand Laura sufficiently well on its own to do her justice.[8]

Although my gut-level response to the phone call was as described above, in the aftermath of the call I questioned my response, wondering if it might not be the overreaction of a mother trying to find a reason for her daughter's bedtime anxiety. In the context of this questioning, it seemed to me that Laura's illness the same day as the council meeting could have been coincidental and that the phone call could have been a spontaneous one, free of innuendo or strategizing, aimed at solving an unexpected hitch in a busy school day. For example, I told myself, the call could have been placed following a conversation in which Laura's fellow officer had noticed Laura's absence and, realizing that the treasurer's information would be needed at that day's meeting, mentioned the absence to Mrs. Matthews. Mrs. Matthews could have suggested, perhaps while she was busily collecting homework or handing back papers or taking roll, that the student make a quick trip to the office and call Laura at home on the chance that the needed information was at school and so would be available even though Laura was home sick. As for my irritation at the phone call, that could have been caused, I speculated, by my own overdeveloped sense of a right to privacy, which may have been so very different from Mrs. Matthews' own attitude that she would not have considered a similar call to her own home the least bit pushy or presumptuous. And even though this alternative interpretation of the phone call did not account for Laura's apparent stress when I first told her about the call, it did fit in with her assurance, after taking the call, that everything was all right. The alternative interpretation could also have explained why Laura snapped at me when I said the call had surprised me and seemed pushy.

Laura's illness did not progress and she went back to school the next day, a development that increased my sense of a link between her anxiety and the treasury. Within a short time—it could have been only a few days or as much as a week or so—Laura woke up feeling ill and wanting to stay home again. Exactly how many more times this happened, whether there were any more phone calls from school or just the one, and whether I made Laura go to school or perhaps let her stay home one or two of the days and then made her go the others, I'm not sure. I don't think, however, that it could have been more than three or four times more, at most, that she woke up wanting to stay home.

Between the day of the phone call and her second round of wanting to stay home, I asked her to tell me about student council, particularly the treasurer's role, and, when the second round began, I brought the subject up again. The first talk was not at all satisfactory. Instead of becoming involved with the topic so that a conversation developed, Laura merely responded in a flat tone to my few questions. Conspicuously absent from her responses was anything the least bit concrete or anecdotal. When I asked her if she liked being treasurer, she said she didn't. When I asked what she did not like about it, she did not have anything to say. And when I asked her if being treasurer was hard or easy, she said it was hard. In response to my asking if there was any way her father or I could help, perhaps by having her tell us about the hardest parts of the job so we could try to think of ways to make them easier, she said there wasn't, and at some point she also made clear that parents did not do student council work. All the while we were together, which was a very short time, she maintained a wooden exterior and seemed to wish more than anything that she were elsewhere. Because my questions seemed to increase Laura's reserve and because I felt she tolerated them only because of her subordinate position as child, I did not press her for more specific answers but let the subject drop.

Our second talk did not bring me any closer to discovering the source of her troubles, but it was a breakthrough in that I told her directly that she seemed very unhappy to me, that I was concerned about her and thought her student council work was unnecessarily stressful, and that I wanted to have a talk with one or both of the teacher-advisors but that I wanted her to know I was going to call the school before I did so. I said that I hadn't forgotten what she'd said about parents not doing student council work but that her father and I simply could not accept that anyone needed to go through what she appeared to be going through. I added that our experience with the school suggested that once her teacher-advisors knew what a rough time she was having, they would agree that some action needed to be taken. I explained that my plan was to call the school and leave a message for one of the advisors to call me, and then, if talking over the phone was not enough, I would make an appointment to have a conference at the school. When I asked Laura for her opinion of my plan, specifically whether she thought it was worth a try or if she would rather I forget the whole thing, she said she thought it was worth a try. My impression was that though the thought of a conference filled her with apprehension, she was also unutterably relieved to have had someone speak to the frightened child behind the emotionless, robotlike mask.

The secretary at Laura's school took my call, and Mrs. Matthews called me back the same day. I told her I was concerned about the difficulty Laura seemed to be having with the treasury, and I summarized her home behavior, adding that I would like to get a concrete description of Laura's duties in the hope that it could help uncover the source of Laura's trouble. Mrs. Matthews acknowledged my concern and then spoke forcefully (she was an ardent speaker, clearly involved with her teaching and concerned about children and their education) about Laura's performance. She said the performance had been problematic practically from the start, that Laura was behaving irresponsibly, and that nothing she or the other advisor had done seemed to make a difference. I said I felt Laura's problems could be connected to some confusion or misunderstanding about the job. Because Mrs. Matthews had never had Laura as her classroom student and I didn't know if she had spoken with any of the teachers who had, I added that in past school years Laura's performance had been characteristically responsible and that in my opinion she had a tendency to be too conscientious rather than not conscientious enough. I also said that Laura had no history of insomnia or school avoidance and that the sudden appearance of these suggested to me that even if she were behaving "irresponsibly," I doubted that irresponsibility could be the whole story.

It became increasingly clear, as we talked, that the behavior I was seeing at home and the behavior Mrs. Matthews was seeing at school had led us to entertain very different theories about Laura, and so we arranged for a conference. Mrs. Matthews' closing remark was to remind me to bring Laura to the conference—she had mentioned, earlier in our conversation, that she believed strongly that students should be included in parent-teacher conferences. In closing, she also made a comment that she had not made before, which was that the conference would give us an opportunity to question Laura and that, on the basis of her answers, we would—between us—be able to tell whether or not she was being irresponsible. My closing remark was one of confirmation or assent, something like "Yes, okay, see you in the library tomorrow at four." I remember this closing particularly well not only because of Mrs. Matthews' tone, which had had that "wrap-up" quality we tend to use when a plan of action has been agreed upon, but also because I had no sooner hung up the phone than I realized, on the basis of Mrs. Matthews' closing remark, that for all intents and purposes I had agreed to a grilling of my daughter.

To tell myself, as I eventually did, that in the final moment of the conversation I had stopped listening for information that might bear on Laura's difficulty and had turned my attention to the formality of concluding the conversation with a polite confirmation of the arrangements we had made did help me understand that my assent had been to the time and place of the conference and not to its structure as an examination. And this understanding of the way my culture's customs could structure my attention did quiet the anger I had been feeling at myself for having been so "stupid" as to assent. But it did not change the fact that Mrs. Matthews was expecting me to bring Laura to the school library for a conference in which mother and teacher-advisor were to be the questioners and Laura the suspect. Nor did it change my sense that Mrs. Matthews' closing reference to Laura and to the questioning had been made in the apparent confidence that the function of the conference—to question Laura—had been implicit in the very agreement to have the conference in the first place. Obviously, given the pending conference, I was going to have to sort out where I stood in relation to Mrs. Matthews' expectation.

Although at the time I did not know Michel Foucault's work on
the phenomenon of examination, if I had, I hope that in my effort to
gain my bearings I would have recalled his comment that "the
examination combines the techniques of an observing hierarchy,
and those of a normalizing gaze. It is a normalizing gaze, a surveillance that makes it possible to qualify, to classify, and to punish"
(1977, 184). And if I had been familiar with his comment, I hope I
would have personalized its generality and abstractness by envisioning myself and Mrs. Matthews meeting in the school library,
where the suspect would be brought, by her mother, so that the
observing hierarchy of mother and teacher could elicit behavior
through questions, survey the elicited behavior, and pass judgment.[9]

My reasons for such a hope are two. First, I think it is necessary
that we try to see the ways in which we ourselves, as specific human
beings in specific contexts, are implicated in such observations as
Foucault's. Second, in my experience, it is when we personalize the
abstract and general through such envisionings that we make additional discoveries ("additional" in the sense that they are added to
the initial discovery that we ourselves are implicated in the abstract,
generalized theories we encounter), discoveries about aspects of
reality that are all around us but that we can easily miss when we
think mostly in the third person and mostly in general and abstract
terms, and also discoveries that can help us gain our bearings. For
example, in the present case, I can think of two discoveries I made
through a concrete envisioning of the examination in the library but
that I doubt I would have made if I had let Foucault's comments
(when I did read them) remain impersonal. One discovery involves
Mrs. Matthews' comment that by questioning Laura we would be
able to tell whether or not she was being irresponsible. The problem
with the comment (a problem invisible to me until I actually pictured
the examination in the library) was that it assumed that Laura's
answers would be transparent: that is, the comment did not allow
for the possibility that Laura's answers might prove inconclusive.
As for why an adult might make such an assumption, I would
guess, on the one hand, that it could be because as adults we tend
to take for granted that we are experts who by definition do not
obscure the truth but who discern it. On the other hand, I would
guess that it could be because the norms we have been taught to
use to help us "see" often have a structure that discourages the
perception of ambiguity or complexity or multiple possibilities and
encourages the perception of simplicity, clarity, or the single or "one
true" reality.[10]

The second insight is that though a time and place had been set for a semipublic examination of Laura's performance as treasurer, no time and place had been set for a similarly public examination of Mrs. Matthews' and my performances as guides or nurturers of Laura. Considering the question of why only the one examination had been arranged, I would guess that the scheduling, like the assumption that Laura's answers would be transparent, was connected to our culture's concept of adulthood. In this instance, I mean to our conception of it as a plateau that we reach, one that brings with it the privilege of administering examinations to those in our control (that is, to those who are in some respect defined as our inferiors) rather than the responsibility of being examined on their behalf.[11] I would also guess that no examination had been arranged for Mrs. Matthews and me because, as an elementary school teacher and a mother, we had already been held responsible—blamed—for so much for so long, or, to put it another way, we had so consistently been subject to the normalizing gaze of those "higher" in the hierarchy (school principals, school district superintendents, secretaries of education, doctorates in psychology, sociology, education, and human development, and so on—in other words, to the normalizing gaze of "wise 'men'") that we had learned to survive, though it might sicken our spirits, by making their gaze our gaze and turning it on the children in our care.

Not having read Foucault did not render me helpless, however, and I think this was because I had something else to call to mind, something that Mrs. Matthews did not have and something that gave me a definite advantage as well as a definite responsibility. This something was the personal experience of having witnessed Laura's response to the few questions I had already asked her at home. The image of her wooden "cooperation," of her presence before me as a child who wanted to escape me and my questions but who held still nonetheless, perhaps out of an habituated deference to my authority as an adult and as her mother, was one facet of the experience. The other was my projection, on the basis of my own memories of childhood and the memories of friends, acquaintances, and writers, of the anguish a child can be living beneath the woodenness. Taken together, these two facets created one image powerful enough to make me stop and consider what I was about. If Laura had responded with so little show of trust and so great a show of passive resistance to an "examination" conducted by her mother in her own home, the aim of which had not been to accuse her of anything but to try to understand the workings of the treasury in enough detail to identify areas that might be confounding Laura's intellectual understanding or her emotional way of being, then how was she likely to respond to an examination to be conducted in a place as public as the school library by her mother and her teacher-advisor, the aim of which was to judge her innocent or guilty of the accusation of irresponsibility?

Though the above question may sound rhetorical, the word *likely*, one of many qualifiers I have used and that I know are not popular among those who associate them with a weak and irresolute mind, is meant to undercut the rhetorical flavor of the question and emphasize my awareness that I could not with certainty predict Laura's response. In fact, I did consider that the conference could conceivably benefit her, particularly if, once the three of us sat down together, the chemistry of the situation turned out to be such that we all set aside the expectations and the scripts we had brought with us, perhaps after acknowledging their existence and contents to each other, and "wrote," or perhaps it would be better to say *lived*, the conference then and there, with the kind of openness and sense of connectedness that would have demonstrated to Laura and to Mrs. Matthews and me that home and school could come together not as conspirators against children or as adversaries fighting over children but as mutual nurturers of children, children who, through the example of the conference, might learn something about nurturing others as well as themselves.

It seemed to me, however, that such a transformation of original intent was a remote possibility in the present case and that an adversarial or, particularly, a conspiratorial conference would have done further damage. And so I decided I would talk to Laura about the phone conversation—tell her that a conference had been scheduled, that Mrs. Matthews wanted her to attend, and that I had agreed to bring her but that after hanging up I had realized that she should have been consulted about participating. If Laura chose to attend, I could call Mrs. Matthews back and explain my objection to a questioning of Laura. If Laura chose not to participate, I could explain her absence when I met Mrs. Matthews for the conference.

Though at the time I was satisfied with my decision and still accept it as pretty much the most I could realistically have expected from myself at that point in my life, I was struck, during the writing of Laura's story, by a thought that did not occur to me when she was treasurer and that, though it will probably seem a rather fine distinction, I want to explore before moving on to describe the con-

ference itself and its aftermath.[12] The thought was that if I had taken
Laura in for the conference as agreed on in the phone conversation,
Laura would have been subjected not only to an examination but
also to one she had not known was going to take place.[13] This realization is not the same as the one I made immediately after talking
with Mrs. Matthews on the phone. The distinction is that my first
realization enlightened me as to the nature of the agreed-upon conference (it was to be an examination), whereas my more recent
realization brought home to me the fact that if the conference had
gone ahead as planned, *Laura* would pretty certainly have arrived
at the conference ignorant of its nature. In other words, while writing,
I realized that just because I had talked with Mrs. Matthews and so
knew the form of the conference, it did not follow that Laura knew.
    Given the agreement made on the phone, I do not think, fur-
thermore, that there is much basis for assuming that a teacher and a
mother, on making such an agreement, would realize that Laura, as
child, was ignorant of the structure of the conference. Nor do I
think that I had much reason to assume, if it had somehow occurred
to a teacher and me, that we would have told Laura the structure or
even that we would have wanted her to know. In addition, I do not
think it likely that a teacher, having arranged a conference such as
Laura's, would automatically assume that the mother would naturally tell the child what the structure of the conference was to be.
An alternative at least as likely is that questions such as Laura's
knowing or not knowing would not have been raised by the teacher
or by me, not even to ourselves. Not having raised them, we would
not have been in a position to raise the additional questions that
would have emerged as a result of asking these basic ones. The
questions I have in mind are (1) why we would or would not have
wanted Laura to know the structure of the conference; (2) what our
wanting or not wanting would have said about our conception of
the child, the adult, and education; (3) how we would have communicated the nature of the conference to her if we had wanted her to
know; and (4) how Laura's knowing or not knowing would have
influenced, from our point of view, the structuring, content, and
tone of the conference.
    A second alternative I think we must consider is that Laura's
not knowing could have been lived by either the teacher or me, or
by both of us, as so implicit to the strategy of examination that the
choice of strategy itself was equivalent to our having taken for
granted that Laura was not to know. If I assume for the moment

that this second alternative accurately describes the position of teacher and mother in such a situation, there are two answers I think the teacher and I would likely have given to the question of why it was a forgone conclusion that Laura should be kept in the dark, both answers in my opinion suggesting a self-justifying and sentimental concept of the child. One answer is that we would have wanted Laura kept in the dark for her own good, that is, that we would have wanted to save her the anxiety often associated with accusation and examination. The conception of the child I see embedded in this answer is that children are so fragile, so vulnerable, that they need to be protected from the truth and also that children are gullible enough—or adults expert enough—for children to be successfully kept in the dark.

The second answer is that the success of the examination depended on Laura's ignorance: that is, the power of the examination to reveal the truth of her guilt or innocence would have been compromised if Laura had known about it. The conception of the child I see embedded in this answer is that children are so sophisticated, such dissembling little devils, that their guilt can best be exposed through entrapment. As for the fact that these two conceptions suggest either a contradiction or an oversimplification arising from the abstraction and generalization of one extreme (that is, of one half of a dichotomy), I do not think such issues often occur to adults, at least not in the heat of a busy workday. Instead, I think we tend to adopt whichever conception, or extreme, seems most likely to facilitate the control we seek at any given moment.

Regardless, however, of the questions raised or not raised concerning the conference and of the reasons for raising or not raising them, the fact remains that if I had proceeded with the conference as originally agreed upon, it would almost certainly have been a proceeding in which Laura remained an outsider to knowledge. The image that pops into my head is from television and the movies—but does have a counterpart in real life—and is of the police detective who says to the suspect in a criminal case, "I'm sorry, Ma'am (or Sir), but I'm afraid I'm going to have to take you downtown for questioning." In contrast to the suspect in a criminal case, however, who arrives downtown knowing that questions are the agenda, Laura would have arrived at the school an innocent (*dupe, patsy,* and *dummy* are three synonyms speakers of English have generated that connote disdain for a person susceptible to being deluded because of innocence or naiveté). Presumably, that is, she would have arrived expecting the conference to be a *conference* (a meeting for the purpose of consultation or discussion, from the verb *confer*: *com*— together + *ferre*—to bring) when in reality the teacher-advisor and I had agreed on a meeting for the purpose of examination.

Turning to the question of how Laura would have experienced the "conference" had I proceeded to take her, I see five possibilities as most probable:

1. She could have remained innocent, with the examination being successfully conducted "over her head," so to speak, which would have made it yet another version of the situation in which adults talk about children in their presence as if they are not there, a situation that I think would have made a mockery of the philosophy of including children in parent-teacher conferences because, though present, Laura would not really have been *included*.

2. Laura could have sensed an examination was taking place (and I think most children would have sensed this), have felt betrayed (no matter how fine the examiners' intentions), and have suffered an erosion of any trust she may have had in Mrs. Matthews or me.

3. Laura could have sensed the examination, have felt like a criminal, and suffered an erosion of her belief in her own capacity for "goodness" or authenticity.

4. She could have sensed the examination, but, because she trusted us not to trick her, she could have doubted her own sensing, a doubting that could, among other things, have led her to mistrust herself—to lose confidence in her ability to perceive reality with accuracy[14]—and to feel guilty for suspecting two so obviously caring and trustworthy human beings as her teacher-advisor and her mother.[15]

5. She could have experienced the examination as some fluctuating combination of possibilities 2 through 4 above, a fluctuation that could have made her feel like an incompetent, a criminal, and a victim, by turns or all at once.

It is true that in the end I consulted with Laura about the conference and so avoided the outcomes described above. But I do not think that my success in that one instance meant that I had "arrived."

In fact, my failure to note that Laura was ignorant of the planned examination, even though I knew about it, was itself evidence that I had not arrived. Although I do think I learned from the experience, I also know that I remained (and always will remain) susceptible to obliviousness, presumptuousness, and complacency in relation to Laura's position as a child (or in relation to anyone's position as an *other*). Yes, I had managed to question the wisdom of an adult plan and found it wanting, and eventually I had even managed to question two conceptions of the child embedded in the plan and found them wanting. I think, however, that such questioning is a solid breakthrough in the effort to nurture only if nurturers accept the susceptibilities mentioned above as essentially human, concluding neither that such susceptibilities can be outgrown once and for all nor that their ever-presentness means they must be expiated through perpetual guilt.

When I told Laura about the conference Mrs. Matthews and I had scheduled, it took Laura about half a second to say she did not want to participate. On the day of the conference, she and her brother waited for me on the school playground, and I met Mrs. Matthews in the library. She was alone, and as I recall, Mrs. Coulter, who was her co-advisor, had a commitment elsewhere. Mrs. Matthews asked immediately where Laura was, and I explained that I had invited her to attend but that she had chosen not to join us and was waiting on the playground with her brother. Mrs. Matthews did not approve of Laura's absence. She repeated what she had said on the phone about children, particularly upper graders, being included in parent-teacher conferences, adding that without Laura she could see no purpose for the conference. Her attitude surprised me, because, as I thought I had made clear on the phone, I had been hoping she would fill me in on the treasurer's duties, something that did not require Laura's presence. I told her that I, too, liked the idea of including children in conferences, but not always if it meant forcing the participation, and that in this case I had accepted Laura's decision because I felt she would have experienced the conference as equivalent to being asked to testify against herself.

Mrs. Matthews did not respond verbally to my explanation, but she looked startled, as if I had said something truly odd. In retrospect, I think she was as surprised by my remark about Laura's attitude towards the conference as I had been by her remark that the conference was purposeless without Laura. In addition, though I have nothing to go on here except Mrs. Matthews' body language and my intuition, I think she may have been startled because it had not occurred to her that a child could mistake a dedicated teacher, which she certainly was, for an ignoble inquisitor or that Laura, one of the children to whom she dedicated herself, might have feelings other than those that she had intended or assumed Laura would have. Given this chasm between Mrs. Matthews' self-image (as I understood it) and the image implied by my remark, I think her instinct was to dismiss it out of hand as hopelessly extreme.[16]

Though it did not occur to me until much later, I also think that Mrs. Matthews' and my outward agreement about parent-teacher conferences (we both favored including children) could have masked differences that contributed to a sense of each other as misguided. For my part, I had taken for granted that her motivation for wanting to include children in conferences grew out of a desire to create an open and trusting relationship with children. Though I have no doubt that she valued openness and trust, her primary motivation could just as easily have been a desire to cultivate a sense of responsibility in children. Consequently, even though she could have valued openness and I responsibility, our primary motivations could have been different, and this difference (masked by a common belief in inclusion) could have interfered with communication between us and accounted for our radically different perspectives on Laura's absence from the conference, despite our apparent sympathy of viewpoint. For that matter, I certainly could have compromised the potential of inclusion to encourage responsibility by not requiring Laura to attend the conference, just as Mrs. Matthews' insistence on inclusion could have compromised the potential of choice to encourage trust. In addition, we both may have paid too little attention to the ways in which widely valued characteristics can conflict in specific cases. I also think, however, that such conflicts have their source in the accumulated impact of a history of specific instances in which we have miscalculated how best to encourage trust and responsibility (and also in our inability as human beings ever to perfect this encouraging) rather than in any inherent conflict between these traits.[17]

After explaining Laura's absence to Mrs. Matthews, I repeated what I had said on the phone about the possibility that confusion, not irresponsibility, was the source of Laura's trouble. Early in the conference, I also said something I had not thought to mention on the phone, and I think I remembered it at the conference because Laura's classroom teacher happened to walk through the library on her way to the teacher's lounge just as the conference got under way. What I remembered and told Mrs. Matthews was that, in talking with Laura's fourth-grade teacher (at the individual parent-teacher conferences the school held routinely each fall), I had asked how Laura seemed to be handling the treasurer's job. Her teacher had said that she couldn't tell for sure but that sometimes when Laura finished assignments early she would ask permission to leave the classroom and go to the office to attend to council business and that she seemed pressured when making these requests.

Although I mentioned these trips to Mrs. Matthews because I thought they suggested Laura's concern for her duties, Mrs. Matthews was upset by the information and interpreted Laura's requests as pointing towards irresponsibility. She said that all student council members were aware that classroom work came first and that they were not to use their duties as an excuse to get out of the classroom. She added that using class time was against the rules, that the classroom teachers knew this, and that Laura had been out of line in making such requests and her teacher in granting them. She also emphasized that one aim of student council was to help children learn firsthand the importance of making individual sacrifices for the good of the school community and that students who were allowed to use class time for student council business could hardly be expected to learn the importance of giving up free time.

My immediate reaction was to feel as if I had "tattled" on Laura and her classroom teacher. In addition, although the logic of the rule Mrs. Matthews had cited was clear enough, it seemed to me she was taking a rather hard line on very little evidence and had jumped to the conclusion that because the rule had been made to prevent the avoidance of classroom work, avoidance was automatically the motive of any students who broke the rule. Later, after the conference was over, I would wonder if the hard line had been more a defensive tactic, perhaps one acquired through years of dealing with parents, than it had been a sign of rigidity in relation to rules; that is, I would wonder if Mrs. Matthews had spoken so firmly because she anticipated that I had been about to complain that Laura's work as treasurer was interfering with her regular academic work and she wanted me to understand that the school had taken steps to prevent this. At the time, however, this possibility did not occur to me, and I merely tried to clear the air and make amends for my tattling by saying that I had not known about the rule. I also said that though I could see the rule's purpose, Laura's classroom work did not seem to be suffering and that her teacher could have been exercising discretion rather than disregarding or spurning the rule.

As the conference proceeded, I again brought up my hope that Mrs. Matthews would fill me in on the details of the treasurer's duties and that I might be able to identify possible sources of confusion, sources that might show us a way to help Laura perform more satisfactorily. Mrs. Matthews listened attentively. Then she made clear that she did not think my point of view on Laura's performance had any real substance. She did so by responding to my request for information with a very concernful and eloquent version of what I have since come to think of as the "If you only knew what I know" speech, a version I do not remember well enough to quote exactly but that I want to paraphrase as dialogue. If we imagine that I concluded my request for information about Laura's duties with the words "And so, Mrs. Matthews, I think it might help me understand what is going on with Laura if you gave me a concrete description of her actual duties as treasurer," then I would approximate Mrs. Matthews' response as follows:

> You know, I would really like to help you out here. And I certainly would if I could. I mean, you're obviously concerned about Laura. Anyone can see that. But, well, it's just that there is simply nothing about the treasurer's job that would cause a student the least difficulty. And I think *if you only knew* how really elementary Laura's duties are, if you were right there working with her and the student council, you would see that there isn't anything for me to describe, that it would be, well, silly, actually, and not a very helpful use of our time, to try.

Though I believe that no task is so simple that it cannot appear complex and even impossible to a given child and furthermore that as the given child's mother I had a right and a responsibility to inform myself about a task that could be connected to the kind of anxiety I was witnessing at home, I did not press Mrs. Matthews further for details but instead let my request be swept aside by her earnest eloquence. And in addition to being "charmed" by her forceful and charismatic manner of speaking, I think I desisted because her comments cast me as the outsider. As I said above, I have since come to think of Mrs. Matthews' response to my request for information as a version of the "If you only knew what I know" speech, by which I mean a speech in which an expert or "insider" appeals to an ignorant person or "outsider" to accept or defer to the insider's point of view because it is knowledgeable and therefore to be trusted as authoritative.[18] At the time of the conference, however, I had neither named nor defined this kind of speech, at least not in the context of the parent-teacher conference.

Nor, I suspect, had Mrs. Matthews named or defined it, which is another way of saying that I think she used it earnestly and not as a technique reflectively chosen for its potential to intimidate me by underscoring that my ignorance rendered me an outsider. Instead, I think she used it as the kind of speech that the "syntax" or "grammar" of the situation elicited from her, a syntax that, like the syntax of a native language, we as a rule learn from birth through immersion in culture and have little call to question unless we become observers of ourselves and our speech behavior, perhaps through perceiving its implications or witnessing its consequences, or perhaps because someone else brings it to our attention.

In other words, I think that during the parent-teacher conference we both thought we were doing what was best for Laura but that our efforts were hampered by a sort of subterranean drama in which we were both implicated but of which neither of us was aware. In this drama I played the outsider, the person, that is, who had neither witnessed Laura's school performance (remember, Mrs. Matthews' knowledge was of Laura's highly visible *public* school performance whereas mine was of Laura's private, or relatively invisible, home performance) nor managed to comprehend its meaning (irresponsibility). Mrs. Matthews, on the other hand, played the insider—the accurate interpreter, the expert eyewitness, the public or worldly person who, with great earnestness, was trying to prevent me from intervening and wasting time with a request whose ludicrousness was apparent to her, as insider, but not to me as outsider.

What is more, it was not simply an insider-outsider drama in which I want to argue that Mrs. Matthews and I were caught but also a drama in which I played the more specific role of the overprotective or interfering mother who threatened to cripple her daughter's growth towards independence and in which Mrs. Matthews played the more specific role of the delivering father (the knight-errant or heroic wise man of action) who would wean or rescue Laura from my debilitating influence and ready her for entry into the "real" world of independence, responsibility, and productivity outside the home. In the context of this experiencing of roles,

I think Mrs. Matthews' "If you only knew" speech could have been part of a well-intentioned and perhaps intuitive or nonreflective effort to keep me politely, gently, diplomatically in the dark concerning Laura's duties. Yes, she would humor me by noting my concern for Laura and so on, but no, she would not provide me with any information. And here I in no sense mean to imply that Mrs. Matthews thought there was anything the least bit complex about Laura's work as treasurer or that she was trying to hide the complexity from me. Instead, I want to suggest that she may have felt that Laura's salvation—her growth towards independence—hinged on doing the work of the treasury, and similar tasks, herself (without any help—any interference—from home). According to this script, if I gained a concrete knowledge of Laura's work, I might, with the best of motherly (overprotective) intentions, make the mistake of confirming Laura in her irresponsibility and inhibiting her growth by helping her with her work, or perhaps even by doing the work myself.

Ironically, overprotection was the very behavior I had, since attending Back-to-School Night, been making a special effort to avoid. But I did not think to bring this up at the conference. After all, it was the subterranean drama in which this issue figured. And in this instance of my request for specific information about Laura's duties, as in the earlier instance of my explaining my reasons for not bringing Laura to the conference, I think Mrs. Matthews perceived me as a mother whose judgment was distorted and whose intervention could only harm Laura—in other words, as a mother whom it was her duty (as a professional teacher or rescuer) to discourage.

Furthermore, though when I arrived at the conference I had not been perceiving myself as an overprotective or interfering mother but as a neglectful one who had allowed school avoidance and insomnia to develop before acting, I think that as the conference progressed I did to a degree begin to *behave* as if I were perceiving myself as an interfering mother. I do not think, however, that this was because I had stopped seeing myself as neglectful, but rather because the situation of the conference and the long and complex history of the relations between mothers and teachers (and also between mothers and children and teachers and children) that informed the situation or brought it to "life" (what I earlier referred to as the "syntax" of the situation) began to feed me my lines, lines that did not press further for the information I had intended to obtain but that deferred to the authority of the professional teacher.

I also think, in looking back, that I let my request for information be swept aside because I was afraid of being defined by a second stereotype, one equally as negative as that of the interfering mother and one that sometimes overlaps with it. The stereotype is that of the shrill or harping woman, and I think my fear was that if I persisted in the face of so eloquent and sincere a speech as the teacher-advisor's, I would appear, or reveal myself to be, the sort of woman who persists in asking questions after their absurdity has been aptly demonstrated and the sort whose views have traditionally been dismissed on the basis of the perceived shrillness alone. Such a dismissal could have cost me whatever power I did have to make myself heard and, through being heard, ease the strain Laura was experiencing as treasurer.

If my above analysis has been mainly accurate and if one function of Mrs. Matthews' speech was to silence my request and keep my helping hand at bay, then I think she was operating from a point of view (in this one instance) that, given the knowledge I eventually gained of her, she would have had little sympathy with had it been spelled out to her. The point of view is that of the professional teacher, specifically the professional teacher who has been schooled by a social science that early in the twentieth century "laid claim to the child and identified the devoted mother as a threat to normal social development" (Grumet 1988, 44).[19] It is a view that can become so overly confident, so patronizing, and so imperious all at once, particularly when adopted in relation to any mothering person who is not also a twentieth-century social scientist (or one schooled in the social sciences), that it fails to grasp the possibility that situations sometimes arise in which a mother's help is not a threat to the child's growth but is instead instrumental in nurturing it and in which a mother's intervention—her stepping between her child and the school—is one of the few existing ways of preventing, ending, or beginning to repair the damage that can occur when a teacher or a school has misjudged a child's need for help.

If, in addition to my being mostly accurate about Mrs. Matthews' viewpoint, I have also accurately assessed my own, in other words, if, as the conference progressed, I did let the syntax of the situation undercut my effort to obtain information, then I played the very role that Mrs. Matthews' speech, and a great hunk of twentieth-century social science, had designed that I should play, a role that I would have had little sympathy for had it been spelled out to me.

Furthermore, though before the meeting with Mrs. Matthews I had taken a step to prevent the conference from assuming the structure of an examination, I think there is room to argue that an examination of sorts did take place. It was, however, Mrs. Matthews and I who were placed under surveillance or "put to the test," and not Laura. And instead of being examined on behalf of Laura's well-being, we were, as I see it, examined on behalf of the survival of the status quo. In addition, because we were such conscientious pupils and had learned so well the roles that would be expected of us as grown-ups, the status quo did not have to send out official examiners to observe us but instead could rely on us to monitor our own performances. Ironically, for all my belated insight into Laura as a child who would have been cast in the role of dupe if I had taken her to the conference as originally conceived, it was teacher-advisor and mother, caught up in a subterranean drama of mothering person at odds with delivering father figure, who were in my view the true dupes.

Think about it: there we were, two women—a mother and a public elementary school teacher—occupying positions that have historically been associated with powerlessness and subordinacy in relation to much of the rest of the adult world, and yet we were interacting in accordance with the very traditions that had subordinated us in the first place. And though we were both women, my conference with Mrs. Matthews illustrates quite well Madeleine Grumet's observation that "until teachers and mothers acknowledge the ways in which schools perpetuate the asymmetry in class privilege and gender that is present in both the home and the workplace, they will not interrupt the patterns of their own complicity" (1988, 56).

Though from Mrs. Matthews' point of view Laura's absence had undermined the purpose of the conference and though after her "If you only knew" speech I made no further effort to obtain the concrete description of Laura's duties that I had originally sought, we nonetheless talked on past our initial disappointment. The remainder of the conference was very similar to our phone conversation. I emphasized Laura's history as a model student, the anxiety she was experiencing at home, and the possibility that her unsatisfactory performance was due to disorientation rather than irresponsibility. And Mrs. Matthews emphasized the scope of Laura's deficiency and the fact that Laura had, from the very first, received special help. Recalling an introductory student council meeting, Mrs.

Matthews said that she and her co-advisor, Mrs. Coulter, had both noticed that Laura was literally wide-eyed (with awe) and that after the meeting one of them had said to the other, "Did you see those [Laura's] eyes?" and that the other had agreed. In response to Laura's awe, Mrs. Matthews said that she and Mrs. Coulter had taken it upon themselves to adjust the treasurer's duties to ensure that they would be within Laura's grasp.

Though I could appreciate their sensitivity, I wanted to ask what specific adjustments had been made. I also wondered how Mrs. Matthews and Mrs. Coulter could have been sure their adjustments were ones that placed the job more within the reach of *Laura*, a child they had only just met, and whether they had taken into account the possibility that in adjusting the job they might have sacrificed some aspect that had contributed to its logic, coherence, or meaningfulness. I kept quiet, however, perhaps because to pose a great flood of questions after being told that Laura had been shown special consideration would have been to appear ungrateful. Of course, my silence, though it may have made me seem the model of politeness, meant that I could not evaluate the possible impact of the adjustments made because, not knowing what had been eliminated and what retained, I had nothing to evaluate.

In describing the scope of Laura's deficiency, Mrs. Matthews reiterated that Laura was lax about keeping the accounts and making her reports. She also said that Laura did a poor job of organizing the weekly Popsicle sales and that, instead of heeding repeated reminders to choose different salespeople each week, Laura over and over again chose the same few students. Mrs. Matthews did not spell out what made this method of choosing problematic, but I assumed the inadequacy lay in Laura's not following simple directives and also in using her treasurer's power in a way that could be construed as favoritism in that the Popsicle sellers were not rotated so that everyone got a chance to share in the responsibility as well as the fun and privilege of the sales. At some point, Mrs. Matthews also observed that, in all her years of working with student council, no parent had ever come forward as I was doing. And lest I create a misimpression here, I want to add that Mrs. Matthews did not make these observations in a tone that seemed either defensive or offensive but rather in the same earnestly concernful tone that had marked most of what she had previously said and as if the singularity of Laura's trouble and my intervention was information that had an obvious place in our conversation. As for any questions readers may have about my tendency to intervene on Laura's behalf at school, I can remember only this one intervention during her elementary years, although I intervened a second time, with more indignation than dexterity, during her high school years.

For my part, I did not comment on her observation that Laura and I had performed a first, mainly, I think, because for me her comment was a penny that did not fall immediately, and, by the time it did fall, the conference was part of the past. I remember thinking, when she made the comment, that it was an incongruous thing for her to say; given my own positive feelings about my intervention and her apparently negative ones, the comment seemed nonsensical. To explain further: when Mrs. Matthews singled me out as the *only* parent ever to have come forward, my bent had been to take her remark as a compliment that hailed a positive distinction, in the sense, say, that to be the only bystander to speak up about a possible injustice might be positive. In light of her position on Laura's performance and her comment that no child had ever had difficulty before, however, it seemed inconsistent for Mrs. Matthews to congratulate me for my intervention. Though it would later dawn on me that she probably had been suggesting that the student council's perfect record should be my cue to look somewhere else than the school or the council program for the source of Laura's troubles, at the time of our talk I experienced an impasse in relation to her comment and so simply leapt over it. Restating my thesis, I said that Laura's shortcomings could as easily be caused by disorientation as by irresponsibility and that her long history of conscientiousness seemed to me to suggest perfectionism and a preoccupation with rules that meant she put a lot of pressure on herself to "measure up." I also said that if Laura had shown signs of relaxing her rule-consciousness, I would have been more relieved than alarmed, but that on the basis of the anxiety she was experiencing, I thought that, far from relaxing, she was feeling haunted by her poor performance.

As we continued to express our respective viewpoints, one of us mentioned the upcoming winter holidays. Mrs. Matthews said she had not realized how little time Laura had left as treasurer. Two weeks would be taken up by vacation and then, in January, the fall semester and Laura's tenure would be all but over. I had not realized how little time was left, either, and though it made me think how many weeks Laura had been having trouble, the realization of an end in sight was undeniably a relief and seemed to ease the sense of impasse between us. Observing that there was generally quite a stigma attached to "quitting," Mrs. Matthews suggested it would be better for Laura if she did not simply resign but went ahead and finished out her term with the understanding that she would be under no pressure to transform her performance.[20] Having come to the conference hoping to receive information about Laura's duties that would help clarify the source of her difficulties, I had not thought about resignation or benign neglect as options. Given my altered expectations and the winding down of the semester, however, I said that I would relay her suggestion to Laura and let her know if there were any complications. She said she would talk in a casual, friendly way with Laura about the remainder of her term so that Laura would know the conference had created no hard feelings.

Then, though I cannot remember how it came about, Mrs. Matthews suggested that we make our way out of the school together. When I indicated that that would be fine, she led the way towards the door to the teacher's lounge. Without understanding why, I suddenly felt a strong aversion to entering the lounge and would have begged off if my aversion had not seemed so much silliness.

Once we were inside the lounge, where I continued to feel uncomfortable, Mrs. Matthews introduced me to everyone present. There were four to five staff members, as I recall. Although I knew most of them only by sight (Mrs. Coulter, co-advisor to student council, may have been among them), one of them had been a primary-grade teacher of Laura's. After the introductions, which felt elaborate, Mrs. Matthews took a minute to attend to something in an adjoining room. While she was gone, Laura's primary-grade teacher took it upon herself to speak to me. Either Mrs. Matthews or I must have mentioned the nature of our conference (perhaps we had been discussing Laura when we entered the lounge) because Laura's former teacher expressed disbelief that the efficient and well-organized child she had had in her class could be having any trouble as treasurer. Her remark could have been solely diplomatic or tactfully sympathetic, I suppose, but it was made in the direct, matter-of-fact, almost brusque style I had come to associate with her, and I accepted it as genuinely skeptical. However, though I welcomed a spontaneous endorsement of Laura's capabilities, her remark took on an almost surreal quality for me, and I think this was because her direct, almost blunt manner contrasted so greatly with Mrs. Matthews' concernful eloquence that I had some trouble negotiating the distance between the two styles. I responded to the primary-grade teacher's remark by saying something about not having noticed Laura's difficulty soon enough, and then Mrs. Matthews rejoined me and headed towards a door on the far wall opposite the library, a door I had not noticed before.

Although I had done volunteer work at the school since Laura was a kindergartner, and may even have been in the teachers' lounge before (though I don't think so), it had not occurred to me (or I had not noticed) that there would be a door that led from the lounge to the administrative complex and on to the front entrance of the school. As Mrs. Matthews moved towards this door and I realized that we were going to pass through it instead of backtracking through the library, it dawned on me with unusual force that this section of the school (particularly the teachers' lounge but also the administrative complex we were moving towards), a section that Mrs. Matthews and the rest of the staff knew so well and moved through so naturally, was mostly a mystery to me, mostly, I suppose, because it "belonged" to the staff and, with a number of exceptions (some well defined, others less clear-cut) was "off-limits" to everyone else. In fact, it struck me that the presence of Mrs. Matthews (as a person who had an official right to be in the lounge and so legitimized my presence) was all that kept me from being labeled an alien or intruder. In other words, I was feeling the uncertainty of the stranger who not only questions the "correctness" of her own whereabouts but who also experiences the awkwardness of unfamiliarity with the rules or layout of her present landscape. Though I was an adult woman, I think my uncertainty in the teachers' lounge had much in common with the uncertainty children at the school sometimes felt for areas that were mostly off-limits to them or that had at one time been off-limits but which some change in status had suddenly opened to them.[21]

My awareness that uncertainty often accompanies transition had figured in the concern I felt early in the semester when Laura first announced she was going to run for treasurer, but my concern at that time had not been the same as the concern I began to feel as a result of my walk through the teachers' lounge. Whereas my concern at the semester's beginning had been largely abstract and therefore much easier to minimize or dismiss as insubstantial, my experience in the teachers' lounge had given me a tangible sense of the disorientation that the complex geographical and personality boundary system of the school could generate. I began to think again about

Laura's fourth-grade schedule, about the fact that, not counting her homeroom teacher, she interacted with six adults each week (the band teacher, the gifted-program teacher, and—in relation to student council—the two teacher-advisors, the principal, and the school secretary) in at least as many settings (the multipurpose room, the cafeteria anteroom, the library, the fifth- and sixth-grade classrooms, the principal's office, and the secretary's office) and that her schedule lacked any consistency in that no two days were necessarily alike. For the first time I began to consider in a bodily way the opportunities for stress that so fragmented a schedule could create, particularly for a child who took rules as seriously as Laura did when she was nine.

Walking ahead of me through the door I had not known about before, past the principal's office and into the school office, Mrs. Matthews introduced me to the secretary (I already knew her vaguely in my role as parent and school volunteer), pointing out to her that I was the school treasurer's mother and to me that the secretary sometimes helped Laura with the student-council accounts. The secretary acknowledged her connection to Laura not by making any reference to student council or the accounts but by saying, at least twice, that, yes, she did know Laura and that she was really a very sweet little girl. Though the walk through the teachers' lounge to the secretary's office could have entailed additional content, I remember it as a cordial and graciously executed gesture that gave a sense of conclusion to a conference that had left me knowing very little more about the concrete workings of the treasury than I had known before it.

My talk with Laura after the conference differed markedly from the talks we generally had after the routine fall semester conferences with her classroom teachers. After the fall conferences, Laura would seek me out as soon as I got home, greeting me with a confident and interested "Well Mom?" or an "Okay, Mom, what did you and my teacher talk about?" These greetings would be my cue to spill the story of the conference. Depending on what was going on at home, Laura would either follow me around the house while I talked with her or we would sit down, sometimes with her father and her brother, and I would tell her all about it. When I had finished, and Laura had poured over the report card I often received at the conference, she would usually round out our talk by asking questions, two frequent ones being what I thought of her teacher and whether or not the teacher had shown me where her (Laura's) desk was.[22]

In contrast, after my conference with Mrs. Matthews, Laura did not request any information but waited for me to broach the subject. When I did, she was not passively resistant or wooden, as she had been the day I first tried to engage her in a talk about the details of the treasury. Instead, she was visibly alive to what I said. However, though visibly alive, her attention was not that of a confidently assured child who knew she had "measured up" and could count on good news. Rather, she attended with what I would describe as the silent and apprehensive expectancy of one who knows she has failed to meet the standard, who is waiting to find out what is to be done with her, and who fears the worst while at the same time hoping that the worst will, somehow, be averted. As I told Laura about the conference, her apprehension gave way to a quiet and unceremonious relief. Though far from appearing jubilant or exhilarated, she looked physically refreshed or revived in that her body seemed to have been released from the strainful alertness of apprehension. Without any puzzling over of options, she decided to finish out the term.[23]

Actually, Laura resolved on a course of action so rapidly that the word *decided* above is probably a poor choice. So far as I could tell, there was no evidence that Laura had been entertaining resignation as a possibility or that she even noted my reference to it. If she did not notice it, one explanation would be that she had never thought of resigning as an option for elementary school student council officers. In other words, though Laura had found the treasurer's job awful enough to keep her awake at night and to make her feel ill and want to stay home from school, and though I am sure she wished that she had never run for the office, I doubt that the concept 'resignation' existed for Laura in the context of student council.

In addition, I think the absence of this concept could have meant that Laura was experiencing the boundary separating the adult world from the child's world as a rigid one. More specifically, I mean that she may have been influenced by a prevalent cultural view that has decided advantages as well as disadvantages. The view is that the child's world is a practice-pretend world, and the disadvantage I am concerned with here is that the view can distance us from children's real suffering because it makes way for the conclusion that the child's world, unlike that of the adult, is not important or consequential enough to generate real conflict or suffering. This conclusion can in turn encourage us to think that such "adult" concepts as resignation are superfluous in the child's world. One alternative to my thesis is that, instead of considering resignation as open only to adults, Laura may have experienced it as open to some people of all ages but not to a competent and conscientious person such as herself.

I also think the absence of the concept could have meant that a discrepancy existed between the way Laura herself viewed her choices in relation to the treasury and the way Mrs. Matthews viewed them or assumed Laura would view them.[24] And here I do not mean to imply that Mrs. Matthews believed that Laura's suffering was extreme enough to call for resignation but rather that she may have assumed that a child in Laura's position would be attracted to resignation as the easiest way to escape responsibility. Regardless of whether Laura experienced resignation as an option for student council members or for herself, however, Laura's apprehension was relieved when I told her about the conference, and she did say without hesitation that she intended to finish out the term. In addition, though Laura was no more talkative about her work as treasurer after the conference than before it, her insomnia and her school avoidance did not recur.[25]

In the day or two following the conference, while I was working in the school library, Mrs. Matthews took a moment to confirm, with warm good feeling, that she had spoken with Laura and that the postconference transition was proceeding smoothly. I was glad for the news, and I guess I could have taken it as a signal that the agreed-upon plan had been put into effect and that the case of Laura's difficult tenure as treasurer could be closed. However, despite the fact that Laura's unhappiness had been brought into the open and aired, that her anxiety seemed to have been alleviated, and that she had chosen to finish out the term, nothing that had happened had gone very far towards helping me understand the specifics of the relationship between Laura's anxiety and her work as treasurer, and about these specifics I continued to wonder.

Partly, I expect, I continued to wonder because Laura's anxiety constituted a puzzle that intrigued me. But in addition, it seemed to me that guidance is most successful when it is grounded in an understanding of the child's reality and that it was therefore important to try to discover specifically what could have unnerved a child to the degree that the treasurer's job had unnerved Laura. Her decision to apply for the job of commissioner of tutors in the spring semester also helped keep my interest alive. Among other things, this job, for which she was accepted, meant that she would continue to attend student council meetings but that she would be directly responsible to her third-grade teacher, who supervised the program and with whom Laura had had a very positive relationship. One thought I had about Laura's choice was that she was making an effort to reaffirm her sense of her own competence and self-worth by reestablishing contact with a teacher whom she knew and trusted and who had previous experience with her competence. Probably Laura also liked the distinction of being on student council and did not want to give it up.

Something else that fed my desire to discover the specifics of Laura's difficulties was her continued silence on the subject of the treasury even after the conference. She not only did not include it as part of her after-school chatter but, if someone else should mention it, which rarely happened, she kept her remarks to the barest minimum. As well as intensifying my desire to know more, however, Laura's silence also commanded my respect; though I believed the silence indicated that her spirit had been injured by her experience, I also felt that time would have to pass before she would be able to sort through what had happened to her and that to ply her with questions or try to coax the information from her would have been harassment. At nine, Laura would not necessarily have understood what had happened to her well enough to articulate a personal position to another person, even if she had wanted to. Questioning her under this circumstance would have been to ask her to supply information on faith (without knowing what picture of herself or others the information might paint for the asker or to what purpose the information might be put). And so, though I remained curious about the specifics of her anxiety, I did not question her but limited myself to mulling over those bits and pieces of information that turned up on their own.

One such piece of information came from Laura's classroom teacher. Stopping to speak to me in the library within a few days of the conference, she mentioned that she had noticed my conference with Mrs. Matthews and had assumed we were discussing Laura and the treasury. I related the gist of the conference, and she offered an observation of her own, which was that Laura's troubles might be connected to the school secretary's role in the treasurer's work. Explaining that the secretary traditionally helped the treasurer handle the student council's earnings and accounts, she said that the present secretary, though perfectly competent in her own work, was relatively new to the school and did not have the knack for working with the children that a secretary who had worked at the school for years had had.

Two other pieces of information turned up much later, about a year and a half after Laura's tenure ended. One of them came by way of another mother who did volunteer work at the school. The other mother said something one day that made clear that she believed Laura had thrived as treasurer. Although Laura's right to privacy was a concern, it also seemed to me that to let the mother's remark pass would be to verify an impression I knew to be false. In addition, I thought that to verify this particular false impression, if only by remaining silent and letting the other mother's remark pass, would be to forsake both Laura, as a real-life and therefore less than perfect child, and the student council program, as a real-life and therefore less than perfect program, and in the process to endorse their public image. Probably I was also curious to know how the mother would respond to the news that Laura had had an awful time as treasurer. And so I told her that Laura had been miserable in the job and that in my opinion it had been the most negative experience of her school life. The mother responded by saying that her daughter (a very competent student) had been treasurer, which I had not known, and that she had hated the job but had gotten through it as best she could and then let that be the end of it. Although this information strikes me as the kind I would have relayed to Laura, I don't remember doing so.

The other piece of information came to me from Laura and also concerned a student treasurer. I don't remember if she communicated it before or after my talk with the volunteer mother, but I do remember Laura's communication as one of the only two she ever initiated that dealt with her work as treasurer. The first, which I mentioned earlier, was her disappointment at the subdued congratulations she received from her family when she won the election, and this second was something she burst in with one day after school, a year or more after her tenure was over. Greeting me with a "Guess what Mom?" she said all in a rush that the student who was currently treasurer and who had held another office as well had told her that the treasurer's job was terrible and that since winning he could see why she had had a bad time with it. As an excellent student who was older than Laura, his speaking up about his own trouble with the treasurer's job had obviously meant a lot to Laura. What is more, the fact that she had come in the door and made the announcement with such exuberance so long after she had left office suggested how depressing an experience the treasury had been for her. In addition, in a recent conversation, Laura recalled the treasurer's speaking up by saying that she would remember his comment until the day she died. She added that he had made her feel as if she wasn't the only person who could have trouble with the job and that he had been particularly convincing because of his age and experience.

The discovery that two students besides Laura had had a rough time brought to mind the comment Mrs. Matthews had made during the conference about Laura's difficulty and my intervention being firsts in the history of student council. I began to consider that though Laura's difficulty may have been the most visible, other treasurers had also had problems, and I also realized that a view of the council program as invulnerable to criticism because only one officer and one mother had ever "complained" rested on a couple of questionable assumptions. One assumption is that a task no one speaks up about as difficult is equivalent to one that is not difficult. Though it seems too obvious for words when voiced, a possibility that gets lost in the shuffle of daily life despite its obviousness is that people can be experiencing difficulty even when they do not say so and even when they appear to be doing all right. This possibility, to which teachers are generally sensitive, but in the slightly different context of teaching a new lesson in the classroom, is illustrated by the two treasurers besides Laura who had trouble but said nothing to the staff in charge. On occasion all of us have no doubt heard a teacher point out that one student's confusion invariably means that others are confused, too, and that students should not sit silent out of a fear that everyone else understands. At some point all of us have no doubt also been the confused student who sat silent, convinced that he or she was the only person who did not understand. And yet, in the context of student council, the possibility that Laura was not the single exception to a long-standing rule did not seem to occur to Mrs. Matthews, or to Laura or me. At least it did not occur to Laura or me until others actually spoke up about their own troubles.

A second assumption suggested by a view of the council program as invulnerable is that a program that has never proved difficult for anyone in the past will not prove difficult in the present. One possibility this assumption overlooks is that the performance of student officers elected in the past may not reliably indicate how officers elected in the present will fare and that at any point in time a child may come along who is just different enough in sensibility, academic skill, expectations, and so on from all the other children

who have come before that this new child will experience a task as
the very essence of difficulty whereas previous children will have
experienced it as the essence of a breeze. A second overlooked possibility is that a task, especially one involving interaction among
people, can change substantially through time. In the case of the
treasurer's office, two staff members who worked with the treasurer
(the school secretary and the principal) were relatively new to the
school when Laura took office and could have affected the program
without its being noticed. Given such staff changes, it does not
seem quite accurate to equate the council program Laura participated
in with the one that predated the arrival of the new staff. And, if the
programs could not be equated, it hardly seems fair to characterize
Laura and me as exceptions to a rule associated with the earlier
program.

   In exploring the above assumptions, I began to see that the
student-council program was more vulnerable to criticism than
people seemed to think. It also seemed to me that a vicious circle
could have been at work and that the program's reputation for
excellence could have discouraged students and parents from
speaking up (if and when difficulties did arise) and that the silence
of students and parents could have contributed to a staff impression
that the program was beyond reproach. In addition, because the
treasurer who spoke to Laura about his difficulty had been older
and more experienced than she and had also held a council office
besides the treasury, it occurred to me that the treasury may not
have been the least complex of the four offices. Though in general
(and despite Laura's and the other treasurer's troubles) the council
program had been put together with great care, I think it is possible
that fourth graders could have been allowed to run for treasurer on
the basis of status rather than complexity. What I mean is that because in terms of status the treasury was the lowliest of the four
offices and fourth grade was the lowliest of grades 4 through 6, it
may have seemed only natural to make the treasury the one office
that fourth graders could run for. Or, to put it another way, more
attention may have been paid to matching the status of grade levels
with council offices than to analyzing which of the four offices would
have been the most appropriate for a fourth grader in terms of
skills required. Of course, these two hypotheses are largely conjec-
tural. Even though the three pieces of information that came my
way after the conference did strengthen my basic thesis that Laura's
difficulties as treasurer had arisen from confusion or disorientation

rather than from a frivolous irresponsibility, they did not conclusively verify it.

When I chose to write about Laura's tenure as treasurer, I knew she would be able to clarify many of the broad and impersonal aspects of the office. For example, I knew she would be able to describe the election process for me as well as the structure of student council. But because of her long silence about her own participation, I did not expect she would have much to share in the way of concrete memories about her personal experience as treasurer. In fact, I assumed that support for my basic thesis would have to remain mostly hypothetical.

As I mentioned earlier, however, Laura eventually had more to say than I expected she would, answering not only my broad and impersonal questions but also, once I had gotten well into the writing (sometimes she would stand quietly just inside the door of my room and watch me working on her story), some of the questions that had to do with the specifics of her personal performance. Although I am not saying that I think she has poured forth all that lies buried in relation to this experience or that what she did pour forth exactly matched my theories, I am saying that on several occasions, usually when we had come together without any sense of urgency or any highly specific goal, and once or twice when we were talking about something else altogether than the treasury, she shared memories and observations and opinions about the work that demonstrated that her tenure was marked, practically from the beginning, by a central confusion concerning a key task of the treasurer's. In addition, I think that because her confusion came at a time (fourth grade) when she was supposed to be evidencing increased independence, the confusion may itself have alarmed her to the point of rendering her *unresponsive*. Her unresponsiveness, grounded in confusion, was in my opinion quite distinct from what we generally term "irresponsibility" and think of as an unresponsiveness grounded in a shirking of duty or lack of conscientiousness.

The first memory Laura communicated with a real sense of intellectual and emotional engagement (as opposed to the flat and detached responses she had made in the past whenever the subject of the treasury came up) concerned the account book it had been her job to keep up. Singling out the keeping of this book as the task that had given her the "hardest time," she not only pinpointed what had confused her about the book, but she also critiqued the account book's suitability for fourth graders in general and for herself in particular, suggesting an alternative to the account book that she felt would have been more suitable for fourth graders. And she did all of this in one mouthful, or one outpouring, so to speak, with hardly a pause, so that it seemed as if the pinpointing of difficulty, the critique of suitability, and the suggestion of an alternative had been simmering for a long time and were, even as she spoke, coming together in a way that enabled her to take a stand on her own experiencing, perhaps for the first time.

After wondering over the years about the specifics of the anxiety I had witnessed when she was a fourth grader and wondering whether she would ever speak openly about them and also after spending hours at the typewriter trying to argue a point of view for which I had very little concrete evidence, I was delighted to snatch my tape recorder and simply sit quietly and listen to what Laura had to say. Her comments, which I am going to quote in their entirety and which I have tried to punctuate to best convey the tone and rhythm of her speech, ran as follows:

The thing that confused me the most and gave me	1
the hardest time about the treasurer's job was	2
the book problem, and the biggest problem was,	3
there were too many columns that dealt with too	4
many words that I could not understand, like *net*,	5
gross, *debt*—all those words I really didn't	6
know what they meant and nobody took the time out	7
to explain them to me, and so when they [those	8
involved with student council] would talk about	9
things like that and *profit* and things like	10
expenditure, how was a fourth grader supposed	11
to understand that?—unless somebody sat down	12
with them and said—"Okay, here's the vocabulary	13
you need to know and here is, if you just learn	14
these words." I mean, if I had just learned	15
those words, *everything* would have been so much	16
easier. Except for the fact that this stupid	17
book had all those dumb columns. I mean, it	18
would have been easier just to make your own book,	19
when you just take a piece of paper, rule it out	20
and in certain columns put for certain things,	21
and for each transaction you have like a piece of	22
paper and it says, "previous balance," and	23
then you have to put, then you subtract it and	24

you get that, and then on the same piece of paper 25
after whatever is done with, you can come back 26
to put the profits from that on there—*THAT* TYPE 27
OF SYSTEM. And then you just staple all the 28
pages together at the end of the semester or at 29
the end of the day or the end of the week or 30
whatever. That would have worked so much better 31
for working with kids because it would be so much 32
more easily explained and easy for them to 33
understand and because that store-bought book 34
with the little—I COULDN'T EVEN FIT THE NUMBERS 35
IN THE SPACES!—THERE WASN'T ENOUGH ROOM FOR ME 36
TO WRITE!—and so it was a totally confining book 37
because,[26] (a) there wasn't enough space (b) I 38
didn't understand the purpose or the reason or how 39
to use the column system that was set up in the 40
book, which was probably a very efficient system, 41
but not for fourth graders.[27] 42

In contrast to any image of the treasurer's duties as so elementary as to preclude description, Laura's description of the account book indicates that there had been an aspect of the job complex enough to disorient her. Of course, I suppose it would have been easy to assume that because Laura had the school secretary to help her, the account book would not have been a source of confusion. Laura's comments suggest, however, that she had experienced the school secretary as a further source of confusion and that the fourth-grade teacher had been on target when she suggested, that day in the library shortly after the conference, that the secretary may not have been easy for Laura to learn from.

As Laura perceived her, the secretary was competent at office work and could handle tasks involving children that were part of her routine—such as receiving messages and paperwork from teachers that students might deliver to the office—but, as Laura put it, she had "minimal finesse at those duties" that "had to do with kids" and "that wouldn't be in a normal secretary's job." Laura also said that the secretary did not know how to talk to kids "that well" and that she "made other people feel kind of stupid sometimes." Other comments Laura made were that the secretary was hard to understand because she spoke with an accent and that she seemed "ornery" and also "dingy" (not *dinj'é*, but *ding'é* as in "dizzyheaded") when it came to working directly with children.

When I asked Laura if the secretary seemed interested in work that centered around children rather than adults, Laura answered, almost vehemently and in a voice that underscored the "no's" and distorted their vowel sounds, "*Noooah, nooah*—NO, a resounding no!" And when I asked her if the secretary seemed like a busy person, she said, "Yeah—she was *very* busy," a comment I include not only to suggest that Laura probably felt as if she and the treasurer's account book were a nuisance or an interruption of the secretary's "official" work but also to suggest that this particular secretary's apparent lack of interest could have been a way of expressing frustration at being asked to take on more and different types of responsibility than seemed fair or appropriate.

In a later conversation, Laura added to the picture of her relationship with the secretary, an addition that suggests how little understanding of the account book Laura gained from the secretary. I had asked Laura if she had any of those kinds of memories about her work as treasurer in which she could picture herself back in fourth grade and on the job. And I had tried to encourage the formation of an image by recalling the braids she had worn in those days. At first, she answered, "not really." But then, as I was about to change the subject, she said, a little as if she were talking to herself—

> I can picture myself sitting next to [the school secretary]. . . . she was trying to explain it [the account book] to me, but I didn't understand. . . . well, I just sat there at the desk and she tried to explain it to me and then she usually ended up mainly doing it all herself 'cause I sat there and watched in bewilderment. . . . I just didn't understand what they [the student council in its use of the account book] were trying to do—I mean—[the way I can understand it] *now*—

Because in recounting her memory Laura did not explicitly state whether she had been conscious of her own bewilderment as a problem and because much of my support leaves room for multiple interpretations, I pressed her a little by saying, when she had finished, "So you knew you were having problems?" She looked at me as if I had asked a question unbelievably—almost unforgivably—obvious, and then said, in a tone that was reproving, emphatic, and distressed and that I will try to convey through spelling and punctuation, "Oh!—Yes! *Ma-awm—Gawd!*—I don't know—it was just like constant, constant problems. I was always having problems."

If Laura's comments make clear that the account book remained a source of confusion even given the secretary's effort to explain it and that Laura was aware of herself as a child who was having problems and of the account book as something that she would have needed to understand to do a competent job, her comments also suggest that the secretary was the person who actually kept the accounts and that for the most part the entries would have been in her handwriting. On the one hand, I was struck by the irony that while Laura's father and I had made an effort to respect the school's philosophy of the upper grades as a time when children should rely less on their parents and other adults for help and also had taken seriously the fourth-grade teacher's comments at Back-to-School Night, the school had created a situation, no doubt unwittingly, in which the secretary was doing Laura's work for her. Instead of getting the kind of help we would have had the time to give Laura at home, the kind that I hope would have enabled her to keep the accounts herself and so have had a choice between behaving responsibly or irresponsibly, Laura sat and watched in bewilderment while the secretary kept the books.

In addition, I think the sitting and watching would have humiliated most children and also would have startled a child such as Laura, whose school identity centered around a consistent history of competence and conscientiousness. The sitting and watching, furthermore, could not have been made any easier by the fact that they did not take place on Laura's own turf but in the secretary's office, which was a kind of grand central station for the staff and which had the additional distractions of the telephone and the front counter with its influx of messages and inquiries from the classrooms as well as from parents and the community at large. On the other hand, I was struck by the possibility that Laura's "failure" to keep her own accounts may have been a reason for Mrs. Matthews' view that Laura was irresponsible and that the teacher-advisor may have concluded that Laura frivolously ignored the account book until the last minute and then expected the school secretary to do her work for her—to "bail her out."

Given that Laura found the account book incomprehensible and that she gained no understanding of the book from the secretary's attempts to explain it, the question that seems to me to become important is why Laura did not tell anyone about her confusion and ask for some additional help. Keeping in mind her history of competence, it seems probable to me that the confusion provoked by the account book would have been a new experience for her and that the strangeness of the experience of confusion could itself have further disoriented her. In addition, her history of competence meant that she rarely needed to ask a teacher for help and that, as a result, she may not have had much idea about *how* to ask for help. Though it is true that there must always be a first request that marks the beginning of our experience in asking for help, I also think that as we go about our lives we draw on all manner of experience to fashion scripts for ourselves and that we work on those scripts we perceive as meaningful *for us*. Because Laura's identity as an independent worker could have led her to view "How to Ask for Help" scripts as superfluous to her way of being, I think she may have been caught short when she was faced with the account book and could make no sense of it on the basis of the secretary's explanations.

I also think that even if Laura had known how to ask for help or had managed to fashion a script on the spot (perhaps one that reached into the far periphery of past experience in which she had seen others ask for help or perhaps one that drew from a refocusing of her attention on those facets of her present that could give her some clue about the "how to" of asking for help), she would have been reluctant to act out her script, to announce her confusion and ask for help. And I think this because to ask for help would have been to risk her identity as a competent and conscientious student and the place at school that such an identity had earned for her. After all, she was valued by her teachers as an *independent worker*, as a child who could complete assignments with very little help or supervision beyond the teacher's introductory instructions. It was this ability that had qualified her to be assigned to the first- and second-grade combination class when she was a first grader, an assignment that, though she may have preferred to remain in the classroom in which she had spent the first two weeks of first grade, nonetheless distinguished her from other children. Her ability to work independently was also commented on at parent-teacher conferences, conferences that, as I have already mentioned, Laura was eager to hear about and that I told her about in considerable detail.

In addition, Laura's ability to work competently and conscientiously brought with it certain privileges, for example, privileges such as taking messages from her teacher to another teacher or taking paperwork, perhaps an absence list or the day's lunch count, from her classroom to the school office. As Laura indicated in one of our conversations, running clearly defined errands for the teacher (for instance, delivering a note to the office and then returning to the classroom) was not only a privilege in itself in that errands were run by those children who finished their work early, but was also a privilege that she valued because it brought a chance to experience the school from new and interesting angles, angles that, except for her privileged status, she would not have had a chance to experience unless she broke school rules, something she was not inclined to do. In the following comments made by Laura, lines 1–15 focus on errand running as a privilege, lines 16–27 focus on the bonus of experiencing the school in new ways, and lines 18–19 and 21–25 reveal her awareness of and concern for school rules:

Usually people who finish[ed] their work	1
earlier did it [ran errands to the office for	2
the teacher] because they would like, if they	3
were done with everything, I mean, why should	4
someone who is in the middle of something go when	5
somebody who was done with something could go?	6
And so I was often done, *finished*—excuse me.	7
Not necessarily first. But in the top three or	8
four. Top ten anyway, for sure. So then, um, it	9
would often be, it's always the, the people who	10
finish first who take that sort of thing up [to	11
the office] when it's needed. . . . it was like a	12
privilege because since you were finished with	13
work, you were allowed to leave the classroom,	14
and actually go somewhere, even for a minute or	15
two. And you could kind of mosey along down the	16
hall, and just kind of peer in the classrooms,	17
and you had a pass, so you couldn't get in	18
trouble. . . . it was weird to be in the halls	19
when there was nobody there because I never	20
really experienced it like that, 'cause the halls	21
were off-limits during any time when there was	22
no one going to be there—like lunch they're off-	23
limits but everybody's outside, but then like	24
when they're not off-limits, it's like	25
everybody's there [filling the halls while	26
passing to and from recess, etc].	27

The competence that earned Laura a chance to run errands did not define her only for her teachers but also to some extent for her peers. As I have already said, it was not unusual for classmates to call after school to clarify assignments, and in my observation, her school identity helped get her elected to class senator in third grade and to school treasurer in fourth. Consequently, I think that for her to ask for help would have been to jeopardize her identity in the eyes of her fellow students as well as her teachers. I further think that she may have experienced her inability to understand the account book as equal to breaking the promise of her campaign speech. In her speech, which she took very seriously, she had cited her past experience on student council and her good grades, especially in math, as evidence of her qualification. I think that when she took office and discovered the account book was beyond her grasp, she may have felt, at least part of the time (for example, at those points when her confidence in her own abilities would ebb), that she had not been qualified at all and that she had misrepresented herself to her fellow students. And even if she did not go so far as to see herself as a fraud, I expect she would have wondered if her peers would have viewed her as such. Would they, in other words, have understood that she had had no idea, when she decided to run for office, that there would be such a thing as a store-bought account book that would bewilder her and that, in spite of all appearance to the contrary, she had run for office in good faith?

As well as feeling distressed by her own confusion and by the threat to her identity, a wide variety of other feelings could have discouraged Laura from asking for help. For example, I think she may have felt demoralized in her own being when she discovered that the arithmetic she had learned in the primary grades was not powerful enough to solve the mystery of the account book she was supposed to keep as treasurer. In other words, she very understandably may have assumed there would be a connection between the math she had learned in the primary grades and the math required of the school treasurer. But when she took office and discovered no such connection, she could have felt demoralized—as if the world of school did not function as its spokespeople had led her to believe it would—and her demoralization could have undercut her resilience. In fact, when I think back to her sharing of her campaign speech at home before she gave it at school and to her citing of her primary-grade experience as the source of her qualification to become treasurer, and if I further recall the willingness with which she accepted the first- through third-grade curriculum as authoritative and worth her effort and also the way she seemed to experience her relationship with her primary-grade teachers as a collaboration in the adventure of learning, I am left thinking that it is not only possible but also probable that the account book would have struck

Laura as some sort of bizarre error or insufficiency on the part of the adults in charge of student council and one that would have undermined any inclination to place in them the kind of trust we place in those we ask for help. In other words, I think the reality of the account book was discrepant enough from her expectations prior to taking office to erode her confidence in her ability to understand the world as well as in the world's ability to follow through and realize the expectations that it raises. In addition, I think this discrepancy is comparable to the one she experienced when she won the treasury and her father and brother and I responded quietly rather than with our usual boisterousness.

That Laura had not had any previous experience with the two teachers who advised the council and that she typically liked to orient herself to new people and places before opening up could also have diminished the chance that she would turn to them for help. In addition, I think that at times Laura felt angry at and frustrated by the adults in charge of the council, feelings that also could have discouraged her from asking for their help. Anger is certainly suggested in her reference to the account book (see Laura's description of the account book, pp. 158–159 above) as that "stupid book" (lines 17–18) and her reference to the columns in the book as "those dumb columns" (line 18). And frustration as well as anger and perhaps indignation are suggested, in the same description, by her detailed criticism of the account book's vocabulary and layout (lines 4–16 and lines 34–42), by her observation that no one had taken the time to explain the vocabulary to her (lines 7–8), and by her argument that the treasurer should have been allowed to fashion a "homemade" system (lines 18–34), one that, as described by Laura, would not have confronted a fourth grader with so great a discrepancy between past learning and present tasks as was created by the store-bought book.

Given the high premium traditionally placed on the loyalty and gratitude due adults from children, I think that Laura, even though she did not have a high opinion of the school secretary, may also have felt it would hurt the secretary's feelings or appear ungrateful or insubordinate to ask for help from a third party. Taken in combination, these feelings (confusion, fear of lost identity, demoralization, a reservation about trust, anger, indignation, fear of appearing ungrateful, and perhaps shame at having broken the promise of her campaign speech) could have been experienced by Laura as a great storm of conflicting, fluctuating emotions that rendered her mute when it came to saying to one of the teacher-advisors into whose midst the election had thrown her, "I am confused about how to use the account book you have given me, and I do not understand what the secretary tells me to do. Will you help me?"

Although Laura's comments did not verify all that I have been suggesting, they were in keeping with my general thrust. One observation she made when I asked why she had never told anyone about her confusion or asked for help was that she hadn't asked because of the people she worked with, because, as she put it, "of the way they *were*." When I asked her what she meant, she said that the people she had worked with on student council never would have understood the trouble she was having with the account book and that if they had known about it they would have concluded she was an imbecile (*imbecile* was her word). Although it could be argued that her view indicated her own lack of confidence rather than accurately reflecting the attitudes of the people she worked with, and though I expect someone with a good grasp of Laura's predicament as well as of the council's viewpoint could have fostered understanding between Laura and the council, it seems to me that Laura's lack of confidence was not wholly without basis. For one thing, that two treasurers besides Laura had had trouble with the job but had not spoken to anyone in authority could have meant they felt a similar lack of confidence, or at least a sense of powerlessness. For another, that Mrs. Matthews did label Laura irresponsible also supports Laura's view that the council would not have been sympathetic.

Because Laura had not mentioned, in response to my original question, anything about her father or me as sources of help and because I felt that our adoption of the school's definition of fourth grade could have discouraged Laura from coming to us, I asked her why she had not told us about her confusion, perhaps even brought the account book home and had us go over it with her. I also asked her if she thought her silence could have had anything to do with the emphasis that had been placed on independence when she was in fourth grade. Laura said she couldn't remember anything about the school's definition or whether her awareness of it and our support for it might have kept her from coming to us but that, regardless of how she had felt about us at the time, she never would have brought the torturous (her word) book home with her. She explained that her struggle with the book and the whole treasurer's job had been so awful that she had needed home to be a place where she could escape from the account book and all the rest of the stress of the treasurer's job. Relying on a shared knowledge of cultural types, she said, "You know what I mean, Mom," and then compared herself as treasurer to adults who are so miserable at work that they shut out all thought of it at the end of the day, and she reiterated that the last thing she would have wanted was for the account book to have followed her home from school.[28]

Laura's comments about wanting home to be a refuge made clear that she had craved a getaway and might have appreciated an on-site "escape" that functioned in the way an employee or a teachers' lounge does for adults. Her comments also suggested that my original opinion that the school's phone call to Laura at home could have been experienced as invasive was not entirely off-base. In addition, it was good to hear that she, at least in memory, had not shied away from asking her father and me for help because she thought that we, like the people on student council, would have thought she was an imbecile.

I think, however, that her memory is much too generous regarding her home world and that there were obstacles besides the torturousness of the book that kept her from asking her father or me for help. Perhaps a better way to put this would be to say that I think the torturousness of the account book could have encompassed an unacknowledged worry that to bring the book home would have been to evidence dependence or incompetence (traits her culture frowned upon)[29] and also would have been to risk disfavor at home at a time when she was already experiencing more disfavor at school than she could bear.[30] Despite any effort her father and I may have made to avoid imposing certain patterns of the culture on her (for example, the pattern of treating dependence as an abstraction and declaring it absolutely negative or the pattern of allowing model children no latitude), I know that we sometimes endorsed these patterns without fully realizing it (as when we adopted the school's definition of fourth grade or when we became intensely exacting about homework). And so, though we may at times have separated ourselves from those adults who embraced such patterns overtly and taught them as rigid truths, we also lived the viewpoints we opposed. And Laura, in her human susceptibility or openness to the world around her, could easily have picked up on this and worried that we too would reject her or think less of her (despite what we might say) if she brought the book home and asked for help.

As for whom Laura meant by the "people" she worked with on student council, she said she meant the council as a whole or unit that included participating staff members as well as the other student council officers. Although Laura could not remember specifically who had held the other offices, she did experience them in total as a group that was proud of itself and its image and as one that would have had little use for or patience with a member who did not perform up to standard or who hampered the student council's progress or detracted from its image. Her memories of the individual staff members, however, were much more distinct. In discussing her memories of staff members besides the secretary (already discussed above), Laura left no doubt that she had perceived the school principal and Mrs. Coulter as peripheral compared with Mrs. Matthews and that she had perceived Mrs. Matthews as a presence whose extreme forcefulness had negative as well as positive implications.

In commenting on Mrs. Matthews' forcefulness as a classroom teacher rather than as an advisor to student council, Laura described her as awesome in her ability to undertake ambitious and highly creative projects and see them through and as someone whose students were at an advantage in that they got to have a hand in these projects and help bring them to completion. Later, Laura would describe the power of Mrs. Matthews' physical presence as follows:

> The way Mrs. Matthews works things is that . . . if she's doing anything in her room that requires action, especially if it required talking, [it was] the way, partly the way, she moved and the way she, um, kind of *flowed* through things, but mainly the way she talked, and—. The way she expressed herself through talking could absorb anyone's attention span so that nothing else in the room could even hold a remote amount of interest, other than Mrs. Matthews—because of the way she was.

When I commented that lots of parents thought Mrs. Matthews was the best teacher their children had ever had, Laura said, "She probably drew, she probably got something out of their kids that they had never gotten . . . out of them before, because of the way she taught." Then Laura added, "But some kids don't need that," and she went on to describe a classmate of hers who had been quite creative and assertive and who Laura said would have clashed with Mrs. Matthews if she had ever been in her class. Laura also said that Mrs. Matthews could be "slightly condescending with some of her students" and that some people would find this offensive. And, becoming caught up in the subject of Mrs. Matthews' influence, Laura related one long anecdote too far removed from Laura's story to include here that illustrated Laura's sense of the way Mrs. Matthews' persuasiveness and ability to create a feeling of intimacy with her own students sometimes had a negative side effect in that children occasionally perceived the groups she supervised as being cliquelike and as receiving special privileges that Mrs. Matthews' forceful presence won for them. In general, though, when it came to Mrs. Matthews' role as a classroom teacher, Laura seemed to view her as a very powerful and creative teacher who knew how to get things done but whose very powerfulness could be a liability as well as an asset.

When I asked Laura specifically about Mrs. Matthews' way of working with student council, Laura's comments focused mainly on the negative potential of her teacher-advisor's forcefulness. For example, when I asked about the respective styles of the two advisors, Laura said that Mrs. Coulter "was less involved than Mrs. Matthews," and then, as clarification, added that Mrs. Matthews tended to offer help in a way that did not always leave students much space for their own ideas, whereas Mrs. Coulter left them plenty of room to figure things out for themselves. Laura attributed this difference to Mrs. Coulter's perception that student council "was for the students to be part of the school—*not* for the teachers to be part of the students being part of the school."

In comparing Mrs. Matthews' and Mrs. Coulter's way of making suggestions, Laura observed that "when Mrs. Coulter made suggestions, she said, 'This is just a suggestion, that I thought maybe you could try something like it.'" Laura also said that "Mrs. Coulter never jumped in on a meeting unless she had a suggestion" but that "Mrs. Matthews would jump in, I don't remember over what, but I remember her jumping in over things more than [making] suggestions." And in describing the body language of the two teacher-advisors, Laura further developed the contrast between Mrs. Matthews as an advisor who jumped right in and made her presence fully felt and Mrs. Coulter as an advisor who maintained a distance:

> They both would sit at the back [of the meeting room, usually a classroom], but Mrs. Coulter would just kind of gesture a little and say something and Mrs. Matthews would probably have sat straight up in

her chair and projected her voice and stuff like that. They were very
different. She [Mrs. Matthews] had extreme posture, she could draw it
up more, like draw herself taller—that's the way it always affected me.

After Laura finished her comparison, I asked her what it had
been like to speak at student council. I prefaced my question by
repeating Laura's observation that Mrs. Matthews tended to be the
center of attention and asking if that meant she drew some of the
attention away from student speakers and that speaking at the
meetings—giving the treasurer's report, for example—was therefore less stressful. Laura answered emphatically that it did not make
speaking easier. Explaining that Mrs. Matthews always focused her
own attention intently on whoever was speaking and that the focus
of the group usually followed her lead, Laura said that when she
spoke she felt as if the council's attention was always fully on her.
Repeating her earlier point about Mrs. Matthews' involvement at
meetings, Laura commented that "Mrs. Matthews was . . . student
council advisor, so even though the student council president was
supposed to lead the meetings, if something wasn't going the way
she wanted it to, she'd jump right in and make it right." When I
said, "So Mrs. Matthews participated a lot?" Laura answered, "Personally, it was more like she usurped the authority." Further developing her view of Mrs. Matthews' participation as negative, Laura
said (in a later conversation) that when she gave her treasurer's
reports to the council (Laura's format was to write the previous
balance, expenditures, and new balance on the board and read these
figures out to the council), Mrs. Matthews would invariably ask so
many questions and make so many comments and suggestions that
her dissatisfaction with the reports was unmistakable.

Because Laura's organization of the weekly Popsicle sale was a
subject Mrs. Matthews had brought up at our conference (Mrs.
Matthews had described as irresponsible Laura's habit of asking
the same council members to be salespeople week after week even
though she had been reminded repeatedly to rotate the salespeople),
I asked Laura about the sales. She couldn't remember always choosing the same students or being repeatedly reminded to rotate her
choices. But she did say that the procedure had been to ask for
volunteers for each of the two lunch periods (the primary-grade
lunch period and the upper-grade lunch period) and that plenty of
students had always raised their hands to volunteer, especially for
the primary-grade lunch because these salespeople got out of class

early. Laura's feeling was that as a lowly fourth grader she never would have ignored the raised hands of volunteers and "ordered" fifth and sixth graders who did not have their hands raised to be salespeople.

I suppose this hesitancy about giving orders to children older than she might be viewed as unsatisfactory behavior in a leader, and perhaps even as irresponsible, but it seems to me that deference to age is an integral part of public schooling and that in Laura's case she may have felt caught between the conflicting protocol of at least two hierarchies—the hierarchy of the four student council offices, in which the president is the top person but in which each office has its respective power, and the hierarchy of class or grade level that she had been subject to and had been expected to observe since kindergarten. Rather than labeling Laura irresponsible when the problem may have been that she did not know how to juggle protocols, I think it would have been helpful to assume that she was experiencing the pressure of the beginner and also to have spoken with Laura or the council, or both, about the potential of protocols to conflict and create the stress of divided loyalties. It also seems to me that Laura may have found it especially difficult to issue orders to older children—or anyone—because she did not have the support of a fine performance to encourage her to exercise authority with confidence.

As well as appointing Popsicle salespeople each week, Laura was also responsible for making certain that the school principal remembered to buy the Popsicles each Friday, and so I asked her what it had been like to work with him. Laura said that she had liked the principal as a person, that he had been friendly and relaxed and not awesome or persistently eager and pressing as Mrs. Matthews had been, but that because he was THE PRINCIPAL or BOSS of the school (the person who presided over school assemblies, who "patrolled" the lunchroom, who was associated with punishment, and so forth) she had felt intimidated by his role in spite of liking him personally. Recalling that it had been her practice while treasurer to leave notes on his door reminding him to buy the Popsicles, I asked her if the notes had been her idea or if someone had suggested them to her. She said, "He did. He did." Then she explained about the notes in a way that suggested how thoroughly pressured or boxed in she had felt by the guidance of Mrs. Matthews.[31] According to Laura, the principal suggested the notes "because he was forgetful." About her response to his suggestion, she said,

> I figured that's [the notes on the door] a good idea because if he
> forgets it's going to be my ass—with Mrs. Matthews. Not with him!
> He would have said, "I'm sorry—it was my fault." He would have
> "confessed" to it, I guess you would have to say. But Mrs. Matthews
> would never have let me live it down. . . . She would just, she, every—
> then every week she'd like check up on me. "Are you telling [the
> principal] to get the Popsicles? Are you making sure that they're being
> gotten?" And she might even do that to [the principal] too, so maybe
> he was kind of like—"God, that woman, she's probably going to get
> me if I don't get those Popsicles."[32]

Laura's comment that Mrs. Matthews was someone who might
try to "get" the principal in the same way that she was trying to
"get" Laura indicated as conclusively as anything she said that while
treasurer she had experienced Mrs. Matthews' forcefulness as essentially negative. However, because this comment of Laura's, as
well as some of her others, may give the impression that Laura's
negative experiencing of Mrs. Matthews was the singular experiencing of a child under stress, and as such to be discounted, I want
to add that as my children moved into the upper grades and as I
got to know more parents at the school, I found that, though greatly
admired by the majority of parents, Mrs. Matthews was not univer-
sally admired. Among the admiring parents, most regarded Mrs.
Matthews as a teacher with a green thumb who could make children
bloom or as a talented director with a knack for eliciting fine performances. These parents admired her sense of mission, her ability to
help shy or quiet children find their voices, and her ability to generate a sense of community or intimacy in her classroom and an
attitude that responsibleness can be vital and exciting instead of
dull and constrictive. On the other hand, a minority of parents
questioned her teaching style and were put off by her personal
manner, characterizing them as somewhat stifling in their forcefulness and as excessively self-aware and solicitous.

One parent who admired Mrs. Matthews greatly was a mother
who said that her son, who was very quiet as well as bright and
artistic, had never been able to relax at school until he entered Mrs.
Matthews' class and she gave him an opportunity to pursue his
artistic bent in a way that had never seemed possible at school
before. And one parent who was not admiring would make herself

scarce whenever Mrs. Matthews came into the library because she found Mrs. Matthews' way of interacting with people uncomfortably patronizing. A third parent who was a longtime admirer of Mrs. Matthews expressed a blend of the two extreme views when she commented that Mrs. Matthews had been a crucial and positive force in her child's life and that over several years Mrs. Matthews had gradually settled down and become less intense although it remained true that she was always, as the mother put it, "on stage."

As for my own view, on the basis of my observations and interactions in the years following Laura's term as treasurer, I would say that Mrs. Matthews was intense as well as dedicated, that she could do all that her admirers said she could, and that in addition she made a more conscious and sustained effort to help children relax with their errors than any other teacher I had contact with. She also became elated when a child who had previously been reticent began to gain the confidence to venture in new ways, and she made a point to encourage inclusiveness and cooperation in her classroom and also to recognize and integrate minority points of view and ways of being.

In addition, however, though she was very conscious of her own style, she did not seem to me to fully realize the power of her style to disaffect some people—children as well as adults—and I think this relative unawareness that her personal style was double-edged meant that she sometimes came on strong enough to overwhelm or alienate the very person she had set out to win over or help bloom. I also think that her great confidence in her teaching style could have made her prone to interpret the alienation of a child in her care as unreliableness or irresponsibility and that, given the high premium she placed on responsibility, she would have gone to great lengths to transform such an "irresponsible" child into a responsible one.

Returning to Laura's description of Mrs. Matthews as someone who "got" people, I think that Laura experienced Mrs. Matthews as the very antithesis of the teacher with the green thumb or the director with the knack. It seems to me, in fact, that Laura's experiencing of Mrs. Matthews had more in common, say, with Mark's experiencing of the big bad wolf in Chapter 2 and David's experiencing of the piranhas in Chapter 3 than it did with the experiencing of a trusted nurturer or guide. Or, if I keep my focus centered on Laura's own life history, I would compare her experiencing of Mrs. Matthews to three of the experiences from Laura's early childhood that I mentioned in my introduction. These three are the wave that engulfed Laura the day her father and I introduced her to the Pacific Ocean, the experiencing of the air force jets that broke the sound barrier as Laura played in her backyard when she was three or so, and the experiencing of the wolf that appeared and growled at her from the back of the station wagon in the dream she had when she was sick in bed with flu and fever.

Described by Laura as having extreme or *very* good posture and as being able to draw herself up even taller when the occasion called for it, as having a voice she could project from the back of the student council meeting room, as tending to jump right in on a meeting if something wasn't going the way she thought it should, and as being someone who was unyielding in her efforts to elicit prescribed behavior, Mrs. Matthews was a sort of monster-person for Laura. As a monster-person, Mrs. Matthews had the power to loom forth and disrupt the world of the treasurer's duties just as the ocean wave had welled up and disrupted Laura's introduction to the ocean and just as the sound of the air force jets had borne down on Laura and disrupted her backyard play.

As for Laura's dream, the wolf that growled at her could not be seen or heard by the children in the back seat of the station wagon or by the two women who were engrossed by their adult talk and by the task of driving the car and finding their way. Similarly, Mrs. Matthews, as a menacing, intrusive presence in Laura's life, could not be seen or heard by Laura's fellow student council officers; to them Mrs. Matthews was the director with the knack, the gardener with the green thumb, the wonderfully charismatic teacher-advisor who could foster a rare intimacy among the individual members of a group and who could lead them towards worthy achievements that would be widely valued and admired.

In addition, just as the Laura of the dream was separated from the two women in the station wagon by the boundaries mentioned above, so Laura-the-treasurer was separated from the adults in her home world, the adults of her primary-grade years, and the adult who was her fourth-grade classroom teacher (all of whom Laura knew better than she knew either Mrs. Matthews or Mrs. Coulter and all of whom knew Laura better) by the boundaries between home and school, lower and upper grades, and regular and extra-curricular activities, and also by the boundary between the portable and the permanent classrooms. I suppose we could say that Laura's isolation was in part a side effect of specialization or of a rigidity of boundaries that does not allow for much overlap or integration of the various moments and geographies of a child's life. Another way of putting this would be to say that when Laura's separating-out occurred, when she was judged irresponsible, there was no adult (no person with power or authority) near enough to Laura whom she knew well enough and trusted sufficiently to turn to in her neediness. Nor was there an adult near enough Laura who knew her well enough to stand up for her, whether or not Laura asked for help.[33]

Her isolation was no doubt also related to the fact that she had been imprudent enough to experience her first great confusion and need for extra help during the very year the "experts" had defined as the year in which she should become more independent and responsible and less dependent on adults. And so, in the context of an activity as apparently mundane or unextraordinary as the student council program of a public elementary school, Laura lived through weeks and weeks of isolation and hopelessness: on the one hand she had been singled out as irresponsible and felt herself "dogged" by a teacher-advisor determined to transform her irresponsible performance into a responsible one, and on the other, as only Laura knew, the transformation that could have drawn her into the intimate circle of responsible student council officers hinged on the keeping of an account book whose layout (all those empty spaces that were too small for Laura's numbers) she found constrictive and whose logic and vocabulary she found bewildering. Not until her tenure was nearly over did anyone think to intervene, and then it was a *mother*, a person whose point of view was suspect and who herself was so implicated in the traditional and complex relationship between mothers and teachers, home and school, that she effected only a bit of first aid or emergency care that eased her daughter's anxiety but did not penetrate to its source.

If we are going to do more than provide emergency care to our children when they are distressed, if we are going to work to create a relationship between home and school that aims at preventing such lonely hopelessness as Laura's, then I think we are going to have to examine our personal performances as nurturers or guides. At one extreme, I think we are going to have to pay particularly close attention to our potential for guiding imperiously, for behaving as if our age, experience, expertise, and education, or our sense of mission or the worthiness of our cause, can somehow render us incapable of error. At the other extreme, I think we are going to have to attend to our potential for passively following or deferring to those who guide imperiously.

Specifically, it seems to me that when we are tempted to dismiss a child's less than model behavior with abstract negative tags, or to accept the dismissal by another, we have a responsibility to pause and explore less negative alternatives. For example, taking Laura's case, we have a responsibility to pause and explore the possibility that a child who appears to be behaving irresponsibly may actually be a child who is confused or alienated but too frightened, angry, and mistrustful, too tired out from worry and too desperately in search of a little respite, to ask for help. In such cases, it seems to me that we also have a responsibility to consider that it is the very world we adults endorse, the very world towards which we lead our children and towards which we teach them to behave responsibly, that has made them desperate in the first place. Furthermore, I think that if we fail to explore alternatives, if we indulge our temptation to behave imperiously (like the stereotype of the traditional "Dad" or top person in the hierarchy) or our temptation to defer to imperiousness (like the traditional "Mom"), then it is we adults, and not our children (or, at least, not only our children), who are behaving irresponsibly.

Of course, I may be oversimplifying here, by which I mean that I may be overlooking the possibility that when we adults behave imperiously or passively defer, we are, like the Laura who behaved "irresponsibly," merely confused or, if not confused, then in hiding from confusion. My guess is that this is often true. There is, however, an important difference between the adult and the child, which is that the adult has great power over the child, whereas the child is relatively powerless in the face of the adult. It is this difference in power that I think makes it imperative for all of us who bear the label *adult* to let go imperiousness as well as timidity and to do so even though these ways of being may appear the perfect pair of hiding places, the two points of view that can best insulate us from confusion and save us from exploring alternative perspectives, perspectives that might compromise our own views and reveal to us the need for change.

III

Looking Back
Two Adults in Childhood

A child's drinking glass, a keepsake from the past.

5

When Daphne Was a Girl

Henry sighed. He wanted a bicycle now. He could see himself riding up and down Klickitat Street on a shiny red bike. He would wear his genuine Daniel Boone coonskin cap with the snap-on tail, only he wouldn't wear the tail fastened to the hat. He would tie it to the handle bars so that it would wave in the breeze as he whizzed along.

Beverly Cleary, *Henry and Beezus*

In a cardboard box of old black and white photographs I keep next to my desk, there is a picture of two small girls, about five and seven, dressed for church on Easter Sunday morning. The girls have been posed so that they stand facing each other in front of a willow tree whose branches weep clear to the ground and whose leaves are so dense that only a few patches of sunlight show through. Both girls are wearing spring cotton dresses with gathered skirts, short puffed sleeves, and bodices with some decorative touch—a row of lace around the collar, a spray of flowers at the waist—that suggests a special occasion. The older girl, whose head is bent slightly and who is smiling down into the face of the younger (I would call her smile "fond"), is adjusting her companion's hat. A close-fitting small saddle shape secured by a length of dark velvet ribbon tied under the chin, the hat is light colored with more dark velvet ribbon for trim and a single row of roses stitched lengthwise across the top. The wearer appears to welcome the attention she is being paid. Her bright, slightly crinkled eyes are turned up towards the older girl's while her head is held level and her lips are pressed closed but upturned at the corners. To me she looks as if she might like to express her full appreciation by breaking into a grin, or perhaps even by giggling, but is trying hard to hold her face and head still so that the hat can be adjusted, and perhaps also to accommodate the photographer, her father, who doubtless called out a "Hold still" or a "Don't move" just before snapping the picture.

The girl having her hat adjusted is Daphne. I have known her practically forever, and, though her name did not appear in Chapter 1, not even peripherally, she was at the picnic along with David, Mark, and Laura—as an adult, however, and not a child. Having known Daphne for such a long time, I know a lot about the way she was as a child, some of which comes through in the photograph and some of which does not. For example, I know that the spiritedness hinted at in the bright eyes and ready-to-burst-through grin, the receptivity to the attention of others, and the cooperativeness the photograph implies were characteristic of Daphne when she was a girl. From the time she was very small, she was a spontaneously warm and affectionate child who was uncommonly sensitive to the feelings of those around her, noticeably concerned when others were unhappy or crabby or blue, and eager to do her part to cheer them up and generally promote harmony in her world.

On the other hand, I know that the love of feminine attire and dressing up suggested by the Easter dress and hat was anything but characteristic of Daphne as a child. Though nothing in the photograph suggests it, except perhaps the hair, which is cut short and left straight, Dutch-boy style, Daphne had emerged, at about the age of four, as a passionate and committed tomboy who did not wear dresses or girls' hats unless required to do so, as she was, for example, on Sunday mornings. Furthermore, when she was required to wear girls' clothing, she wanted it to be as simple and tailored or as "ungirlish" as possible, which the hat in the photograph definitely is not. With its roses and velvet ribbon, it is much too fancy to have been chosen by Daphne. My guess is that it was a hand-me-down that she agreed to wear because it saved her from having to try on hats in the girls' section of a department store. As for why she looks so happy in the photograph if she did not like to wear girls' clothing, I would guess that she had become so caught up in the spirit of Easter and in her enjoyment of the older girls' attention that she had forgotten any of the displeasure she might have felt, or perhaps expressed, when dressing earlier that morning.

Because as a child Daphne's great vitality and enthusiasm had seemed to be rooted most essentially in her tomboyishness, I would also guess that Daphne felt nothing but relief when she got to change from her Easter dress and hat back into her tomboy clothes. At least I would have guessed this until fairly recently, when Daphne confided that, despite what people may have thought, her tomboyishness had not been without its drawbacks and that, in addition, it had been implicated in a devastating experience she had had as a child but never talked to me about before. Because I think readers will have the best chance of grasping the import of Daphne's experience if they first get to know her as I and others knew her during her childhood, I want to provide a concrete picture of the ways in which the above-mentioned traits (sensitivity, spiritedness, affectionateness, cooperativeness, tomboyishness, and so on) exhibited themselves and were viewed by others before I explore the childhood experience she recently shared with me.

As I said above, at about age four Daphne emerged a passionate and committed tomboy. In saying this, however, I want to clarify that though she had the boundless physical energy and enthusiasm for physical activity that people have traditionally associated with boys, she did not physically resemble a boy or have the masculine features we often associate with boys. Actually, she was short for her age as a child, and she had large brown eyes and long thick lashes that a boy might have been teased about. Instead, her tomboyishness was a way of being that she herself sought out and cultivated, so to speak, and that consisted most noticeably in dressing in boys' clothing, pursuing traditionally male activities, taking boys and men for role models and heroes, and playing as much or more with boys than with girls. Although Daphne's sisters and some of the other girls she played with often wore boyish clothing similar to Daphne's, for these other girls such clothing was usually a compromise or a matter of practicality tied to the inheritance of an older brother's hand-me-downs, the ruggedness of some game, or the semirural nature of their landscape.

The house that Daphne lived in until she was seven was one of five or six built almost city-close, but it was situated on a country road that was itself surrounded by olive, orange, and almond orchards, pastureland, poultry farms, and open fields that would gradually, as Daphne grew up, be divided into large lots and sold to families who wanted to build a house and live in the country or to developers who wanted to build subdivisions. One consequence

was that though Daphne's road had enough houses to provide playmates and a sense of neighborhood, it was also rural enough to
make boyish clothing a practical choice for both sexes, something
that would also be true of the house her family would move to
when she was about eight.

For Daphne, in contrast to her sisters and the other girls she
knew, girls' clothing was the compromise, whereas boys' clothing—
whether her brother's hand-me-downs or clothing purchased
firsthand for her at a department store—was what she liked best to
wear. And here I would isolate the word *liked* and add that it would
not be exaggerating to say that Daphne felt affection for her boys'
clothing and became emotionally attached to specific articles. Her
preferred daily attire, from about the age of four, included blue
jeans, often cuffed, and a long-sleeved flannel shirt buttoned at the
neck and sleeves. With her blue jeans and flannel shirt she might
also wear suspenders or a boys' belt buckled at the side. In warm
weather she usually wore the same jeans but often substituted a
short-sleeved, round-necked T-shirt for the flannel. At night she
wore boys' pajamas, which she says she *loved*, and there is a photograph of her wearing a flannel pair that she became particularly
attached to. The flannel is patterned with sailing ships, compasses,
and pirates, some of whom are digging busily for buried treasure
while others are lugging discovered treasure to a ship or facing off
in pairs with drawn swords. Even now, Daphne refers to these
pajamas as her "pirates." By way of contrast, her sister, who sits
next to her in the photograph (the two girls have squeezed themselves into an overstuffed Naugahyde chair to look at the storybook
Babar), is wearing a long flannel gown decorated at the yoke with
zigzagged embroidery thread and patterned not with pirates, compasses, and ships but with tiny rosebuds.

As a small child Daphne had no use for shorts, even in warm
weather (she did not begin to wear them until she signed up at her
local recreation district for tennis lessons when she was about
twelve), and she wanted nothing whatsoever to do with the sleeve-
less blouses her sisters and other girls wore in summer. The one
exception to the rejection of shorts was that until age eight or nine
she wore cutoff jeans to swim in. Her shoes during these years were
lace-ups (leather oxfords or canvas tennis shoes), and she had her
straight, brown, baby-fine hair cut at home or in a men's barbershop in the Dutch-boy mentioned above until she was ten or eleven,
and then in a pixie cut.

This pixie cut, which her mother may have suggested, had come into fashion for girls but was acceptable to Daphne, perhaps because a woman teacher she especially liked wore a pixie or perhaps because Daphne was just beginning to get a glimmer of the difficulties adolescence was going to pose for her, but also because the hair was cut short—shorter even than a Dutch-boy—and shaped to be left uncurled and combed straight forward to resemble a pixie's cap. Like almost everything else traditionally viewed as signaling femaleness, Daphne dismissed curls as dumb. In fact, she became so committed to her tomboy styles that if anyone suggested a haircut or a pair of shoes or an article of clothing that struck her as markedly feminine— the offensive aspect could be the color, the curve of a collar, an ornate button, or any small decorative touch—Daphne would give a rejecting shrug, a sort of twitch of the shoulder and upper arm, that came to be taken by family and friends to mean "This article of clothing or style of shoe or haircut you are suggesting I wear is totally unacceptable. What is more, I would think that by now you would have learned better than to suggest something so obviously silly to a tomboy like me."

When Daphne began kindergarten (in the 1950s), there was no such thing in her community as a girl who did not wear dresses to school. Even so, Daphne stuck to her boys' clothing and recalls vividly, and with pleasure, marching into kindergarten on the first day of school wearing the railroad coveralls and white turtleneck shirt she and her mother had bought especially for the occasion. Daphne continued to wear pants every school day after that without any objections from the school until fifth grade (during these years she attended several different schools in the growing district), when the school intervened, requiring that she wear dresses. Although Daphne complied (she really had little choice; her family, though themselves accepting of her preference for pants, decided that the school's decision was not worth protesting), she recalls the intervention with indignation even now and continues to feel animosity towards the fifth-grade teacher who initiated the intervention, Daphne's view being that the teacher's objection to pants arose from a desire to exact conformity from children as a way to satisfy a desire for control and not from any authentic concern for a child's well-being. After the intervention, Daphne wore tailored skirts and blouses to school but continued to favor pants outside of school.

Thus far in her life she has never really explored distinctly feminine styles (in the sense of pretty, fussy, precious, cute, or even sophisticated or elegant), and she has never worn anything that could be construed as provocative. From early childhood Daphne was physically modest and was one of those young people who felt self-conscious when she began middle school (seventh and eighth grade) and had to dress out for physical education in the locker room with other girls. During middle school, however, she did become more flexible in her dress (although sometimes with a moody self-consciousness), wearing skirts to social functions such as parties with her peers, and for a year or so even curling her hair. The skirts continued through high school, and then the women's movement of the sixties began to influence clothing styles, and Daphne's rejection of feminine attire was no longer so conspicuous.

As a child Daphne's enthusiasm for physically energetic play and her enthusiasm for male role models or heroes frequently overlapped. Sometimes, however, the enthusiasms could be observed in the absence of each other, although the boys' clothing meant that on one level she was almost always taking a male role. In relation to physically active play that did not require being male or taking a male role, Daphne was an eager initiator and an enthusiastic participant. She could also be persistent, and sometimes had to be to persuade her sisters and other girls to break away from their "girls'" games and play something more rugged with her. Sometimes there would be trade-offs, and she would agree to play a quiet game indoors or on the front porch or lawn in exchange for a promise that some more active game would follow, maybe baseball in the clearing behind her house or hide and seek or tag. One activity she especially remembers was for all of the kids in the neighborhood (the one she lived in until she was seven) to take the wagon to the top of a steep hill on a little-traveled road a short walk from her house and take turns, singly or in pairs, riding the wagon down the hill.

Another activity she liked was to hike with the neighborhood kids in the area around her house, trudging through fields, poking around irrigation ditches, flooding gutters, building dams, and breaking off branches of wild willow and stripping off the leaves and bark to make switches or crude fishing poles. And during elementary school, Daphne remembers always having plenty of boys to play with at recess, kickball being a favorite sport during the earlier grades and, later, softball and volleyball. In about fifth or sixth grade she also made friends with a girl at school who liked sports as much as she did, and both of them joined a newly formed girls' basketball team, which a new teacher, a woman, organized and coached.

When it came to male role models, Daphne discovered them in books, on the radio and television, at the movies, and in real life. One of her favorites was the combat soldier, a figure Daphne learned about from the stories of the World War II veterans in her world as well as from fictional sources. Between the ages of about five and seven, Daphne and her best boy pal in the neighborhood spent hours playing army. Though he usually wore a T-shirt and jeans and carried a play rifle, she wore all sorts of paraphernalia and has a snapshot of herself wearing what she came to think of as her "full dress" uniform. In the snapshot she is wearing, in addition to her usual long-sleeved flannel shirt and jeans, a necktie (she learned to tie them herself when she was eight or so) and a second long-sleeved shirt with a black and white cowhide pattern enough like camouflage to support an army theme. The shirt is buttoned part-way up (so that the necktie is visible) and is cinched in at the waist with a wide army belt. Over her right shoulder is slung an army canteen and over her left shoulder and across her chest is strapped an ammunition pouch. She is carrying a toy rifle that has her initials painted on the butt, probably with her brother's airplane model enamel or her mother's fingernail polish. Daphne is also wearing an army cap. The sides of her Dutch-boy are exposed, but her bangs have been tucked up under the bill. Though expressions can be deceiving, she is smiling and looks extremely satisfied with herself and very much in her element in her army gear.

Among the real-life men who attracted Daphne's attention was the caretaker of the small local cemetery. The children on her street treated the cemetery like a park, and the caretaker, if memory is accurate, was a widower who lived in a small house adjoining the grounds. He was always willing to talk with Daphne and the other children while he tended the flowers and trees or supervised the workers who dug the graves, and Daphne developed a camaraderie with him. She remembers liking his company particularly because he was "just somebody you could work with." Daphne went on to explain that the caretaker would let her get tools for him from his shed and jump down into the partially dug graves just for fun. She also said that he had a low-key way about him that made it easy to be his helper. In trying to focus in on exactly what made the caretaker so appealing, she added that though she would have been too young at the time to articulate it, he had probably been more her helper—

by accepting so unconditionally her child's way and rhythm of helping—than she his.

The crews that were sent to Daphne's street to work on the phone and power lines, lay county water pipes, and construct frames for new houses (here I mean the street she lived on until she was seven) and who, during Daphne's childhood, were all male, also attracted Daphne's attention. Requesting her mother to pack a lunch in an official-looking workman's pail that her father had used before he took an office job (it was one of those black rectangular lunch pails with the rounded lid that holds a thermos bottle), Daphne would join the crews during their noon break and sit and chat with them, often trading the homemade cakes and cookies and slices of pie her mother had put into her pail for the store-bought sweets the workmen carried in theirs. And when the children on her street had a lemonade stand, Daphne was on intimate enough terms with the workmen of one crew to walk down to their work site and ask them to come up to the stand to buy lemonade, which they did and which Daphne says made her feel very proud and important indeed.

The activities pursued by the males in Daphne's world that interested her were often activities open only to boys. Making no secret of how much she wanted to be in Cub Scouts, Daphne, when she was about six, laid claim to one of her brother's discarded Cub Scout shirts and neck scarves, making them staples in her own wardrobe. Later, when she was about eight, someone convinced her to give Brownies a try, but she hated it. Put off not only by the relative tameness of the girls' projects, she says she also resented the way Brownies cut into the time she had to play with her three best boy pals and that she would much rather have been playing "Eliot Ness" (a game inspired by "The Untouchables," a television series about FBI agents and organized crime) than spending one afternoon a week with a Brownie troop.

Daphne also longed to join Little League. She had played baseball with her family from about the age of three or four and was a natural when it came to hitting, fielding, and catching a ball. Her brother and another boy she had grown up with (his name was Glen, and he was the son of Howard and Kathleen, longtime family friends who lived in the city) were Little Leaguers, and Daphne, who was drawn to the officialness of it all (the regularly scheduled practices and games, the elaborate social structure of coaches, umpires, scorekeepers, team captains, and so on, the team uniforms and caps, the "real" ballparks, and the team names), would listen and watch and soak in as much of it as she could from the sidelines or the bleachers.

Fishing was another sport that attracted Daphne. Although not officially limited to males, it tended in Daphne's family to be dominated by men, particularly by her father. Daphne did fish for bluegill around the home neighborhood, and she got to bait fish for trout from the banks of the streams, rivers, and lakes she camped at in summer with her family. She says, however, that she wanted to fish as an equal when her father and brother would leave camp in the rowboat and that she was secretly intrigued with her father's ability to fly-fish, both from shore and from the boat. Fantasizing about the trips in the rowboat, and also perhaps perceiving the skill of rowing as a stepping-stone to such trips, Daphne would sit in the boat when it was tied close to shore—usually in the middle of the day when the fishing was at its worst—and practice rowing, all the while imagining herself to be on her way out into the middle of the lake, where she would catch strings of big trout like the ones her father brought back from his outings in the boat and that her mother cooked for dinner in the big black skillet at the camp stove.

Another skill connected to her father's fly-fishing that fascinated Daphne was fly-tying. The vise that was screwed to the edge of the old library table in one of the bedrooms was accessible to her view, as were the small scissors, the fishhooks, the floss and head cement, and the box filled with dubbing and hackle material from which her father would cut small bits of animal fur and bird feathers to make the pretend flies (*artificial*, he and the other fly-tyers would have called them) with which he fooled the trout and which Daphne wanted to know how to make herself.

The character from children's fiction that Daphne most wanted to be like was Beverly Cleary's Henry Huggins. Her favorite "Henry" book was *Henry and the Paper Route*. In the same way that she wanted to become a Little Leaguer, a Cub Scout, and a fly-fisherman, Daphne wanted to become a paperboy. She couldn't, though, because even if there had been more houses in her area and they had been close enough together to make delivery by bicycle practical, girls were not allowed to have paper routes in those days. She could, however, learn to ride a bike, and she did, even though bike riding was of little interest to anyone in her family. Purchasing a used bike from a playmate who had been given a new one, Daphne taught herself to ride by pushing the bike up a small hill in her friend's yard one day while no one was home and riding down the hill over and over again until she gained her sense of balance and got the feel of steering. Eventually, when Glen, her friend in the city, got a paper route, Daphne's ability to ride a bike meant that when she visited at his house she sometimes got to help him deliver his newspapers, an activity she says she loved because it brought her about as close as she could come to realizing her dream of being like her fictional hero, Henry Huggins.

In addition to such physically active pastimes as tag, baseball, bike riding, and army, Daphne also sometimes participated in quieter or less male-centered games with her sisters, visiting relatives, or friends from school or the neighborhood, games such as office, house, barbershop, and church. But even in these games she invariably took a male role. For example, in church she always played the priest who said mass and administered Holy Communion, in barbershop she always played the male barber who gave shaves and haircuts, and in house she was either the father or the son. Her favorite variation on the game of house was one that demonstrated her preference for male roles while also revealing her spontaneous warmth and affection and receptivity to being mothered.

The game, which was called "Joey," had only two roles, that of the mother, played by Daphne's older sister, and that of the only child, Joey, played by Daphne. The two girls often played the game at home, but they liked to play it best in an isolated loft room in a small cottage they sometimes visited at the coast. The loft's privacy allowed them to forget all about the other people vacationing with them and become wholly absorbed in the game, and Daphne remembers that her sister-mother would read stories to her, tuck her into the bunk bed for naps, and fix her meals, and that sometimes they would leave the loft room and that her sister-mother would take her by the hand for a walk through the sand outside the cottage. Daphne says that she would become so at home in the role of Joey that she would feel sad when the game ended and would sometimes continue to play it in her imagination. She also remembers the game as coming so naturally to her and her sister that it seemed simply to unfold before them from some invisible place and yet to have been created by someone who knew them intimately enough to get the action and the lines exactly right from the very first.

As I mentioned previously, and as the game "Joey" to some extent suggests, Daphne was, in addition to being a spirited tomboy, an affectionate child who was sensitive to the moods of others and eager that people should be happy and life harmonious. She exulted in the physical closeness of evening story times on the couch with her mother and remembers vying with her brother and sisters to get as close to her mother and the book as she could. She also liked to sit beside her grandmother and chat. Or, if her grandmother happened to be knitting, Daphne might sit on the floor at her feet, pressing her body close to her grandmother's legs while they talked. And though she probably would have balked at having anyone "fuss" over her hair at home, Daphne remembers that when she stayed at Glen's house his mother would sometimes brush her hair while they sat together under the shade of a tree on summer evenings and that the brushing felt wonderful. Generally eager to pay others the small attentions that make us feel we have been noticed and matter to another human being, Daphne might fetch a pair of eyeglasses from her grandmother's bureau, deliver a cup of coffee to a family member or guest, or volunteer her help in some other way, a volunteering that seemed to give her a rush of pleasure, presumably at having expressed her affection and demonstrated her competence, and worthiness.

That Daphne was a great hit with people and that others found her an irresistible child probably comes as no surprise. Asked to spell out the root of her appeal, I would say that she caught and held the attention of those who came in contact with her by simultaneously embodying two images of the child that our culture reveres without giving either much thought, images that we have traditionally conceived of, usually in terms of gender, as mutually exclusive or incompatible, and that we typically do not expect to find embodied in one and the same person, at least not in so pronounced a form as they were embodied in Daphne. On the one hand, because she was such a spirited, lively tomboy, independent, self-possessed, and plucky, she appealed to the nostalgia for childhood or "boyhood" as a time of robust and wholesome adventurousness in the great outdoors unencumbered by adult responsibilities and unspoiled by adult corruptions. On the other hand, because she was a spontaneously warm and affectionate cuddler who cared about others, she appealed to the sense of the child as a tenderhearted, loveable and responsive creature, an appeal that doubtless was enhanced by her shortness, her large brown eyes and long dark lashes, and also perhaps by a blurring of the gender boundary, a blurring that I think gave Daphne the appeal of the mythical or extrahuman or of a colorful, unforgettable character in a classic children's story.

At school, Daphne's sensitivity, her willingness to help others, her physical energy and impressive athletic ability, as well as her all-around spiritedness, made as favorable an impression on others as these traits did at home. And Daphne says that she dearly loved school. She remembers her first day as one that put an end to all the other days before it when she had wanted to climb on the bus and go to school with the older kids but had been told she couldn't. And she says that once she got to school she "loved everything about it" and felt that, with the exception of the fifth-grade teacher who made her wear dresses, she was loved and respected in return. One of her earliest and happiest school memories is of the day she asked if she could take the role of the farmer in the game Farmer in the Dell. Daphne says that though her kindergarten teacher was a little taken aback by the request (at that time only boys volunteered for such roles), she recovered quickly. Answering "Well, why not?" she honored Daphne's request and from that time on chose Daphne to be the farmer as regularly as she chose any of the boys.

Perhaps even more telling than the kindergarten teacher's response to Daphne was the response of her sixth-grade teacher. A strict, no-nonsense, but also enthusiastic and concerned teacher, he had nothing but good to say about Daphne. At parent-teacher conferences he gave glowing reports to Daphne's mother, and at one conference he took it upon himself to express his concern that a boy she had made friends with at school might need a little monitoring. It seemed that this boy had struck him as sophisticated beyond his age and as having the potential to take advantage of the hearty wholesomeness of a girl like Daphne.[1] When the teacher's first child was born, he made clear just how thoroughly Daphne had impressed him by naming his daughter after her and expressing the hope that his own child would grow into as fine a young person as Daphne had.

Though some might speculate that Daphne's popularity with her teachers would have distanced her from her peers, she had a way about her—an authenticity or generosity of spirit—that allowed her to be a favorite among her teachers without earning the title "teacher's pet" and that also allowed her to stand up for those children who were singled out for teasing without disaffecting the teasers or herself becoming the butt of jokes or being labeled "goody goody." Frequently appointed a team captain during P. E., she made sure that poorly skilled and physically timid children did not get chosen last by choosing them early on herself. When actual play began and one of the inept players jeopardized the team's chance to win, Daphne would quell any ridicule or jeering. She also would intervene if she happened on any bullying at school; for example, in third grade she reproved a group of boys she knew when she walked into her classroom for a noontime meeting and found the boys playing keep away with the underpants of a classmate who was forever being picked on and who on this occasion had wet her pants. In middle school, Daphne's popularity with her teachers and peers continued. She was president of her class and president of the school, and she was a high-scoring player on the girls' basketball team.

From a fairly young age Daphne's willingness to promote the happiness of others through her personal effort was experienced by many adults, particularly in her home world but also at school, as evidence that her vocation was to lift the spirits of those around her, not only by exuding the liveliness and warmth that were themselves a tonic for anyone whose spirits were low, but also by taking on odd jobs that eased the burdens and pressures of those around her or nurtured their hopes and desires. Though Daphne was experienced as anything but the traditional girl-child or mother's helper and though her tomboyishness was not only accepted but also celebrated by family and friends (as my earlier descriptions perhaps suggest, she did not get dolls, play refrigerators, aprons, miniature mops and brooms, or tea sets for gifts but instead was given gun and holster sets, baseball gloves, tool belts, rifles, chaps, and cowboy boots), she nonetheless spent lots of time obliging others, especially adults, who thought it was just great that Daphne loved participating in the lives of others in just the way those others needed someone of her sensitivity, concern, and loveableness to participate.

Perhaps for the very reason that she was such a pronounced combination of spirited tomboyishness, affectionateness, and sensitivity to the hopes and needs of others, Daphne's willingness to oblige and the odd jobs she took on involved her increasingly in the world of boys and men. Although this involvement did allow her some access to the male world that so attracted her, an involvement that she would not have experienced otherwise, it also drew heavily on the capacity to support and nurture that is traditionally associated with women, and, in a slightly different sense, with such figures as the manservant and choreboy.

Two jobs Daphne excelled at that brought her into the company of men and boys were massaging the back of Glen's father, Howard, which began sometime between the ages of seven and nine, and polishing the shoes her father wore to work, which began at about the same time. Howard, who had periodic back pain, talked a lot about the pain to family and friends and work acquaintances. He also let people know what a great little kid Daphne was, explaining that she had a real knack for giving back rubs and was always glad to oblige him when she was around and he was in pain.

One result of his talk was that Daphne became renowned as an expert back rubber as well as a sensitive and thoughtful child who was something of a "sidekick" to Howard. It became almost routine, when visits brought them together, for Howard to request a back rub. Waiting until he had stripped off his shirt and stretched out on the floor on his stomach, Daphne would sit on his buttocks and rub away at his back and shoulders while he closed his eyes and dozed. Sometimes he would fall into a deep sleep, and Daphne, who was what is often called "a real trooper," would continue the back rub until some adult, usually Howard's wife, would notice and say something like, "Daphne—I didn't know you were still busy there. You must be awfully tired. It's all right if you go out and play now."

When it came to polishing her father's shoes, Daphne would fetch them and the shoe-shine kit from his closet herself and set up a work area on a piece of newspaper in front of a window or in good artificial light so that she would be able to see well enough not to miss any of the scuff marks or fail to remove with a toothpick the polish that tended to build up in the tiny perforations that had been tooled to form a pattern in the leather. Handling the tins of polish, the buffing cloth, and the soft-bristled brush with the same dexterity she evidenced when wielding a baseball glove or fielding a ball, Daphne could put a shine on a pair of men's dress shoes that met even her father's high standards. And the fact that the shoes were her father's—that is, were a man's and associated with the world of suits, neckties, cuff links, dress shirts, and a career outside the home— made the job seem a natural one for Daphne the tomboy to take on. In addition, that Daphne's father was a man who treasured his weekends and did not like to have them interrupted by tasks that reminded him of Monday morning but who at the same time was quite particular about his personal appearance and the figure he cut at work, made the shoe polishing a natural job for the Daphne who sought harmony and was happiest when everyone else was happy, too.

The rowing lessons Daphne had given herself while her father's boat was tied near shore eventually brought her the job of rowing for her father while he fished. This rowing distinguished her from her sisters (they were more interested in playing under the pine trees than in fishing or in rowing), from her mother (though Daphne's mother knew how to row and fish, she rarely did either once her children were born), and also from most of the other girls and women who vacationed with them or who happened to be staying at the same campground. Leaving behind the fixed foot of the family campsite, with its dishes to wash, children to look after, and tent to straighten up, Daphne would row her father, and often also her brother, out onto the fluid surface of the lake and into the world of fishing that she had so great a passion to know about and that in her family was dominated by her father. However, though Daphne hoped she would come to be recognized as someone who did her share of the rowing and had earned the right to a fair share of opportunities to fish, she did not come to be viewed as a fisherman in her own right but instead as a rower of fishermen. Her father, praising her lavishly and exclaiming over her ability to others, made the most of the opportunity her rowing gave him to fly-fish without having to concern himself with the distraction of maneuvering the boat to keep it in an advantageous position for casting.

A third way Daphne obliged her father when she was small, an obliging that drew on her cooperativeness and her sensitivity to the feelings of others, was to share her warmth and affection with the friends he brought home to dinner. Sometimes the friends were men on business trips separated from their families by the demands of their careers, but more often they were bachelors who had not yet settled down with a wife and started families of their own. Observing how wonderful it was to be a family man and how lonely it was to be a bachelor and to have no wife and children or to be away from home on business, her father would extend his and his family's hospitality. For Daphne, this meant bestowing a hug or a "peck" on the cheek of the dinner guests according to her father's direction: depending on who the guest happened to be, he would usually suggest a hug or peck when the guest first arrived, another as dinner came to a close, and a third when the guest departed or Daphne's bedtime arrived. This bestowing of hugs and kisses, which her sisters also participated in (but more soberly, as they were less outgoing) pleased her father greatly by contributing to the image of his home as a warm and hospitable place.

Another job Daphne took on in the world of home that involved reaching out to someone less fortunate than herself was to befriend

Glen. Increasing Daphne's access to the world of boys, Daphne's befriending of Glen also served the interests of the adults in her world, but particularly of Howard and Kathleen, Glen's mother and father, by supporting their efforts to transform Glen from an unpopular child whose behavior often worried his parents into an active and likeable child more like his friend Daphne. During his toddler years, and with apparent deliberation, Glen would break fragile decorative objects in the homes where his family socialized. As a toddler he was also known for biting and hitting other children. At first people were mainly disconcerted by his behavior and tended to assume, once they had regained their composure, that it was a stage he would outgrow. Though the breakage and the biting and hitting did end, he was unpopular and worrisome for other reasons as he grew from toddlerhood into early childhood. Losing the toddler's physical appeal, Glen developed a weight problem and an awkwardness that put many people off. Nor did it help that though he was hypersensitive to his own feelings, he evidenced little sensitivity to the feelings of others. During this period, a friction also developed between father and son, with the father's spontaneous doting on the infant-toddler giving way to an edgy dutifulness. Teased at school during the early years, Glen became something of a social isolate until high school, when, developing good looks and a small but definite circle of friends, he began to date.

If left to himself during the elementary years, Glen would spend hours reading comic books, watching cartoons, and eating candy or drinking soda pop, and when he did interact with others, he preferred that it be over such activities as board games. Other worrisome traits during these early years were that he lied, seemingly at random, and spent lots of time at such forbidden activities as playing with matches, inventing and detonating small explosives, and teasing the family dog. For example, he would tie the dog to a short rope and, putting its food dish just out of reach, watch the dog struggle to reach the dish. In addition to pursuing these prohibited activities, Glen also liked to take apart and reassemble mechanical devices and spent many hours working with his chemistry set, one consequence being that though his parents were very concerned about him, there was also room to view the worrying as an overreaction and to see Glen as a budding scientist who was simply fascinated with the workings of the world and who loved to conduct his own experiments.

In an effort to help Glen learn to interact more successfully with his peers, his parents saw to it that he learned to do the things other children generally like to do, such as ride a bike, fish, swim, pitch and catch a ball, and swing a bat. They also saw to it that he had definite times and places to practice his skills by signing him up for Little League, planning fishing trips with family, friends, and neighbors, arranging for him to have a paper route, and joining a neighborhood swim club. Family and friends supported the effort to "humanize" Glen by taking an interest in his accomplishments, including him in outings, and reminding their own children to be "nice" to Glen and to include him in their play. Glen cooperated in the sense that with repeated reminders and urgings from others he would go through the motions of taking part, and occasionally he seemed to have a really good time and feel good about himself. Generally, however, he did not initiate such activities himself and seemed most thoroughly engaged when he was sitting in front of a television set with a stack of comic books and a sack of candy from the local drugstore, teasing the dog in the backyard, or pursuing his fascination with matches and small explosive devices.

Daphne's qualifications for becoming the main child-recruit in the effort to transform Glen were several. As a tomboy who had little patience with comic books or cartoons and who was much more "one of the boys" than Glen, she could be counted on, when in Glen's company, to support the adult urgings for him to be more active. "Glen, why don't you and Daphne go outside and play ball" is one of the refrains Daphne remembers best from her childhood. As the kindhearted, sensitive girl who was almost two years younger than Glen, she could also be counted on not to judge Glen too harshly, not to tease him as children at his elementary school did, and not to physically assault or punch him, as her older brother sometimes ended up doing, usually when he had made an effort to be nice to Glen only to encounter behavior he found contemptible (behavior such as lying, hoarding candy, breaking agreements, and "blubbering" at the threat of minor dangers or hurts). And because Glen was a Little Leaguer with a paper route, the befriending was seen as benefiting Daphne, too.

Commenting on her childhood attitude towards Glen, Daphne says that she was frightened by his activities with the explosives and his treatment of the dog but that during his awkward years she mainly felt sorry for him and thought of him as "the boy who sat in the rocking chair and read comics, ate candy, and watched cartoons." In addition, she says that though she was never awed or impressed by *him*, she was anxious to explore the worlds of the Little Leaguer and the paperboy to which he belonged.

At school Daphne did not take on so many odd jobs as she did at home that could be clearly defined as benefiting adults. But her combination of tomboyishness and sensitivity to the feelings of others did earn her a reputation as someone who would come through when she was needed and who, in addition, would be more than glad to do so. One teacher who called on her was the girls' basketball coach at her middle school. After basketball season ended, Daphne did not sign up for volleyball, partly because she was tired and wanted a break from sports but also because after elementary school volleyball did not interest her. But the coach wanted Daphne on the team and pressured her until she joined, telling her that the team would really benefit from an athlete of her caliber. Whether it was the team the coach was primarily concerned about or her own desire to win was not clear. Either way, however, it remained true that Daphne's own preference, which was not to play volleyball, carried no weight with the coach. Another teacher who saw Daphne as someone who would rise to most any occasion was the boys' athletic coach, who had watched her play on the girls' team and nicknamed her "Tiger." Apparently convinced that it would create a great stir and be a lot of fun for everybody if Daphne joined the boys' team for one of their league games, the coach made all the necessary arrangements. Two results were that Daphne became the only girl in anyone's memory to play on the boys' team and that the coach distinguished himself by orchestrating such a first. A third result was that, though Daphne never said so at the time, she felt as if she had been made an attraction in a sideshow.

Finally, I would argue that the sixth-grade teacher's naming of his daughter after Daphne, which I discussed previously in another context, was also an example, though indirect, of the way Daphne's combination of sensitivity and spirited tomboyishness contributed to her gravitation towards the world of boys and men and also encouraged her to live up to the expectations others had of her. The naming admittedly did not foster any new connections between Daphne and the male world, and it did not call on her to perform any specific task for her teacher. Still, his "borrowing" of her name did share something with the borrowing of her person for such activities as back rubbing and volleyball, particularly in that it constituted an implicit admiration of Daphne as she was—as the sensitive, socially conscientious, and spirited tomboy—and also suggested a confidence or an expectation that she would continue to exemplify the traits and values that had so impressed him during the year she was his student, traits that he would presumably try to cultivate in his own daughter. Such a naming, then, despite any fine intentions on the teacher's part, had the potential to exert a subtle but powerful pressure on Daphne to live up to or deserve the honor, a pressure that could stifle her own sense of the person she might want to become. And I say this even though I do believe in having expectations of children and even though I recognize that on one level the naming could have had a positive impact on Daphne.

Another way of expressing my view would be to say that the naming had the potential to discourage further becoming, except in the directions already in evidence. And at this point I do not mean to imply any value judgment of her direction but rather to argue, as E. Straus has done, that "whatever is in becoming must gradually emancipate itself from what has already become. The terminated prevails in tradition, the family, language, and knowledge; they are with us everywhere. To come into our own immediacy, we must unloosen ourselves from the outcomes" ([1966] 1980, 222). I also want to suggest that, in addition to embracing and honoring our children as they are (and it is admittedly difficult to distinguish the persons they are from the persons they may appear to be), we must also find ways to let children know that they need not feel bound to the *is*, to the *outcome*, as a way of paying us for having honored them. And I think this remains true even when our children's outcomes are as innovative and nontraditional as Daphne's seemed to be. Though a thank-you for recognition may be in order, a lifetime of deference is not.

Given my description of Daphne's childhood, I want to turn to the devastating experience I mentioned earlier, an experience Daphne told me about one day when she called me on the telephone. Not long before the call (a few weeks, I think), she had told me she was seeing a therapist, and during the phone call she said she wanted to tell me about an experience from her childhood that she was working on in therapy but that it was hard for her to talk about. It was only after I asked her a series of wide-ranging questions and tried in other ways to let her know that I would be willing to hear whatever she might want to tell me that she was able to say that between the ages of about ten or eleven and thirteen or so she had been sexually abused by Glen, the friend with the paper route whom the adults in her world had encouraged her to befriend. On the basis of this communication and the many communications that followed, I want to set forth Daphne's story of the abuse.

During one of our first talks, Daphne explained that Glen's abuse began early one Sunday morning. Daphne, who had been spending the night at her friend's house, was doing one of the things she liked best, which was to help Glen deliver papers to the customers on his route. When they finished, one of them suggested a ride over to the ballpark where Glen played Little League. Daphne does not remember who made the suggestion but says that she was eager to go because the visit would give her a chance to see the ballpark up close when there was no practice session or game in progress to inhibit exploration. In fact, Daphne was so eager to go that she did something almost unheard of for her at the time, which was to cross a busy street Glen's mother had expressly told her and Glen not to cross.

Much more like a professional ballpark than the modest county ballpark where her brother played Little League or than the lots and fields around her house or the P.E. field at school where she played baseball, Glen's ballpark had an official scoreboard, sturdy backstops, a built-in concession stand, plenty of bleachers, and real dugouts. As a place where coaches and players enjoyed a clublike relationship that attracted Daphne but that was off-limits to her and as a place that could not be observed very successfully by a spectator, the dugouts held a special attraction for Daphne. It was after she had walked into one of them and become engrossed in looking around that Glen followed her inside and, grabbing her from behind, began to molest her. Except for an occasional instruction to stand still if she tried to edge away, Daphne does not remember Glen speaking at all during the assault. Nor did he move from the position he had taken at her back.

Daphne has no specific memories of the aftermath of the assault. She assumes, however, that when the assault ended, she and Glen rode back to his house on their bikes, went into the house, and did what would have been expected of them after completing the Sunday morning paper route, which was to attend one of the services scheduled at Glen's church, something that would have entailed Daphne's changing into the dress she would have taken along to Glen's house. After church, Glen and Daphne would probably have had several hours to pal around until her mother drove into the city to pick her up (here I am assuming it was a school weekend) or Glen's parents drove her home.

During the approximately three years of molestation that followed Glen's first assault, Daphne's life came to revolve around her efforts to escape the abuse. Once it became clear to her that the abuse was going to continue, her main concern was to try to find places that were safe from him. At one extreme, her effort, which was unsuccessful, illustrated E. Schachtel's observation that the need for shelter and protection "are often involved in the preference for corners." Corners "are perceived by some persons," adds Schachtel, "as offering shelter and protection to a higher degree than the middle of a room or a seat in the middle of a row would offer" (1966, 132). When Glen visited at her house, Daphne would try hiding from him in closets. Or, if she was outside, she would try to slip away when he was preoccupied and take shelter in some out-of-the-way refuge. Glen, however, was not discouraged by her tactics and invariably searched her out. The day she hid in the closet, for example, he simply stepped inside when he did find her, pulled the door shut, and molested her there.

In addition to searching her out on his own, Glen was aided, unwittingly, by the adults in Daphne's world, most directly by his father. Viewing Daphne as a good influence on Glen, his father would often drop by Daphne's house unannounced on a Friday afternoon and invite Daphne to come home with him for a visit. Because she did not know how to refuse these invitations any more than she knew how to refuse his requests for back rubs and because any effort at refusal was swept aside and the invitation repeated until she said yes, Daphne attempted to avoid the invitations altogether by being away from home at those times Glen's father tended to drop in. This did not work either, however, because Glen's father, often with some well-meaning tips from Daphne's mother or sisters or brother about where to look, would drive around the neighborhood, sometimes with Glen, sometimes by himself, until he found her. And when he did, he would apply pressure until she accepted his invitation. Then he would drive her home so that she could pack her things and they could be on their way, her family perhaps waving a casual good-bye—after all, she was only going to Glen's house—and Daphne perhaps waving back.[2]

Failing to find protection in closets and outdoor retreats, Daphne tried to protect herself by sticking close to adults or spending as much time as possible in wide open, highly visible places; in other words, she tried to protect herself by seeking out the opposite of a corner or what Schachtel refers to in the quotation above as "the middle of a room" (1966, 132). This strategy also failed—partly because the adults eventually would direct her and any other children who happened to be hanging about to "go outside and play," partly because the adults themselves eventually would go off somewhere, and partly because Glen sometimes was able to turn even relatively public places into corners in which he would molest Daphne. One extreme example occurred when Glen's family and Daphne's took a trip to the ocean and the accommodations turned out to be so cramped that most of the children had to sleep on the floor of the living room in sleeping bags. While the adults and some of the children were watching television and talking together in this living room-bedroom and before anyone had fallen asleep, Glen edged himself next to Daphne and molested her under cover of the sleeping bags.

Perhaps because of her continued failure to find a place in her physical world where she could be safe from Glen, Daphne experienced, during some of the assaults and at odd moments in between, time loss and a psychological distancing from her immediate surroundings. Ever in search of some place to hide, Daphne continued to be abused in all sorts of places—bedroom closets, shower stalls, the back seat of Glen's father's car while Glen and Daphne waited for his father to finish some errand, the cover created by trees and shrubs, the corners created by the arrangement of furniture or the closing of a door, a strip of ocean beach bounded by a cliff and broken only by a formation of huge rocks, the toolshed in a neighbor's field.

As for the assaults themselves and the life circumstances of Daphne and Glen, these changed in some ways and remained the same in others. For example, the attacks were progressive in that Glen became more aggressive, probing Daphne's genitals not only with his hands but also with sticks and on one occasion arranging for a high school friend to join him in an attempted assault. In addition, during these years, Glen, who was moving into middle adolescence, became taller and stronger, which frightened Daphne, who was just entering adolescence. As I said earlier, his weight problem disappeared in high school, and he made some new friends and began to date. Daphne's memory of her own transition to middle school is that when a sexual-romantic dimension began to color girl-boy relationships, she began to sense a terrible personal loss and to experience a sadness that seemed always on the verge of overwhelming her. Though for a while she was able to ward off the sadness by becoming absorbed in student government and sports, she says that eventually she could barely keep up appearances and that in looking back she has realized that by eighth grade her spirit had been broken.

A major change in the circumstances of Glen's and Daphne's families that developed during the abuse involved the health of Glen's mother. When Daphne was ten or eleven and not long after the birth of Glen's little sister, Glen's mother had major surgery and was diagnosed as terminally ill. As was relatively common at that time, the diagnosis was kept a secret from the patient and from most of the children among family and friends, including Daphne. Because of the birth of the new baby and the surgery, Glen's family became dependent on others, particularly Daphne's family and particularly her mother, for child and nursing care. When Glen's mother became too sick to care for herself or her family, she and her two youngest children would stay with Daphne's family while Glen and his father continued to live in the city, visiting at Daphne's often during the daytime or evenings and often inviting Daphne to spend the night at their house.

Although these invitations were not new, after the change in living arrangements two new pressures on Daphne emerged. One, which was sometimes vocalized and sometimes simply part of a silent understanding, was that her visits would help compensate for Glen's having been separated from his mother and siblings. The other (Daphne does not know if it was spoken about directly or if she inferred it) was that her visits to Glen's house would ease the pressure of so many people living together at her house. Although the terminal nature of Glen's mother's illness was kept a secret, Daphne was quick to suspect the truth and to anguish over the prospect of Glen's mother's death as well as over the secrecy surrounding the nature of her illness. Consequently, in addition to the great interdependency that developed between the two families, which created pressures for everyone to cooperate to make a difficult situation easier (a situation in which the needs of children and adults alike were often subordinated to the needs of the sick woman), Daphne also experienced the strain of being in the presence of a dying person and the strain that develops in situations where secrecy erodes intimacy and the open expression and sharing of such emotions as anger, sorrow, love, hate, and fear.

Despite the changes in the relationship between the two families and in the intensity and details of the abuse, a pattern did emerge. With some exceptions, Glen would attack Daphne when she was preoccupied and her back was turned. And, except to issue an occasional instruction, he would molest silently and invisibly from behind her, so that for Daphne the world seemed to have been reduced to a pair of hands, a voice, and her own violated flesh. In addition, Glen seemed to regard Daphne as some lackey or nonentity whose sole purpose in life was to carry around an object—her genitals or crotch—that had lately come to his attention, as a new candy bar on the shelf of his neighborhood drugstore might, and that he felt entitled to keep near him in case he should have an urge to handle it or, to carry through the comparison with food, in case he should want to sample it.

The molestations were also characterized by a greediness that both disgusted and terrified Daphne; no matter how often Glen attacked her, he never seemed sated, and she came to feel as if she were being forever hoarded or preserved only to be repeatedly gobbled up or bolted down, a feeling made possible by the fact that, unlike a bar of candy that has been eaten, her body was not "all gone" after having been molested. Alarmed to discover, each time she was abused, that so disturbingly large and perverse an appetite could exist in the world and in addition sickened that the appetite should regard her own body as its food, Daphne lost all sense of the world as a stable or trustworthy place. Despite her image as a spirited and plucky tomboy (and also to some extent because of this image), she was left feeling craven and ashamed.

Something else that remained nearly constant throughout the three years of abuse was Daphne's ignorance of sex. Not only has she no memory of any adult or peer ever broaching the subject to her, but neither has she any memory of ever broaching the subject to herself or even of having vaguely wondering thoughts. The one exception she can recall that did bear on the question of human sexuality, an experience that occurred long before the abuse by Glen and that stuck with her—even though it did not generate any thoughts, at least not conscious ones, of the possibility of intercourse—was of lying awake at night when she was small (perhaps as young as three or four) and being frightened at the sight of her father walking naked down the hallway and past her bedroom door on his way to the kitchen.

The only formal information she received that had anything to do with sexuality was a film on menstruation she saw at school in sixth grade, which, though it may have touched on reproduction, did not in Daphne's memory do so in a way that led her to grasp intercourse as a reality that could have had some connection to the molestations by Glen. Daphne does say, however, that even though she had no concrete understanding of intercourse, she felt, as the abuse progressed, that Glen intended something even more hideous (*hideous* is the word she typically uses when referring to the molestations) than the probing she had already experienced. As well as remaining ignorant of sexuality throughout the period of abuse, Daphne, until the final months, remained almost wholly passive in the face of Glen's attacks, a passivity that I will return to later.

A month or two before Glen's final molestation of Daphne, an aborted effort at assault occurred that particularly terrified her. The attempt took place while Daphne and Glen's families were vacationing at the ocean, a vacation that had been planned largely because the health of Glen's mother had worsened and everyone hoped a trip to the ocean would improve it. The accommodation was spacious and comfortable. The adults, a guest or two, some of the older children or young people, and Glen's little sister slept in the several bedrooms in the main house while Daphne and Glen and three or four of the other young people were assigned to sleep in a large dormitorylike playroom that had a row of five or six beds, a television set, and a cupboard full of cards, board games, and hobby supplies. Although the playroom and the prospect of the relaxed adult supervision promised by its separation from the main house was welcomed by most of the children assigned to sleep there, Daphne remembers hating the arrangement because it meant sharing quarters with Glen while at the same time being cut off from the adults and any deterring influence their nearness might have had on his abuse.

Daphne's alarm proved well-founded. Glen assaulted her a number of times in the dormitory, and she kept watch for opportunities to escape from the house without him, one day managing to slip off by herself to surf-fish from a massive formation of rocks that was not accessible unless the tide was out. After fishing for a while, Daphne spotted Glen coming towards the rocks. She says that something in his manner that she cannot pinpoint made her feel immediately terrified and that as soon as she spotted him and took note of the desertedness of the beach, she knew she was in extreme danger and absolutely must find some way to keep away from him.

Her first thought was to rebait her hook and climb up high on the rocks, a position she felt would be safe because it would be so dangerous to maneuver or scuffle about in such a spot. But Glen reached her before she could climb up on the rocks. She told him to stay away from her, that the tide was coming in and that they must head back to the house immediately or risk being trapped. Glen said she was wrong and moved towards her. Daphne seized her fishing pole and gear—to this day she says that it disturbs and angers her that she would have taken the time to secure her pole and gear at such a moment—and repeated that the tide was coming in. Then, because she was too alarmed by the quality of Glen's manner to head back to the house by the usual route along the beach, she started to climb frantically up the sage-covered bluff that separated the beach from the highway.

Becoming even more frightened when Glen started up the incline behind her, Daphne tore through the dense sage, scratching and cutting her hands and face. And even when she realized Glen had slid back down to the sand and must be heading back to the house by way of the beach, she continued to tear through the brush. Arriving back at the house bleeding and overwrought, Daphne explained her condition by saying that the tide had almost trapped her and that she had had to climb up the cliff but that Glen had taken the beach route and should be back soon. Although Daphne was haunted by this experience on the deserted beach and tried continually to escape the memory, the incident, which was much talked about among the vacationers, became a story others would recall at social gatherings as an entertaining "I can remember when" adventure tale.

Glen's final assault on Daphne occurred the summer before her freshman year in high school while she was playing a game of hide and seek in the field behind her house.[3] During one round of the game, Daphne decided to hide in the neighbor's toolshed, and she remembers feeling very pleased with herself, almost smug, for having thought of the shed. As far as she knew, no one had ever thought to hide there before, and she was sure she had hit on a foolproof hiding place, one that would enable her to remain undiscovered by the seeker until she got a chance to run to home base without being caught and yell "Home free!"

She remembers that she had been peering out the shed's one window trying to keep track of the game when suddenly Glen, who was not "it" and who, according to the rules, should have been concealing himself in a hiding place of his own, was suddenly in the shed behind her, pulling off her tennis shorts and underwear and letting them fall down around her ankles like a hobble. As I have already said, Daphne had no knowledge of sexuality, and when she suddenly felt Glen's penis and some liquid touch her skin, she did not conclude that Glen had been masturbating but instead that he had urinated, urine being the only fluid she associated with a penis. The thought that she had been urinated on—something she says she would never have conceived of on her own and could barely conceive of even given the evidence of the liquid—so enraged and repulsed her that she became hysterical.

> I just was hysterical. . . . I thought he urinated on me. . . . I was in a state of shock and hysteria and everything all at once and I turned around and I shoved him down and I yelled at him, said things. You know. I called him a pig, and I told him never to come near me again . . . um—I'll never forget the emotional, the intensity of the emotions that day. I just felt—like an explosion. It was, and I knew right then that was the last time it was ever going to happen—how you could go from one extreme to another one that quickly, I don't understand. It was like—I thought he had urinated on me and that was the most offensive thing I had ever heard of in my life. It nauseated me.

As Daphne's description suggests, she knew in the midst of her hysteria that Glen would not molest her again. She also has said that though the end of the abuse was an inexpressible relief and that at moments she felt euphoric, the relief was largely offset by other feelings, feelings that I will eventually take up in more detail but that included a feeling of revulsion of which she could not rid herself and a feeling of humiliation and anger at herself that grew into self-hatred and was provoked by the thought that she herself had had the power to stop the abuse and need not have suffered as she had the previous years.

After knocking Glen down, Daphne ran past him out of the shed. Leaving the field and the game of hide and seek behind (she does not remember seeing or speaking to any of the other players), she ran through the front yard of her own house and the neighbors, then past their gravel driveway, through a small orange grove, and down a country road to a small creek about a quarter of a mile from her home. Given her conviction that the abuse was over, she no longer had to worry that the creek was one of the places where Glen had previously sought her out and molested her and where his father had sometimes come in his car to find her and take her home with him. Instead, she was now free to run there, and says she did so because she wanted to be in a place where she would not see people (she says that after the assault the thought of people made her sick) and people would not see her. Two additional measures of Daphne's trauma (besides her hysteria, her violent outburst, and her recoiling from human beings) were, first, that when she ran from the shed she became nauseated and believes, but is not certain, that she vomited, once in the gravel of the neighbor's driveway and again in the orange grove, and, second, that after she had buried herself in the creek's foliage, she suffered a time loss that lasted about two hours.

When Daphne regained awareness of herself and her surroundings, she had no memory of what she had thought about or done during the time loss. However, in listening to her tell about her childhood and in remembering those things I did know about her when she was little, I have considered whether this tired and worn-out young girl may not have rinsed herself off with creek water (she has said that she had hated having to pull her shorts up over her wet skin when she ran from the shed) and then perhaps fallen into the lulling rhythm of some familiar activity, such as gathering together rocks and sticks and arranging them to dam one of the creek's rivulets or perhaps simply sitting on the creek's bank and watching the small bluegill move their fish bodies beneath the surface of the creek's ripple or in the pockets of still water along the creek's edge. In listening and remembering, I have also considered whether she may not have lain curled in the shelter of the creek's overgrowth and imagined herself elsewhere, in another time and place, perhaps sitting at her grandmother's feet while her grandmother worked her knitting needles and talked with her, or perhaps climbing over her brother and sisters on the couch in an effort to get close to her mother for evening story time.

Or maybe, during the time loss, Daphne imagined herself to be some other person altogether than the Daphne who had been abused, perhaps some Cub Scout who had a paper route all his own and a penis that in Daphne's mind would have kept him safe from Glen's greediness for a part of the female body that she could not even name. Or perhaps during those two lost hours she recalled the character Joey from the game of early childhood and fantasized that her sister-mother was near and would soon tuck her into the bed in the loft room for a story and a nap. Daphne's own feeling is that any one of these projected pastimes could have filled the two hours, and she says that even as an adult woman she has sometimes taken refuge from the memory of the assaults by pretending she is the child Joey who so loved being mothered. She has no memory of what she actually thought about or did during these hours, however, and says that when she regained her sense of her surroundings, she walked home to find that Glen had left and that the table was set and dinner was ready to be served.

Taking her place at the table with her family and trying to act "normal," Daphne found that she could not eat. After a few minutes of sitting silently and pushing at her food, she asked her mother if she could please be excused. She remembers that her mother looked at her and at the full plate and answered, "You haven't eaten very much—at least drink all of your milk," and that after emptying her glass as her mother had asked her to do, she left the table and went to her bedroom for the night. In addition to the feelings of revulsion, humiliation, and intense anger mentioned earlier, Daphne says that after the final instance of abuse she was no longer able to fight off the sadness that had been threatening to overwhelm her for so long. Nothing interested her anymore, not at home or, in the fall, at high school, and she sank into a depression that was like a solitary mourning for her own death, a depression that was infinitely compounded when Glen's mother died about six months later and a depression that has remained with her in varying degrees of intensity into the present.

In the process of talking with Daphne about her childhood and the molestations, few things have become clearer than that her silence about the abuse had been a complex phenomenon affected by everything from her shifting perception of the nature of the assaults, to her anger at the adults in her world for not protecting her, to her ignorance of sexuality. Daphne remembers the first assault in the Little League dugout as an experience that stunned her and made no sense and that she did not believe could actually be happening. And here I think it is worth noting that because the assault was physical and involved the sense of touch, it would not have lent itself to such dismissive phrases as "I must have been seeing [or hearing] things." Daphne resolved the discrepancy between her immediate sensing or perception and her concept of reality roughly as follows: at the most extreme, she denied her sense of touch and categorized the assault as a bad dream; that is, she concluded that it could not have happened because her sense of reality—of what was possible in the world—told her unequivocally that though there were such things as hands and though hands have the theoretical potential to do what Glen's hands had done, such an assault could not happen, *really*.[4] At a lesser extreme, Daphne accepted her sense of touch but categorized the assault as a fluke experience or anomaly so aberrant that it not only defied explanation and understanding but also, because it was so aberrant, could not possibly ever happen again. And before moving on to discuss the way this initial response influenced subsequent behavior, I want to add that Daphne's categorizing of the initial assault as a bad dream or fluke was not simply cut and dried but was accompanied by an emotional upheaval and shakiness at having to bridge the gap between her concept of reality and her sensory experience.

Daphne's two responses to the first assault have many possible implications, one being that as long as she assumed the incident had been a bad dream or fluke, any pressure to tell out of a desire to protect herself from future assaults would have been minimized. In other words, though she may conceivably have wanted to tell because the content of the molestation (despite her categorization of it as impossible) had so shaken her sense of the world that she felt a need to have someone listen to her story and perhaps validate her categorization or in some other way help her explain it, and though the assaults may conceivably have made her wary of Glen in a way she had not been before (previous to the first assault she had been wary of his interest in matches and explosives and of his cruelty to animals), it would not, so long as she perceived it as a dream or one-time event, have provoked a great urgency to tell out of a desire for protection in the future.[5]

Glen's continued assaults on Daphne challenged the categories of bad dream and anomaly. At first, even with the repetition of the abuse, she says she clung to the broad view that the abuse would turn out to be some kind of mistake or something very temporary that would go away all on its own—without her having to take action or tell anyone. Gradually, however, Glen's persistence and the greediness she sensed in him forced her to acknowledge to herself that the assaults were going to continue. But she says that even at this point she continued "to hope for a miracle," by which she meant that she continued to hope the abuse would go away on its own. By the same token, she began to fear increasingly that there would be no miracle. In fact, the hope for a miracle and the despair that there would not be one became a set of emotional highs and lows that Daphne was continually traveling between. Although she has no memory of a specific moment or situation in which the feeling of despair gave rise to an urge to tell, and though despair itself can provoke silence, it seems reasonable to assume that an urge to tell, which she says she did experience at times, would have been felt when she was despairing or, at least, when she was not hoping for a miracle.

However, as well as giving rise to an urge to tell, Daphne's relinquishing of the categories of bad dream and anomaly would also have confronted her with various pressures to keep silent; because Daphne had never heard of such a thing as sexual abuse, even on an abstract or general level, let alone as something she knew of as having happened to a particular person, she understandably assumed, during the time when she let go the bad dream and anomaly theories, that she was the only person in the history of the world ever to have had such a shameful thing happen to her. In other words, at the same time that further molestations would have pushed her towards accepting the reality of the abuse and the probability that it would continue (an accepting that would give rise to an urge to tell or, at least, to a desire for protection), she also had reason (given her ignorance of sexuality) to experience all sorts of pressures to keep silent, the following three being pressures that she specifically recalls. First, she feared that people would find her story so outrageously farfetched that they would not believe it and would conclude it was a fantasy or a lie. Second, she feared that even if people did believe her story, they would either be so horrified by the news of such a strange occurrence as to regard her as a contaminated person who repulsed them and was no longer loveable or be so morally outraged at her "badness" as to censure her as equally to blame with Glen. Third, she feared others might assume that to have such a thing happen to her meant that she herself must be marked or flawed in a way that attracted such treatment and that in addition meant she was somehow deserving or cut out for abuse.

Though such fears may elicit incredulity among the adults in an abused child's world once the abuse has been revealed (actually, as many readers are doubtless aware, these fears are practically universal among survivors of sexual abuse), I think Daphne's fears make perfect sense if we only remember that for years Daphne had been experienced by others and by herself as a child "cut out" to uplift others with her spiritedness, her warmth, and her willingness to lend a helping hand. Her fears also make lots of sense if we consider the prevalence in history of theories of human nature and behavior that have at their center just such assumptions as the ones Daphne feared would be made about her. In other words, I think that when we adults hear about such fears as Daphne's and respond with such remarks as "How awful it must have been for the poor child—but really, where did she get such notions?" we are responding superficially, the only honest answer being that "the poor child" got "such notions" from the world in which we live.

In addition to hoping that the abuse would go away without her having to do anything or tell anybody, Daphne also hoped that an adult would rescue her.[6] Like the earlier hope, this one also fostered silence, and, though it may seem melodramatic in its passiveness, the hope did reflect her image of adults, particularly parents, as protectors of children, an image that is hardly radical and that she referred to explicitly in one of our conversations. We had been talking about fathers and I had said that I thought a concept of the father as *the* wise man was shallow in the sense of being unrealistic or wishful and also dangerous in that it promoted a division of the world into knowledgeable fathers and ignorant wives and children. Daphne responded quickly, even firmly, as if to set me straight, which surprised me, since such firmness was not typical of her, saying that she did not think of the father in those terms. I asked her how she did think of the father, and she said that he was supposed to protect the child. She added that mothers were also supposed to protect their children and that protecting children was what parents were for.

As well as reflecting her conception of parents as primarily protective figures, Daphne's hope of being rescued by an adult also in my opinion suggested the degree to which she had been shaped by our culture's celebration of the heroic style, particularly by one version of it.[7] By definition requiring a potential victim as well as a potential villain, the heroic style tends, in one of its most popular versions, to conceive of hero and victim (and also villain) as necessarily played by different people or "actors" in any one drama, the perception of what constitutes "one drama" varying widely; to some it might be a single moment, to others an entire lifetime.

One consequence is that those of us influenced by this version may assume that the parceling out of roles is necessitated by human nature, that is, by our *essential* inability to actualize both the potential for heroism and for vulnerability or victimization in a single situation or drama. Such an assumption could prompt us to ignore the possibility that the parceling out is instead tied to the limitations of time and space and perhaps also, particularly among dramatists and other narrative artists, to a desire to clarify the complexity of human potential by separating out the various potentials and embodying them in different actors or characters. As a result, those of us under the influence of this version may step automatically into the role of hero when other people are being victimized but wait passively for someone else to step into the role when we ourselves are being victimized, particularly if we are children or females whose culture not only teaches that we are relatively weak and helpless human beings but that also structures itself to dramatize this lesson.[8] Thus, we may overlook our capacity to play the hero in relation to our own vulnerability: that is, we may overlook our capacity to help ourselves (and here I would include a direct appeal to another for help as one way to help ourselves). Behaving as if our lives are roles in a drama written by someone in possession of the ultimate script, as if the possessor's drama is our only option, we may play our roles as written and in so doing waste the only life we've got.[9]

In Daphne's case, most of her childhood models (the Cub Scout, the combat soldier, Eliot Ness, and the Catholic priest) were father or rescuing figures whom we are taught will save or help redeem us and whom we are also taught to wait for and honor faithfully as well as emulate. Given these models and Daphne's social conscientiousness (as evidenced in her intervention on behalf of outcast children at school and in the various roles she played for adults), I would argue that she experienced herself, on one level, very much as a heroic figure and that, in addition to being crushed when she discovered her own vulnerability (particularly in relation to Glen, whom the adults had in a sense asked her to rescue), she was also crushed when no adult stepped forward to take the hero's role and protect her, even if only by happening in on the abuse the way she herself had happened in on the third-grade classmate who had wet her pants and was being tormented by a group of boys. Regardless, however, of the influences at work in Daphne's hope for rescue, it is true that when her misery went unperceived she felt both anger and despair, not only at the adults who failed to live up to the expectations they themselves had cultivated but also at herself for having been so naive as to trust in their protection.

The single experience that Daphne says most destroyed her hope of being rescued and that provoked her anger and despair took place in the first year of abuse, after she had realized that the molestations were no fluke and while she was very much in the grip of her hope of being rescued. Daphne's memory of the experience is that Glen and his family came to visit one Sunday afternoon and that Glen remarked in the presence of his parents and Daphne's mother that he and Daphne were going to take a nap in Daphne's parents' bedroom.

Daphne had been aware from the moment Glen announced the nap that he intended to molest her, and she says that once in the bedroom he situated her up against the side of her parents' bed and was proceeding with the molestation when his father stepped into the room—apparently Glen's remark about the nap had only just registered with him—to say that they could not take a nap because Glen was recovering from strep throat and might still be contagious. Daphne's mother stepped into the doorway of the bedroom almost at the same moment, and Daphne says that she will never forget the adults' look of alarm and that she had no doubt (though the bed provided some cover) that they had seen what was taking place. Daphne also says that she met their look of alarm with one of utter guilt. Then Glen's father and Daphne's mother left the room, as did Glen and Daphne a moment or two afterwards.

Tremendous relief, not fear or worry, was Daphne's primary response to the appearance of her mother and Glen's father at the bedroom door. She can remember saying to herself, "Oh boy, it's over—they know," and at this point she was certain that the adults' discovery would bring intervention and the end of the abuse. She also says that at this point she did not care at all whether they got angry at her or punished her and that she actually hoped they would sit down with her and outline the precise limits of behavior to which she was to adhere so that she would have felt, first, that she had been given express permission not to suffer Glen's assaults and, second, that she would have been able to rely on and invoke the limits they set down if Glen should ever try to abuse her after the intervention.[10] However, after waiting and waiting for the intervention that she was sure would save her and never hearing a word from either her mother or Glen's father, Daphne interpreted their silence to mean that "they were going to ignore this [the scene in the bedroom].”[11] And Daphne added, quietly, with her head bent slightly and her eyes lowered, “There is a sinking feeling that goes with that [with the realization that the hoped for intervention was not going to take place].”

That Daphne to this day feels anger at the adults for not intervening became clear when I asked her during one of our talks what she thought the adults would say if she were to tell them about the abuse today (at the time of our conversation, she had not told any of them). Noticeably agitated by the question—she sat up straighter in her chair and leaned towards me across the table—she said, “First they would say ‘I never knew.’ Then they would say, ‘My God.’ After that, they would say, ‘If only I had known.’” After attributing this response to the adults, Daphne leaned across the table even farther. Looking straight into my eyes and gripping her own shirt collar in her fist as if it were the collar of the adults from her childhood, she said, “I would have pulled them [the adults] up by the shirt and said, “You *should have known*.” My impression was that this hypothetical rebuke, delivered in a hostile voice and with each word fairly spat out, was intended to make clear that she would give the adults from her childhood no quarter and that, so far as she was concerned, the adults were not, would not be, and should not be forgiven for their failure to attend to the primary responsibility of protecting her from the devastation of Glen’s abuse.

Although Daphne’s hope of being rescued by the adults in her world had understandably fostered silence, the end of this hope did not increase the urge to tell the story of her abuse. Instead, because she interpreted the adult silence as meaning that they did not want to know about the abuse, Daphne experienced an erosion of trust that increased the pressure to keep silent. And even at those moments when she was not entirely despairing over the behavior of her mother and Glen’s father or entirely under the influence of fears already described, new or previously unarticulated fears always seemed to emerge and overwhelm the urge to tell. For example, Daphne says that though she sometimes did feel that people’s opinion of her would not matter so long as the abuse ended (a feeling she had experienced when Glen’s father and her mother walked in on the molestation), there were also times when she wanted more than anything else, as she has put it, “to be exonerated,” to have others understand that though she had not fought back during the actual attacks, at least not until the final attack, she had never in any sense been a voluntary participant in the molestations but instead had felt herself controlled not by Glen but by some power whose source she could not identify.

As much as Daphne longed for exoneration, however, she was convinced that appearances were against her, and she feared that if she told her story people would conclude that she could have stopped the abuse if she had really wanted to and that, since she had not stopped it, she must have wanted it to go on. The two appearances that she viewed as the greatest obstacles to exoneration and that she still views as obstacles today were, first, that she was perceived as Daphne the spirited and independent tomboy who could take care of herself and, second, that Glen, far from being an adult, was only about two years older than she was and therefore was not someone who should have been able to so thoroughly dominate her. A circumstance complicating Daphne's situation was that at times she admonished herself in the very way she feared others would admonish her if she told her secret. For example, she can remember getting angry at herself and saying over and over again, "I should be able to handle this myself. I should be able to get this little creep away from me. I'm only two years younger than he is."

Daphne's self-admonishment and her fear that others would admonish her seem to me to be anchored in reality in much the same way as were the fears already discussed. In this case, as in the case of her fear that she would be regarded as a liar or as a bad or contaminated child, I think she had picked up on certain widely held and very abstract principles (people are wholly responsible for their own destiny, needing help is a sign of weakness, nearness in age evens the odds) that our culture constantly invokes but whose subtleties she did not grasp and had never been taught. Applying these principles out of hand to her own situation, she never took into account that within the context of her world Glen had numerous psychological and strategic advantages, advantages that could have contributed to the power she felt was controlling her and that far outweighed any advantage her age or spiritedness might have given her. Specifically, these advantages included such things as that she was female and physically smaller than Glen, that Glen was a "needy" and worrisome child whom she had been encouraged to befriend and "normalize," that she was valued for taking on tasks that were a bother to others and was viewed as someone who would not let others down, that the adults unwittingly abetted Glen by actively seeking Daphne out so she could "babysit" him during his mother's illness, that her job had traditionally been to lift the spirits of others rather than to be the bearer of bad news, and that the adults had promoted an atmosphere of silence and secrecy in relation to painful information by themselves keeping the terminal nature of Glen's mother's illness a secret.

A further reason Daphne says she kept silent is that she could not imagine how she would have gotten through the actual telling of her secret even if she had found the courage to approach someone with the intention of confiding. Another way to put this would be to say that she was held back by an impoverished vocabulary, one that reflected her ignorance of sexuality and the silence of those around her on this subject. Phrases such as *sexual abuse* and *sexual molestation* did not have the currency during her childhood that they do today, and in her home, as was not unusual at that time, talk about sex was as good as taboo. In perhaps the only reference he ever made to sex—and this when Daphne was an adult—her father observed that "sex is not something to be talked about. It belongs behind closed doors."

In addition to lacking the words that would label Glen's action, Daphne did not have any name for the part of her body Glen was molesting. Words such as *vagina* and *genitals* were foreign to her. But even if she had known these words, they probably would have seemed much more forbidding (given the prevailing attitude towards sex) than the few words she did know—such as *breast*—but that she never said herself (not even when she was being silly) and would rarely have heard anyone else say. Among other things, Daphne's impoverished vocabulary meant that a decision to tell her secret would have confronted her with two main options, both of which alarmed her. One option would have been to state that she was having a problem with Glen and then to have relied on her audience to gradually draw the secret into the open by asking questions. The other option would have been to state that she was having a problem with Glen and then explain the problem with such language as "He's doing bad things to me" or "He's touching me where he's not supposed to," and perhaps clarifying by pointing at her "lap."

An additional pressure to keep silent, one tied directly to the circumstances surrounding the first instance of abuse, hinged on Daphne's crossing of the busy street leading to the ballpark. On the one hand, crossing the street had broken Daphne's own code in the sense that she generally liked rules—both those made to keep her safe and those made to ensure a social order—and tended to abide by them out of a respect for safety and order. On the other hand, she was afraid that if she told the adults about being at the dugout, they would dismiss the molestation as her own fault for having broken Glen's mother's rule. In addition, Daphne was particularly worried that if Glen's mother discovered the transgression, she would not like Daphne anymore. Daphne had a special feeling for Glen's mother, who was as warm and affectionate as Daphne and who paid her a certain kind of personal attention (such as the hair brushing described earlier) that people generally assumed Daphne the tomboy would not like and that Daphne herself found it difficult to accept from just about everybody else. What is more, Daphne says that as a child she had liked the idea that Glen's mother cared enough to make the rule against crossing the street and that she had worried his mother would stop caring if she discovered Daphne's disobedience.

Daphne's special feeling for Glen's mother and the changed circumstances her illness brought created at least four additional pressures to keep silent. First, because the illness was such a strain on Glen's mother and everyone else, it intensified a fear Daphne had already experienced to some degree, which was that the news of the abuse would devastate Glen's mother, and everyone else involved. During one of our conversations about the pressures to keep silent, Daphne lost her train of thought just as she was about to add a pressure to the informal list we had been keeping. She became irritated at herself, and after a moment or two I said that perhaps the reason was not a crucial one and that it might come back to her later. At this point she regained her train of thought and said, "Oh—it's real important. I think I always forget it because it's so painful. Um—I did not want her [Glen's mother] to know what Glen was doing. I just—I could not imagine her having to deal with that on top of everything else." When I asked Daphne what she thought would have happened if she had told the already burdened families about the abuse, she said there had been no question in her mind that "we would all go under." And then, using the pronoun *you* rather than such alternatives as *I* or *one* or *a person* and referring to Glen's family and her own with the phrase *these people*, she added, "You could not do that [inform them of the abuse when they were already burdened by the illness] to these people."

Although I know many people would interpret Daphne's use of the pronoun *you* as a way to distance the self from painful material by avoiding the first person or simply as conversational usage, and though I am willing to recognize some of this distancing and conversational quality in her choice, I do not think these two interpretations exclude the possibility that her use of *you* is one sign that her remark was equivalent to the citing of a widely held principle, commandment, or maxim that she experienced as an instruction to keep silent. In the context of this argument, I see Daphne's statement "You could not do that to these people" as her paraphrase or application of a commandment whose standardized version might read, "Thou shalt not strike a person who is down," a standardized version that could be elaborated to read, "Our culture considers it unethical (cruel, unusual, and unacceptable behavior) to strike a person who is already down (literally or figuratively), mainly because a person who is down is defensively at a disadvantage." To illustrate the commandment's wide applicability, the elaboration could in turn be rephrased to read "Thou shalt not heap more bad news on people who have already received bad news." That Daphne did not view herself as a person who had been struck again and again after she was down seems to me further evidence of something I argued earlier, which is that she had been greatly influenced by our culture's concept of the hero as someone who rescues *others* and as someone who can be counted on to come through against all odds.

A second pressure connected to the special feeling for Glen's mother (one already referred to briefly) was that Daphne could not bear the thought of losing her esteem. When I asked Daphne if Glen's mother's death had affected the pressure to keep silent, Daphne's answer suggested just how important this woman's good opinion had been to her. Daphne first responded to my question by saying that after the death she "particularly focused on how [Glen's mother] would feel now [that she was dead]—wherever she was." Then Daphne added, "I know this sounds silly because I was older then, [but I would wonder] if she knew about it [the abuse] now, if she had access to it because she was dead—how she interpreted it and if I was a bad person and, you know, if she was crushed about Glen or if she already knew what he was." Though it does not bear directly on my point here, I want to add that I asked Daphne what Glen "was" and that she answered, "a sick, sick, sick child."

The third pressure growing out of Daphne's relationship with Glen's mother was that Glen exploited his mother's illness by telling Daphne that his mother would want him to be happy (implying that the molestations would make him happy), that it was not fair that he had to live alone in the city with his father while everyone else lived at Daphne's house, and that it was only right that Daphne should help compensate for the unfairness by submitting to the assaults. The final pressure I want to mention is that in a desperate effort to transform the negativity of the abuse into a positive, Daphne made a contract with God in which she agreed to suffer through the abuse in silence if God would cure Glen's mother. And it was while Daphne was being pressed by Glen for compensation and was being influenced by her contract with God that Glen assaulted her in the storage shed and she shoved him over, called him pig, and fled, nauseated, through the orange grove and down the country road to the shelter of the creek.

As I have already said, the end of the abuse, though a relief, did not prevent Daphne from falling into a severe depression. Nor did it end her conflict over whether to tell or keep silent. Daphne says that she continued to long for exoneration and understanding and that (just a few months before Glen's mother died) she broke down completely during a private conference with a woman teacher who was trying to understand why she had become such a behavior problem in class. Though Daphne was able to confide her anguish over Glen's mother's illness and the secrecy surrounding it, she could not bring herself to reveal the secret of the abuse, and she eventually lost the opportunity when the teacher transferred to a distant school. Years later, Daphne would try again to confide her secret to a woman in a position of care and authority, her gynecologist. But even when her doctor directly invited confidence by saying, "Daphne, if you can't talk to me, who can you talk to?" Daphne did not tell about the abuse.

Instead, after asking her doctor's opinion, Daphne consulted a psychiatrist. This first therapist did not work out for Daphne, however, and it was not until she consulted a second therapist that she was finally able to open up about the molestations. And even with this second therapist, Daphne says that she is not sure she could have introduced the subject herself, and certainly would not have done so as soon, if she had not been asked to fill out a health history asking if she had ever been sexually abused. Given this opportunity to take a first step towards telling her story by making a simple pencil mark on a printed form, Daphne took it—but not without making one qualification. Marking the form to indicate that yes, she had been sexually abused, she added an "I think" in the margin, a qualification that in my opinion evidenced her persisting concern that such things as the comparatively small age difference between her and Glen would prevent others from taking her abuse seriously. I also think that the qualification was connected to a fear that her layperson's categorization of Glen's assaults would be at odds with the official or "textbook" definition employed by professionals, making her look ridiculously ignorant, or, even worse, making her appear an interloper or fraud who had the audacity to try to secure for herself the attention and care that by rights did not belong to her.

Once Daphne had marked the history yes and added the qualifier, she did not refer to the molestations until the therapist introduced the subject, which she did one day after Daphne had gained a degree of equilibrium in the office setting (gaining this equilibrium itself turned out to be a major task) by asking the question, phrased approximately as follows, "What do you mean you *think* you were molested?" The therapist's request for clarification of Daphne's qualifying "I think" on the health questionnaire began a period of therapy focusing on the assaults and on the consequences of the abuse (the severe depression, the inability to trust, the fear of rejection, and the time losses Daphne had experienced, for example). Then, about a year or so into therapy, Daphne began to recall previously forgotten incidents from early childhood, incidents that she said came back to her in rushes or floods.

At least a flood of recollections is what Daphne initially said she experienced. And a flood of recollections is what I communicated in the initial text of this chapter.[12] In this earlier text, I wrote the following:

These recollections, which I learned about from Daphne some time after she began working on them with her therapist and that I do not want to explore in any detail here because she is still very much in the process of working them through as I write her story, raise the possibility that Daphne may have experienced two additional pressures to keep silent about Glen's abuse, pressures which she would not have been aware of at the time of Glen's abuse. However, going far beyond a suggestion that there may have been additional pressures to keep silent, the recollections, which she says came in rushes or floods, also confronted Daphne with the possibility that the sensitive, socially conscientious, and spirited tomboy everyone had found so irresistible had emerged more out of an urgent need for protection than out of a sense of who or what she herself might have wanted to become if the need for protection had not been so great.

I also wrote that the recollections had made clear that

> despite others' perception of her, she had not been a child (even in
> early childhood, before the abuse by Glen) who should have provoked
> nostalgia for childhood as a time of robust and wholesome
> adventurousness unspoiled by adult corruption.

I then described the childhood incidents briefly before going on to
discuss, among other things, their possible implications for Daphne's
experiencing of the abuse by Glen and for the development of her
tomboyishness.

Some time after I had completed the full draft of Chapter 5,
however, and the rest of the book, Daphne had a serious emotional
crisis during which she qualified her initial telling of these incidents
from early childhood, saying that the initial telling contained embellishments. Expressing, in the aftermath of the peak of her crisis,
a desire to set the record straight, Daphne communicated specific
qualifications, both orally and by annotating a copy of the initial
text. Because the qualifications are of a nature that I feel needs to be
set forth in the text, I am going to incorporate them here while
retaining the earlier telling as backdrop.

One qualification Daphne has made is that the incidents from
early childhood had not been forgotten ones, as she first said they
had. This qualification, of course, also means that the incidents could
not have come back to her in rushes or floods. During the qualifying
process, she also has communicated other details about her current
life and the progress of her therapy, some of which have clear implications for the text and some of which do not.

But here I feel as if I am in danger of getting ahead of myself, as
if the desire to disclose in an instant (that is, with a simultaneity of
telling that could achieve an evenhandedness that sequence cannot)
all that remains to be laid out may send me racing ahead pell-mell
in a way that will impair coherence.

I therefore want to pause a moment to say that though I cannot
tell what remains except as a sequence, the order of presentation
can itself be highly influential. I also want to point out that to include
even a small part of the detail available in relation to what remains
would take me far beyond the scope of the present work and that I
have had to make choices in this regard, choices guided by a number
of factors. One of them is my feeling that though Daphne's story
has on one level begun to seek the broader scope that a new context

would allow, its origin in the present context also needs to be affirmed. A second is that, despite the story's continuing development, I would not want to pursue it beyond the present context. Having said this, I want to move on to describe the childhood incidents in question—first those involving Daphne's relationship with her father, and first minus the initial embellishments.

The incidents include two sets of actions by her father that, though ambiguous, Daphne says she experienced as sexual molestation. The first set of actions occurred between the ages of approximately three and six and centered around a chronic skin rash affecting Daphne's buttocks. Taking the role of doctor, a role he frequently played in his family, Daphne's father medicated the rash with a salve or liquid prescribed by a dermatologist. In addition, Daphne's father instituted a treatment not prescribed by the doctor. This treatment was to have Daphne lie for some set period of time so that her buttocks could be exposed to air and sunlight. Sometimes this would be on a bed in front of a large window in a bedroom and other times it would be in the living room, where Daphne says that anyone "could see me or walk in on me from the front door."

Daphne does not remember the frequency of these treatments (nor do those others I have consulted), but she does say that she experienced her father's medicating of the rash as sexually invasive, that her father's enthusiasm for both the medicating and the sun treatment frightened and disturbed her, and also that she believes her father's intent was to molest her. In discussing these incidents, however, she has also acknowledged, with what struck me as a certain impatience-despair tinged with an irritability difficult to hold in check, that she has no way to objectively verify her sense that her father was using the rash as a cover for molestation. And more recently, in an exchange that touched on some of the comments she had made before her crisis and on others made in its immediate aftermath, she posed a question phrased approximately as follows: "What if he [her father] didn't molest me and he was simply medicating the rash—what about that?" After posing the question, she added that she felt great confusion about her father's actions and commented that there was little or no chance that she was ever going to know for sure whether a molestation had been intended or not.

The second set of actions by her father that Daphne experienced as molestations involved his teaching her to swim. Specifically, she has said, both before and after her crisis, that she is convinced he fondled her during the lessons. Here again, however, she has added (after her crisis) that because physical contact is routine to swimming lessons, she has no way to objectively confirm her sense of her father's intent.

Regarding the embellishments—initially, Daphne presented the first set of actions as unqualified molestations, fabricating details to support the unambiguousness of her father's intent. The majority of the details, which I did not enumerate in the initial text and which it does not seem necessary to enumerate here, are those that figured in Daphne's description of the molestation as a physically invasive act. Another fabricated detail was that a gun had been in view during some of the medications.[13] Although she described them as less aggressive and fabricated only one supporting detail, Daphne also initially presented the set of actions involving the swimming lessons as unqualified molestations.

Commenting generally, Daphne has written in the margin of her annotated text that she embellished the childhood incidents because of "the need/want for more reason to stay with" her psychiatrist. That her attachment to her doctor was strong had been clear from the time Daphne first began to talk about her therapy and that the attachment had the quality of an infatuation or obsession had become increasingly clear in the months before Daphne's emotional crisis. Speaking adamantly and with some elation, as well as with a certain pride of ownership, about her doctor's great competence and professionalism, Daphne would point out the superiority of having a *psychiatrist* for her therapist as opposed to, say, a clinical social worker or psychologist. At one moment she might be wishing that everyone she knew could enjoy the benefits of a doctor such as hers and at the next be expressing her jealousy of the doctor's other patients and "confessing," usually with dubiousness or surprise over her own behavior, such things as that she scheduled her appointments so that she would not have to cross paths with these other patients and could thus cultivate the illusion that her doctor attended only to her.

Daphne's life also came to revolve increasingly around her therapy: if she was not on her way to an appointment, she was wishing she were on her way to an appointment or killing time until she would be on her way to an appointment; if she was not calling her doctor on the telephone or leaving a message for her, she was waiting for a return call from her doctor or from the doctor's receptionist; if she was not talking to others about her doctor and about the issues that had come up in therapy, she was defending her doctor from any reservation others might express. And on those rare occasions when Daphne ventured to criticize her doctor, it was for such things as her lack of affection and her rule against sharing any information about her personal life with patients. And here I do not mean to defend a distant style of therapy but rather to suggest Daphne's preoccupation with eroding the boundaries between herself and her doctor.

In speaking of her doctor's office as a specific therapeutic setting, Daphne repeatedly said, previous to her crisis, how much it had meant to a person like her to finally find a completely safe place to be. And she seemed to regard any suggestion that there are no *completely* safe places as rather embarrassingly ignorant, that is, as something she knew to be false on the basis of her experience with her therapist. In addition, when family and friends, concerned by such developments as an increasing use of medication and a pronounced decline in mental alertness, began to suggest that Daphne consider a consultation, she would respond with hostility, alarm, or coolness, making clear that she was not going to do anything that might offend her doctor or jeopardize a relationship that had made her feel safer than she had ever felt before.

The fabrications began, Daphne has said, about the time her therapy turned from Glen's abuse to other issues, particularly her relationship with her father, and she worried that the new issues would not be interesting enough to hold her psychiatrist's attention. Daphne has also said that the fabricating took on a life of its own and that eventually she was fabricating a wide variety of experiences and symptoms (and being prescribed a variety of medications for these fabricated symptoms), both inside and outside the therapeutic setting. In other words, as Daphne has explained it, though the embellishments that found their way into the initial text are few, this is not because the embellishments were limited to these but because the text focuses mainly on the abuse by Glen and not on the actions by her father or on any number of other issues that she brought up in therapy as her fear of losing her psychiatrist began to grow.

One of the saddest things in all of this to me, the thing that at this moment tempts me to a wild, pervasive rage, that makes me almost want to shake into consciousness this woman about whom I write, is that it never seems to have occurred to Daphne that an overwhelming craving for protection, in and of itself, without the slightest adornment, not even a snippet of ribbon or a wisp of lace, was symptom enough to render her deserving of professional help.[14] But perhaps a craving as great as hers, nurtured by a culture as valuing as ours of achievement and its trappings, takes up all the slack of being and allows for no such consciousness, in which case my sadness and near rage, my temptation to violently shake, become so much sentimentality.

In light of the fabrications, which placed Daphne in the position of impersonator in relation to her psychiatrist, her family, and her friends, it seems appropriate to refer back to several comments I made earlier in the chapter. One is that when Daphne first entered therapy, her penciling in of the "I think" on the psychiatrist's questionnaire suggested her concern that she might be regarded as a fraud. Another is that one reason she kept silent about Glen's abuse was that she feared people would think that she was lying if she told the truth. Given the fabrications, any concern Daphne may have had about being regarded as a fraud becomes strikingly ironic. In pointing up the irony, however, I am not implying that Daphne's fabrications necessarily negate the earlier observations. Of course, the earlier observations could simply be wrong, which has been a possibility all along. But it could also be that as therapy progressed Daphne's attachment to her psychiatrist overwhelmed the standard she typically ascribed to; after all, there is nothing to say that a person will not behave according to some standard at one moment in her life, whether it be a personal standard achieved through many years of conscious effort or a cultural standard absorbed from birth through immersion and never really questioned, and at another abandon the standard, especially where passion or infatuation is involved. And those of us who have not learned this from personal experience have only to read the daily newspaper or some great novelist, Proust or Flaubert, for example, to witness the change in behavior, the shattering of the code, the decision to sell the diamond for the crust of bread—or to redefine the crust as diamond—that a passionate attachment can work.

For that matter, if we will settle for a less-well-known story, a story not about such celebrated nineteenth-century European adult characters as Charles Swann or Emma Bovary but about a neighborhood American child in our own time, and if we will focus for a moment simply on the breaking of a code and not on the many differences between the stories, we have only to recall the young Daphne, the passionate tomboy who broke her culture's code when

she marched proudly into kindergarten wearing the railroad coveralls and white turtleneck and who sought for herself, at home, at
school, and everywhere, the roles traditionally reserved for boys.

A related possibility not explored in my earlier observations
about Daphne's attitude towards fraud is that from a very young
age her concern had been about being *regarded* as a fraud or, in a
broader sense, about being perceived negatively, rather than about
behaving "fraudulently." In other words (and here I am greatly
oversimplifying, my aim being to raise a range of possibilities rather
than to explore any one of them in detail), from early childhood a
desire to please others, to enjoy the intimacy, the good graces, the
power and the protection accorded the pleaser or endearing one,
could have absorbed Daphne to such an extent that any distinction
between being percieved as a fraud and actually behaving fraudulently never fully registered with her. Such absorption would also
suggest that she has experienced herself throughout much of her
life essentially as a public image or reflection rather than as a person
who can distinguish herself from the person she believes others
take her for or want her to be. Another possibility is that a desire to
please and a preoccupation with public image left her feeling personally "unrealized" and that an apprehension about being regarded
as a fraud was intertwined with a vague but persistent sense that
she, like many of us, was a "fraud" in the sense that though she had
lived each day of her life in relation to people, places, and things,
she had not as yet focused on finding, creating, or choosing herself.

With respect to the presentation of pleasing, protective imper-
sonations, Daphne's tomboyism was itself an impersonation of sorts,
one that endeared her hugely to the majority of her world. It is also
true that a possible motivation for her tomboyism was a perception
of femaleness as insufficient, undeserving, and highly vulnerable,
in other words, as both no-account or unesteemed and dangerous.[15]
As for her impersonation of an unequivocal victim of incest, a victim suffering from a complex array of very stubborn and disabling
symptoms, Daphne could have experienced this as a pleasing as
well as protective role in that the fabricated symptoms would elevate
her to the status of "star" patient, thus giving her doctor the satisfaction of a great challenge while giving Daphne the insurance of
their continued relationship and the sense of absolute security she
experienced when with her doctor.

As Daphne proceeded to qualify her initial telling of the incidents
from early childhood and as it became clear that it would be impos-

sible to let the initial text stand because to do so would be to present a father's ambiguous interactions as outright molestations, I expressed the impossibility to Daphne. She responded by pointing out, specifically in relation to the embellishment involving the gun, that her father had been a horrific presence all through her childhood and that given his interest in guns and hunting and the rage he exhibited in the home, she had experienced him as a highly unpredictable man who was a personal threat to her physical survival. We then spoke briefly about the anger, confusion, and resentment (as well as about the desire for an ironclad case) that such a father might provoke in his daughter, and my sense was that Daphne wanted it understood that she had endured great suffering at her father's hands and that in her mind the fabrications were expressive of her experiencing of him, or perhaps it would be more accurate to say that in her mind the fabrications had the power to convey the quality of her suffering to others, whereas the actual truth did not.

Though in our conversation I made a remark suggesting the helpfulness of valuing actual experience if we are to create a firmer ground for understanding humanness, my remark seemed not to engage Daphne beyond a polite attention, and it struck me that, at its core, the deep sense of personal inadequacy that seems to plague her could have been intertwined with a profound lack of confidence in, and perhaps also contempt for, the perceptual powers of those around her. That such a sense of herself and of her world could have its source (through personal experience, an inherited perspective, or both) in a refusal of humanness, of mortality, of imperfection and all that it entails, seems as apparent to me as that her world, our world, widely encourages such refusal. It also occurs to me that such a sense could contribute to a person's becoming caught up in a puppetlike relation with others, a relation in which one attraction is the satisfaction of "pulling the strings" so that others "dance" their fallibility and another attraction is a momentary surge of appreciative gratitude towards the dancers.

In an early conversation, we also spoke, but only briefly, about the pitfalls of victim psychology (particularly the victim's temptation to "bed down" in the victim's role and the ease with which the victim can become the victimizer) and about the anger, confusion, and resentment a daughter, son, or other intimate, perhaps a husband or a mother, a sister or a brother or a friend, might feel in relation to fabrications such as Daphne's. Daphne expressed horror and remorse over any pain her fabrications might have caused others, but these emotions seemed overshadowed by the urge to reiterate and focus on her father's awfulness, on her sense that he had indeed molested her, and on her own pervasive misery and sense of absolute lostness. I later found myself wondering if the expression of remorse was in part one of those conversational tokens we sometimes offer instinctively when we want to sustain a listener's tolerance for a return to the topic of our choice, Daphne's choice in this case being her childhood suffering. And I found myself thinking that Daphne would have experienced her fabrications as benign to the same degree that she had experienced them as compelled and her childhood as extenuating or "awful." That these highly personal impressions could reflect my own complex intellectual and emotional response to Daphne's embellishment of her story, and, through its embellishment, to her demonstration of my fallibility as listener-narrator is, of course, possible.

I next want to take up the one other incident from childhood that Daphne initially said had been long forgotten until therapy. But this time I want to begin by discussing the initial, distorted version. Daphne first presented this incident as her attempt to confide, specifically and exclusively, the sense of molestation by her father to a trusted adult. In the initial communication, Daphne said that she had asked the adult about the badness of certain kinds of touching and had been told that as long as the person to be touched did not permit the touching, it would not be bad. Daphne also said that because her father had already done the touching and because she had not stopped him, the trusted adult's response filled her with guilt and revealed her own badness to her.

Subsequently, however, Daphne has qualified her first telling by saying that though she clearly remembers approaching the trusted adult and speaking about, as Daphne has put it, "a sexual matter I was confused and upset about," she cannot remember the specific sexual matter that sent her to the adult. She has also qualified her first telling by saying that she does not remember the adult's specific response to her approach but only remembers that she already felt guilty when she approached the adult and that the response did nothing to relieve her sense that exploration of the body was taboo. She has further said that the skin-rash treatments could have prompted or partly prompted the approach but that an experience she had with some neighborhood boys, or perhaps both experiences, also could have prompted it.

Given Daphne's comment, related earlier in the chapter, that she had no memory of any childhood exploration of sexuality, I want to take a minute to focus on her more recent reference to an experience with some neighborhood boys. Daphne blurted it out, along with some other childhood memories, when I asked her (in one of our first conversations after I learned of the embellishments) if her original statement about having no childhood memories of sexual exploration had been accurate. Indicating by the blurting out that it had not been, Daphne described the experience with the neighborhood boys as one many of us would categorize as routine and as involving her and the two boys lowering their pants so that they could see the difference between male and female bodies. It seems, however, that such exploration provoked boundless guilt in Daphne, who said that she has felt deep shame about anything and everything having to do with the sexuality of the body for as long as she can remember. Even though she had not forgotten the child-hood explorations, she said that she felt too ashamed to speak up about them when I first introduced the topic.[16] Although she has not said so, I have wondered if a desire to admit a previously denied reality and take a step forward in a search for a long-elusive well-being prompted Daphne to brave her shame and speak to another person about her exploration with the neighborhood boys.

I also know, however, that I want the above to be true and that there are other possibilities. Among these is that Daphne makes up her story as she goes along, replacing fabrications that no longer please (here I mean *please* to include a connotation of *persuade*) with fabrications that she believes have a better chance, perhaps mixing in elements of truth while at the same time attending to the essential of saving a created face and perhaps also experiencing me, and various others in her world, as her "champions" or helpers in this saving, which (however unwittingly) I have been. I commented ear-lier that Daphne recently posed a question phrased approximately "What if he [her father] didn't molest me and he was simply medi-cating the rash—what about that?" and that, after posing the ques-tion, she added that she felt great confusion over her father's actions, commenting that there was little or no chance that she was ever going to know for sure whether a molestation had been intended or not. And yet Daphne's fabrications make it impossible to get a clear sense of the significance of such a statement. Was it the statement of a victim of molestation suffering from a lack of confidence in her own perception? Was it one step in an effort to gradually retract a story that she knew to be false in its entirety? Was it an expression of concern for the possible innocence of a projected molester? Was it an expression of anxiety at the thought of having to live with ambiguity? Was it none of these? Was it some combination of these, and others, in flux and minglement?

Another way to frame the difficulty would be to say that Daphne's fabrications impart a disturbing awkwardness to an unverifiable story and that the scope of the awkwardness will not be limited by Daphne's statements about where the fabrications begin and end, or by my sense, as narrator, of these boundaries. She has said with great feeling that the fabrications began when she turned from the issue of Glen's abuse to her relationship with her father, a time when she was desperate to ensure her therapist's interest, and though there is logic and the feel of the authentic in this, there is no certainty. "But how will you know about any of it?"—this was the gist of one friend's response when I spoke to her of the fabrications, and, because I am no seer but an ordinary woman, I won't know but will simply have to accept Daphne as she is, as, at present, indeterminate. However, though the making up of a story as she goes along, or something equally as difficult to penetrate, is a possibility, my concern is not to try to see through the ambiguities.[17] Instead, in addition to acknowledging the ambiguities and communicating Daphne's qualified telling of the incidents from early childhood, I want to relate her sense, and mine, of the bearing the qualifications have on the initial text. I also want to note that the communications, whether embellished or plain truth, are hers as told to us through me. As such they are in some sense expressive of her being and, at least in my opinion, also of ours. She speaks. I listen, remember, and write. You read. We each of us make sense, or not.

Returning for a moment to Daphne's story about her experience with the two neighborhood boys, I need to add one further detail, which is that she blurted it out in the same breath with another less routine experience. The less routine experience is one Daphne has said she could neither forget nor accept. And I am including it here not for any shock value it may have but because it seems important to convey the range of material Daphne has communicated (if for no other reason than to keep track of possible concrete sources of her great craving for protection), and also because it calls into question the myth of the pastoral childhood. The experience was of tromping off into the woods with a group of neighborhood children and of witnessing the oldest boy urinate into a bottle and drink from it.

Having presented Daphne's qualified telling of her father's actions and of the interaction with the trusted adult, I want to discuss the impact of the qualified telling on several questions raised at a point parallel to this in the initial text. I also want to cue readers at the outset of the discussion that I will be incorporating more and more of the initial text into the present one.

The first of the several questions concerns the impact that the incidents from earlier childhood may have had on Daphne's silence during her described abuse by Glen.[18] In the initial text, I wrote that the actions of Daphne's father and the possibility of a gun could have increased the pressure to keep silent about Glen. Basically, my argument was that Daphne might have been frightened, consciously or unconsciously, that her father would become alarmed for his own safety if she told about Glen's molestations. I also wrote, however, that Daphne's silence had made complete sense to me before I learned of her father's actions.

In Daphne's qualified telling, she did not comment on her father's actions as a possible source of increased pressure to keep silent, except to acknowledge that it had been raised on the basis of her fabrication of an unambiguous molestation. Given her stated belief that she was molested, however, and her statement that her father was a terrifying figure in her childhood and that his interest in guns contributed to her terror, it seems possible that her relationship with her father could have contributed to her silence about Glen's abuse.[19] Regarding my statement in the initial text that Daphne's silence had made complete sense before she told me of her father's actions, Daphne has written, in the margin of her annotated text, "seems very important, and certainly very important to me." My understanding of this comment is that she found the statement important because it suggests that the credibility of her silence about Glen's abuse did not depend on her embellishments about her father's actions.

I also commented, in the initial text, on the possibility that Daphne's approaching of the trusted adult contributed to her silence about Glen's abuse. My argument was that Daphne might have kept silent in part because she had earlier tried, with disastrous results, to approach an adult about her father's actions. Daphne has not commented on this possibility when qualifying her initial telling. My comment is that her qualified telling of approaching the trusted adult is too vague to serve as a basis for raising such a possibility. I also want to point out, however, that a thread running throughout Daphne's story is her preoccupation with her silence about Glen's abuse—with whether the silence is credible, with whether it is fathomable, with whether it will lessen others' opinion of her, and with whether it is forgivable.

That Daphne's tomboyishness may have been rooted in her sense that her father had molested her is another possibility raised in the initial text. I put it there as follows:[20]

> Because the first period of [Daphne's experience of] abuse by her father predated and overlapped with Daphne's emergence as a tomboy and because her tomboyishness manifested itself in the adoption of boys' clothing and costumelike attire that masked her femaleness, Daphne has come to believe that her tomboyishness had its primary impetus in a "decision" that to masquerade as one of her father's own sex would be the best protection against further molestation. She has also come to entertain the possibility that her choice of males for companions and role models was not only part of the masquerade (as well as part of a search to discover a trustworthy male to serve as father figure) but also her way of studying the subtleties of maleness so that her masquerade would be convincing.

In her qualified telling, Daphne has affirmed this passage as still accurate. She has especially emphasized her desire to discover a trustworthy male to serve as father figure, and she has annotated the sentence ending with the words "the best protection against further molestation" by writing: "against the [skin-rash] treatment molests/sexual invasions—whatever they were—and I do believe they were molests!"

Also taken up in the initial text is the possibility that the child Daphne's sensitivity to others was rooted in a hope that someone would reciprocate and tune in to her needs, a possibility expressed as follows:

> Another possibility Daphne has had to confront is that her extreme sensitivity to the plight of others and her willingness to do their bidding was shaped by her father's [perceived] abuse. More specifically, she has found herself wondering, on the one hand, if her helpfulness was in part an attempt to ward off molestation and whether she may not have been acting from the premise that "goodness" would save her because no one would treat a really good and

helpful child as her father had treated her. On the other hand, she has also found herself wondering if her helpfulness was an indirect appeal for help motivated by the hope that if she was sensitive to the needs of others, someone would eventually reciprocate and tune in to her needs.

In annotating the initial text, Daphne has written in the margin next to the above passage, "I don't know what to say about this section or if I need to say anything." Because Daphne has said that she experienced the skin treatments as molestations and because she has said that she is convinced that her father did molest her, my view is that Daphne's qualified telling does not undermine the possibilities raised in the initial text. Concerning Daphne's desire to be saved, I want to recall the quality of her attachment to her psychiatrist described earlier. And I want to add a personal observation, which is that I have rarely known a person so afraid of so many things (but especially of not being loved and of being attacked by an intruder while she is alone), so despairing about how to proceed in light of her fears, and so captivated by the myth of the rescuing knight, whether the knight arrives in the form of a living person, an open-and-shut psychiatric diagnosis, or a sleeping pill, as Daphne for some time now has appeared to me to be.

In the initial text, I additionally commented on some of the ironies and possible implications of Daphne's childhood:

> Daphne has also had to grapple with the irony that it was her tomboy's disguise and her willingness to help others that prompted the adults in her world to see her as the ideal child to help "normalize" Glen. Her gravitation towards the male world not only placed her in Glen's path, it also meant that people tended to view her as a rough and tumble child who could take care of herself and who didn't want much interfering with or fussing over, a view that would have lessened the chance of family and friends thinking of her as a child vulnerable to sexual abuse, if they thought of such vulnerabilities at all.

> Though Daphne believes that her spontaneous warmth and affectionateness predated the interactions with her father, and in fact regards the warmth as the one trustworthy indication of her "true" child's self, she is also having to confront the ways in which her father's [perceived] abuse, as well as the abuse by Glen, has stunted this warmth and distorted her sense of touch to the point that it has become largely a provoker of alarm and painful memories rather than a source of pleasure or joy. Although these new-found perceptions of

WHEN DAPHNE WAS A GIRL

her childhood have been liberating in some respects, they have also provoked panic—panic at the realization that her father's [perceived] abuse and her tomboyishness distanced her from her mother and the world of women at a very early age, and panic at the realization that she has been traveling incognito for most of her life. Only now, as an adult woman, has she begun to ask herself who it is she wants to become.

Daphne has affirmed as still pertinent the discussion of the implications and possible sources of her child's self quoted in the above two paragraphs. In addition, however, she seems to me (although she has not said so) to have been hit hard by a realization that the force of the points raised above will be diminished in many minds (perhaps even including her own) by the knowledge of the fabrications. She also appears to be experiencing a sense of loss for a personal history that cannot now be realized, a personal history, that is, in which she tells the story of her childhood unembellished by the fabrications, as true as memory allows. Though I tell myself that I could feel for such a loss, and though I am not a stranger to regret, or guilt, I have also come to believe that such a mourning need not forever dominate a life, that we can mourn our losses, embrace the history that in fact is ours, explore its surfaces and depths, make amends where such is appropriate, forgive ourselves, and step keenly out of mourning into a present filled with memory and doing, with being and possibility, with repose and thought and liveliness, with silence, with laughter, with love, with talk.

In the initial text, I closed my discussion of the possible sources and outgrowths of Daphne's child's self with a paragraph that does not know quite how to acquit itself in light of the qualified telling— whether, for example, to be glad that it is present to help the text receive the weight of the qualified telling or to flee altogether a text that has doubled back and asked so much of it. The paragraph begins:

> How Daphne will resolve the questions that have emerged during therapy, or if she will resolve them at all, I do not know. Nor do I know what additional questions may yet arise or how they may qualify what I have written.

Though it contains no content tied to the embellishments, the paragraph is one that has drawn a comment from Daphne. Next to my statement that I do not know how she will resolve the questions that have arisen in therapy, or if she will resolve them at all, she has written, "Nor do I." And next to the sentence stating that I do not know what additional questions may yet arise (a sentence she has underlined), she has written, "So many have."

In this same paragraph from the initial text, I continued on to express a personal opinion about Daphne's story. The opinion is that those of us who have heard it "in its current form would be making a terrible mistake if we distanced ourselves from it by concluding that it raises questions only for her." I also suggested, in the same paragraph, that "we would be better off if we took the time, while she struggles with her questions, to ask some questions of our own." I then concluded the initial text by suggesting one question that we might ask ourselves and by describing a scene that I would sometimes find myself imagining after hearing Daphne's original telling of her story.

Though the qualified telling cannot help but impart ambiguity and awkwardness to my initial conclusion, I nonetheless think that the conclusion must stand as originally written. I think this not only because the original conclusion seems to me to be as appropriate to the present text as to the initial text (although with a multiplicaton and shifting of resonances) but also because it seems to me that through living both the ambiguity and the awkwardness of its new context, the original conclusion gives us a chance to perceive the "thickness" or density of our world. Once perceived, I think this density can disclose a routine truth many of us do not think much about, which is the transience of finish, the artifice of closure, the naiveté of thinking that we have ever grasped the whole in anything approximating its full complexity. I also think that if we can accept this density and speak openly about it with others instead of trying to flee from or deny or rationalize it, we will have taken a step towards finding the courage to seek wellness and become ourselves. I therefore offer the original conclusion here, without quotation marks, indentation, or a colon to distinguish it from the present text, but with the lead-in paragraph from the original to bridge the reader's entry.

How Daphne will resolve the questions that have emerged during therapy, or if she will resolve them at all, I do not know. Nor do I know what additional questions may yet arise or how they may qualify what I have written. I do think, however, that those of us who have heard her story in its current form would be making a terrible mistake if we distanced ourselves from it by concluding that it raises questions only for her. Instead, I think we would be better off if we took the time, while she struggles with her questions, to ask some questions of our own.

One question we might ask ourselves is the extent to which we might be raising Daphnes without knowing it—or, if not Daphnes, then human beings who would exploit a Daphne to make life easier for themselves or for someone else. I am suggesting, in other words, that we ask ourselves the extent to which we conceive of children, though we may never have realized it before, as small bodies donated to adult causes. Do we nurture children so they will have the best possible chance we can give them of becoming the human beings they want to become? Or do we nurture them so that they can service our personal fantasies—for example, by becoming vehicles for our projection of a mythology of childhood that may be reassuring but that is largely pretense—or service and console us, on a more concrete level, by polishing our shoes, rubbing our backs, rowing our boats, kissing our guests, tending our deviants,[21] saving our volleyball seasons, entertaining our crowds, or simply by holding ever so cooperatively still—whether the stillness be so that we can snap their pictures or molest their genitals?

And to those of us who find this first question personally offensive, I would propose a second, which is that we consider the source of our feeling of personal offendedness. Could it arise, for example, from a belief that the world is divided neatly into the categories good guys and bad, and could we believe that we belong without question to group 1, a belonging that exempts us from the consideration of all such messy, unpleasant questions? Or are we perhaps so frightened that our lives may already have been touched by sexual abuse in ways as yet unacknowledged or unseen that we are reluctant to risk a closer look, a look that might spoil the landscape, tarnish the mythology? I know that I had not thought of Daphne as someone who could have been sexually abused until she told me her story. And yet my life had been touched by hers since we were small.

I also know that since she told me her story I have thought more than once about all those others who were close to her and did not know (or, if they did know, did not acknowledge the knowing). Sometimes I think, for example, of those children who would have been playing hide and seek with Daphne in the field the day of the final abuse, all of them ignorant of a suffering so near, all of them adults now. And when I think of those children, I also think of the field itself. It would have been spotted with patches of drying weed by that time of year, short where the blade of the disc had turned the soil under in spring, longer in the corners, up against the fence, and around the trunks of the fruit and nut trees where the blade could not reach. Any apricots would have been long since picked and baked into a pie. But the peach and nectarine trees could still have been bearing fruit. And a garden of tomatoes, squash, and string beans would have matured. Blue Jays would have been breaking the shells of the almonds that had not been knocked, and in the southeastern corner of the field, past the garden and the fruit trees, a pair of doves would have been roosting or pecking at seed in a chicken wire and pine slat cage that sat on a redwood picnic table under an almond tree whose branches grew out and down to such an unusual degree that it resembled a gnarled umbrella or an angular, wizened willow.

That southeastern corner with the doves under the almond tree would have made a good place to hide. And when I think of the final day of abuse, I imagine one of Daphne's fellow hide and seekers hunched up under the picnic table, close to its legs, hoping to escape detection. I picture another child crouched behind Daphne's father's rowboat, which would have been lying near the garden, turned upside down to keep out falling leaves, rain, and the neighbors' cats. A third player, the child who was "it," could easily have been tagging a fourth player, who I imagine would have been hiding between the honeysuckle and the Cecile Brunner rosebush. Growing just beyond the top of the driveway, not far from the toolshed where Glen was assaulting Daphne, the honeysuckle would have been all pale yellow and sweet with bees, the rosebush a mass of pink.

Besides Daphne's fellow players at hide and seek, I also sometimes find myself thinking of those human beings who would have been nearby in Daphne's house—at least three adults and one child, I would guess—not Daphne's grandmother, who would have been at her office in the city, and not Daphne's father, who would have been at his office, too, wearing a suit and tie and the brightly polished shoes, but Glen's father and mother, their small daughter, who would have been about two, and Daphne's mother.

Looking back at Daphne's mother from my own vantage point as mother, I picture her tired out by a raucous morning filled with children of all ages going every which way and glad that the older children have found something to do outside. Standing at the kitchen counter, she is quietly slicing a chilled peach from the tree in the field where the children play. Food has been losing its appeal for her patient lately, and she is hoping that a cool, lightly sugared peach, picked fresh that morning, will stimulate the dying woman's appetite. Standing next to Daphne's mother, elevated on a chair to help her reach the counter, is Glen's young sister. She is watching the peach slices fall into the bowl and hoping that she will be asked to help sprinkle on the sugar. Down the hallway, at the far end of the house, Glen's father is sitting in a chair talking with his wife, who lies across from him in her bed. Next to the bed is a nightstand on which sit a lamp, a missal, a rosary, and an array of prescription bottles. Glen's father and mother are discussing the interval that has passed since they last talked. He wants to know what kind of night she had, whether her pain medicine is working. She wants to know whether Glen's father's back is hurting him, how Glen is doing with his swimming, and if they will be staying for dinner or eating at home, perhaps taking Daphne with them for a visit.

Three adults and one child in the house. Three or four children, not counting Glen and Daphne, in the field. Seven or eight human beings in all who lived close to Daphne day in and day out and who were within a short distance of the toolshed on the day of the final instance of abuse. All of them ignorant of the suffering in their midst. All of them evidence of how easy it is to become one among the many whose lives have been touched by sexual abuse in ways unacknowledged or unseen.[22]

Postscript:

One winter afternoon, as I was reading through the first full draft of the above qualified text, a card arrived in the mail from Daphne. The photograph on the front was of a small wooden rowboat floating on a still black surface unbroken by any other object. The boat was empty, the oars had been tucked up under a seat of varnished wood, and a rope secured to the bow extended over the blackness to the edge of the card so that it wasn't clear whether the boat was tied to some stationary object outside the frame of the photograph or whether it had slipped loose from its moorings, a boat caught by watery dark stillness in need of an experienced rower to take up the oars. The note inside was short:

> I am so sorry.
>   love,
>   Daphne

6

An Afternoon Spent
Playing Dress-up

I have all that I lost
and I go carrying my childhood
like a favorite flower
that perfumes my hand.

> Gabriela Mistral, *Selected Poems*
> (translated from Spanish
> by Doris Dana)

In giving me permission to write about an intimate experience from each of their lives, David, Mark, Laura, and Daphne have evidenced a willingness to risk openness. Because we can never know in advance all that such openness may entail and because we so easily fall into the habit of forever examining other people's lives and never our own (that is, of forever letting other people take the risks, serve as our subjects, provide us with our "data," be our fodder), I would like to participate in the venturing by writing about an experience from my own childhood. Influencing my telling of the other children's stories as much as any childhood experience I can recall, the experience I want to tell about—it occurred between the ages of six and eight—was of participating in an outing with a friend from school, Sharon, and then overhearing the outing discussed by my family and some company as I arrived home.

The outing concluded an afternoon spent playing dress-up at Sharon's house after school. I can't remember the specific setting or the roles we settled on that day or a single detail about the clothes we wore. But there was one outfit I especially liked to dress up in. Stored in my mother's cedar chest when I wasn't playing with it, the dress had been my grandmother's. A celery green chiffon formal, it had, as I remember it, a slight V-neck, the hint of a short sleeve, and a bodice covered with small rhinestones. With its great

239

length of gathered chiffon, the skirt was almost more than I could manage, and I would belt the dress at the waist and blouse the chiffon over the belt so that I could walk without tripping over the skirt or catching and tearing it on the heel of my shoes. The shoes, which belonged to my mother, were black suede sling pumps with the toe cut out. As for the purse, I can't remember what it looked like, but I know I carried one because I can still feel my hand gripping the strap as I set off for those destinations—a costume ball, the grocery store, the beauty shop, a movie theatre—suggested by the social landscape of my games.

In addition to remembering that favorite outfit, I also remember that playing dress-up, with one qualification, seemed the most natural thing in the world to me—on a par with waking up in the morning and falling asleep at night. The one qualification was that my mother and father had a way of communicating their negative attitudes towards certain expressions of femaleness that made me feel vaguely self-conscious about being a girl and that prompted me to monitor my behavior, not only in "real life" but also in my games.

My father preferred, for example, that I not use any lipstick or other makeup when I played dress-up, a preference he communicated indirectly rather than through direct instructions or an explicit set of rules that he connected to specific values or principles. And my mother, though markedly tolerant in many respects, had a fierce aversion to female clothing that struck her as inappropriate to a given occasion or setting (patent leather shoes at school, for example) or as generally fussy, whatever the occasion (hair ribbons and ankle chains were two items she had no patience with). Though she would never have thought of herself as prescribing a dress code, she did prescribe one in the sense that she was quick to disparage inappropriate or "silly" styles when we were out and about and would see other girls wearing them. Accepting the authority of her pronouncements as beyond question, I took care to avoid these styles and can even remember how deficient I felt when I discovered she disapproved of bolero jackets, a style that had come into fashion for young girls and that I had been on the verge of asking her to buy for me. Other than these feelings of self-consciousness, however, and the self-monitoring stirred by my parents' preferences, I can remember having only good feelings, until the day I visited at Sharon's house, about playing dress-up.

On the day of the visit I had become thoroughly absorbed in Sharon's and my game. Unaware that her mother had begun to take an interest in our play, I was caught off guard when she spoke to us. Telling us how special we looked, she announced that she was going to drive us down to the main street of our small town so that other people could see how nice we looked, particularly the proprietors of the variety store and another store widely known as the junk shop. In both cases the proprietors were married couples she was casually friendly with (as were many people in our area), and she said that our visit would be a real treat for these couples, who, as I recall, either had no children of their own or had children who were already grown.

Sharon greeted her mother's announcement enthusiastically (my impression was that going downtown wearing dress-up clothes was something she had done before and liked doing), and her mother proceeded as if the trip were settled. I, however, had been panicked by her announcement. My panic arose from my certainty that my own parents would disapprove of such an outing and would take for granted that I, their daughter, would know better than to participate in anything so obviously wrong. Though at the time I could not have explained to anyone how I knew that they would disapprove or what exactly it was that would make such a walk "obviously wrong" in their eyes, this inability to articulate the source of my knowledge did not lessen my conviction.

If my mother had been present, I would simply have turned to her for support. But she wasn't, and so, trusting implicitly in my parents and their values, which at that age I was ever anxious to live up to, I told Sharon, when her mother stepped into the kitchen, that I did not want to go downtown with her, and I think I even suggested that they drop me off at my house on their way downtown. Disappointed, Sharon sought out her mother and told her what I had said. Without making any direct reference to my reluctance, her mother gave me a pep talk, telling me that of course I was going to give the outing a try and that I was going to have a lot of fun.

Her pep talk left me feeling confused and helpless. Given my certainty that my parents would disapprove and my complete faith in the superiority of their judgment, I would have done almost anything to avoid the planned outing and the prospect of disapproval it excited. However, short of outright insubordination, which my parents had taught me was unacceptably rude and which I therefore did not view as an option, I could see no way out. To complicate matters, Sharon's mother sometimes worked at my grade school, a fact that increased the pressure I felt to comply with her plan. Having had my effort to say no swept aside by the person in whose home I was a guest, a person who was not only an adult and currently in charge of child-me but who was also an authority figure from my school and the mother of my friend, I stood silently for a moment in the face of the pep talk, feeling claustrophobic and enraged at finding myself in a position that I experienced as one of utter powerlessness. Then I said that yes, I would go with them downtown, and we went out and got into their car.

If I spoke at all during the ride or interacted with Sharon or her mother in any way, I do not remember it. Instead, I remember feeling physically sick at the prospect of the walk, as if it would literally be my ruin. In addition, my anxiety was intensified by a frantic casting about in my own mind for a possible last minute escape and by a visualizing of the scene I was sure would take place if I could not escape. In the imagined scene I saw myself walking down a public street all dressed up in ladies' clothes while passersby gazed at me in shock and disapproval and while the proprietors of the variety store and the junk shop tried to ease us out of their stores so that the presence of two so inappropriately dressed little girls would not compromise their business.

The actual walk did not turn out at all as I had visualized it. There were some terrible moments: for example, at one point Sharon's mother spotted the priest from my parish walking on the opposite side of the street and made what seemed to me a big commotion about it, announcing his presence, pointing him out to me, and asking if I wanted to cross over and speak to him (I didn't). But none of the passers-by looked at us with shock or disapproval, at least not so far as I could see. Many of them did notice us, and it was clear that our clothing made us conspicuous and that people who saw us were curious about what we might be up to, but some simply bustled by, apparently not noticing us at all. The response both disconcerted me (What was wrong with these people? Didn't they know, as my parents could have told them, that walking down main street in ladies' clothes the way Sharon and I were doing was wrong, something they should be frowning at?) and calmed me slightly (it was a great relief *not* to elicit the scowls and gasps of disapproval I had anticipated and not to be faced with the problem of what to do with my eyes, and with the rest of my body, while I was being censured).[1] Despite some calming, however, I remained sufficiently anxious to prevent full engagement with the reality around me, and I experienced my walk as through a haze. When we approached the junk shop, and again when we approached the variety store, my anxiety returned full force. Though the passersby had expressed no disapproval, I still was not convinced that the shopkeepers would welcome our visit as a treat. Nor had I learned how to relinquish on cue my child's sincerity for a cool instrumentality that would have allowed me to distance myself from my feelings through one of those expedient trade-offs so common in adult-child relations. And so, instead of entering the shops confident of my appeal, greeting the proprietors politely, letting myself be admired for a minute, and then making a beeline for my favorite section in each store—the penny candy case in the junk shop and the aisle with marbles, jacks, and doll-house furniture in the variety store—I entered timidly, sticking close to Sharon and her mother (though I was mad at them and did not like having to depend on them, they seemed my only anchor), and paid no attention to the candy and toys that usually attracted me.

To my surprise, the proprietors of both stores welcomed us with what struck me at the time as genuine warmth and admiration.[2] One of the couples even regretted not having their camera at the store so they could have taken snapshots of us. Their desire to take our picture calmed me in the sense that it allayed my fear that they would be embarrassed or annoyed by our presence. But on another level, the thought of the camera alarmed me, and I was glad they did not have one handy because I was afraid that any photographs would eventually find their way into my parents' hands, perhaps when they stopped in at one of the stores to buy something.

During the ride back to Sharon's house, where I would change back into my school clothes before being driven home, I was flooded with relief, but not so entirely that I did not focus on what had happened, on the discrepancy between my expectation of disapproval and the actual response of the people on main street, which had left me feeling a little stunned but also quizzical. I also kept thinking what a good thing it was that the priest had not seen me and that no pictures had been taken, two circumstances that meant my parents would have little chance of finding out about my walk unless I told them, which, though I did not usually withhold information, I definitely had decided not to do. In fact, the walk down main street was the only time during my childhood that I can remember making a conscious decision to keep a secret from my parents, or perhaps I should say from my mother, since it was she with whom I especially liked to talk over my activities.

When I got back to Sharon's house, the flood of relief ended abruptly. Realizing that our trip downtown was going to make her late in getting me home, Sharon's mother called my house to let my parents know that we were on our way. Instead of simply delivering that brief message, however, as I had assumed she would do, she narrated the outing in detail to whoever answered the phone, even telling about the priest in a way that left open whether he had seen us or not. Though I had experienced the outing as something to keep confidential, Sharon's mother had experienced it as an event to tell about.

The telephone call brought back all my anxiety. On the ride home I dreaded the disapproval I was sure would greet me. But I also kept hoping that I had misjudged my parents, as I had misjudged the shopkeepers and the other people on main street. By the time Sharon's mother dropped me off at the foot of my driveway and I walked up to my front door, it had become all-important to me that I be wrong about what awaited me. I felt myself a different person from the child who had left home that morning. And this different person wanted *more than anything* for her parents and the world of home over which they presided to surprise her, if not by greeting the news of the walk downtown as a strange and provocative adventure, one that they would listen to her tell about and help her sort through, then at least by showing some understanding and concern for the difficult position in which the outing had placed her.

I think if such a practice had been current in our culture, I would have sent a messenger home ahead of me to ready my family for my return by informing them of two things that I felt but did not then know how to put into words. First, I would have wanted the messenger to tell my parents that I had done everything I could think of to live up to their standard and that I had in no sense "disobeyed" them on purpose or thoughtlessly, and certainly not mischievously, since there could hardly have been a less mischievous or more conscientious child than I had been that afternoon. Second, I would have wanted the messenger to tell them that, contrary to everything they had taught me to expect, the people on main street had not been horrified by the appearance among them of two little girls wearing dress-up clothes. And yet, though I hoped that my parents would rise to the occasion of my homecoming and that the "different" child who had come home would be greeted by parents who had become similarly different in her absence, I did not expect the hope to be realized.

I remember standing at the front door of my house trying to work up the courage to open it, my hope that I would be surprised increasing to the point that I think it became momentarily pathological. So intense did it become, in fact, that I did not think I would be able to bear it if they actually expressed the disapproval I anticipated—and so intense that later in life I would immediately recall it on reading these lines of Emily Dickinson's:

> I Years had been from Home
> And now before the Door
> I dared not enter, lest a Face
> I never saw before
>
> Stare stolid into mine
> And ask my Business there—
> "My Business but a Life I left
> Was such remaining there?" (1951, 467)

"But that's exactly the way I felt the day I came home after wearing dress-up clothes on main street," I said to myself, appropriating the poem greedily, as if it belonged to *me* and with no thought at all about whether or not the comparison did justice to the poet or the poem. And by "exactly" I meant that I felt as if I had been away from home for years instead of hours and that I would have changed so dramatically as a result of the walk that the faces of my family would be as strange to me as mine would be to them. Unlike Dickinson's speaker, however, who flees the dread door, I opened mine—not, I think, because my dread was less than her speaker's or because I had more courage, but simply because I was a child with only one address.

It was either after I opened the door but before I stepped into the entryway or just after I stepped into the entryway that I heard the adult voices from the living room, not just the voices of my parents, but also the voices of their company.[3] And, hearing those voices, it was not really necessary to literally see their faces. Discussing the walk down main street, they were too intent on what they were saying, on expressing their shock and disapproval, to have heard me, their audience, come in. They were, in other words, too intent on observing that though such behavior would not have surprised them coming from someone else, it did surprise them coming from me, too intent on singling out Sharon's mother as a person who did not have any more sense than to let two little girls parade down main street in ladies' clothes, too intent on making such distancing remarks as "Well, what can you expect from people like that," and too intent on talking about the priest, on wondering if he had *seen.*

All through the adult talk I held myself silent near the door, not "on purpose" or as a strategy that would make it easier for me to overhear, but because my attention was too consumed with listening for me to have made a noise. Anything but stolid (as is the stranger's face in Dickinson's poem), the emotionally intense adult voices nonetheless gave me a jolt—the jolt of hearing myself talked about as if my behavior (by being other than what my parents had cultivated and come to count on) had rendered me a stranger, a child who was other than the child they knew and valued and whom they had previously had no trouble recognizing as their own. A whole complex of emotions welled up in me at the sound of the adult talk: anger, frustration, disappointment, guilt, and shame. But most of all their talk made me feel desolate, as if my world, a place that had appeared so clear-cut and familiar to me only that morning, had become a maze.

What finally broke the spell of my listening and prompted me to step inside the house and close the door behind me, or what the reunion with my family or the exchange of greetings with the company may have been like, I don't remember. But once I was inside, time seemed to divide itself without any help from me into time spent trying to regain the clear-cut familiarity of the world I had left that morning, time spent in forgetfulness of all that I had seen and heard and felt that afternoon, time spent feeling guilty and ashamed about the awful thing I had done and the trouble I had brought my family, and time spent recalling and puzzling over the events of that afternoon, groping for some answers to the broad question of why those events had made such a difference in my life and to the smaller questions encompassed by that overarching one.

As I grew older, the puzzling would become an overt project that I worked on consciously. But at first it took place silently, nonverbally, and in shadow. It was as if an unusually difficult jigsaw puzzle (I remember I used to like to work on real ones during my spring vacations from school) would seize my attention at odd moments in a basement world and I would try to put it together by pouring over the spread-out pieces and moving them about, trying to form a whole picture that made sense to me, an effort that I became mindful of only because I would now and then catch myself midway in the act of gazing at the pieces or after the fact.

The sense I eventually made was that the difference I felt following the afternoon spent playing dress-up was tied to a change in the way I experienced myself and my parents. Instead of standing submissively before them and experiencing myself as an object defined by their godlike gaze and accepting their perception of me, of themselves, and of everything else in the world (even to the point of adjusting my perceptions when I discovered mine did not quite match theirs), I turned the inquisitor's eye on them. And I think it was the tone of voice they used to discuss my walk, an outing they had not participated in or even witnessed, and particularly the tone of urgency I detected when they wondered whether the priest had seen me, that was instrumental in prompting me to turn the tables, to become examiner and to take them for my object. Up until they spoke of the priest, my attention had been occupied with experiencing myself from their perspective, with taking in how bad a thing I had done and with realizing what a liability a child could be for a parent, and also with comprehending the inferiority of Sharon's family in comparison with mine.

But when they wondered whether or not the priest had seen me, their urgency cut through my guilt and shame, affecting me as a cue that split my attention. No longer *entirely* taken up with experiencing myself as an unworthy child deserving to be shunned, a part of my attention broke free and fastened on my parents' tone of voice, first on the urgency but eventually also on the tone that had marked most of their preceding remarks about me and about Sharon and her family. It was as if I were seeing my parents for the first time and in so doing getting the first glimmer that it was not only my own guilt and shame that were making me feel all small and twisted inside but also the shock and instinctive aversion I felt towards the panic, the intolerance, and the patronage I heard in the voices of these beings I had always assumed were incapable of any baseness.

In time, this first glimmer that my parents were not gods but imperfect human beings like the rest of us would become more tangible, until finally I understood that the adults whose great knowledge of the world and superior standards had made me feel safe as well as warmly and affectionately grateful, as if there could be no greater pleasure than to elicit their approval and no greater pain than to lose it, were as sensitive to being found wanting in the eyes of the world and of being rejected on the basis of their want as I had been sensitive to being found wanting in their eyes and rejected by them. For, as I gradually realized, it was their own fear of abandonment, of losing their place in the world through "misbehavior," that was by all odds at the heart of their condemnation of Sharon's family as inferior and that had prompted them to engage in so intense a conversation with their guests as the one I heard while standing in the doorway of my home.[4]

Though friends, the guests were also representatives of the outside world or public. As such, they could have been perceived by my parents, in their panic, as beings whose good opinion they were in danger of losing, an opinion they might try to retain by distancing themselves as forcefully as possible from Sharon and her mother and also by reacting to my behavior as if it were the behavior of some strange child instead of the daughter they themselves were raising. What I am saying, then, is that I had felt desolated not only by my own sense of failure but also by my realization that my parents were as capable as the rest of the world of casting out another human being to protect themselves and not only of casting out an *other* but also of casting out *me*. This perception of my parents' capacity for desertion, which was the first such perception I can remember, forced me to consider that though they were capable of tending concernfully to my needs and also of opposing public opinion in certain situations, they were also, if sufficiently frightened, capable of disavowing their own child. And I want to note here that though I am presenting my parents' conversation as unique, which on one level it certainly was, and also as a conversation retaining enough of its original power to swell the present moment of this telling with the raw emotion of that day, my aim is not to throw stones at or single out for castigation the parents who loved me but instead to bring home to my own culture the adult capacity (my adult capacity) for such conversation.

The question of why it would be wrong to walk down main street in ladies' clothes, of why it had been that walk, and not any one of all the other activities I took part in as a child, that had so panicked my parents, did not immediately occur to me. When it did, however, I decided that at its core my parents' negative labeling of the walk indicated that they had been deeply influenced, perhaps without any reflective awareness, by the historical fear of the female child's potential to disrupt the social order and shame her family through her sexual conduct.

In the context of this fear, my walk down main street all dressed up in ladies' clothes panicked my parents because it confronted them with the possibility of a daughter as someone who has the power not only to please her parents by growing up into the "right sort" of woman but also to embarrass or shame them by growing up into the "wrong sort," for example, at one extreme, into a prostitute or whore who is so indiscreet as to walk the streets all dressed up in "ladies'" clothes with the express intent of seducing men for pay, men who, as the story goes, would be at home with their wives and children if only it were not for the presence of these daughter-whores. In other words, I am suggesting that my walk down main street shocked my parents not so much because of a concern that it would harm me (by forcing me "on stage" prematurely, for example) but more because of a fear that society or the priest, as authority figure for both the social and the moral order, might view the walk as evidence that my parents were not taking the responsibility of raising a good daughter seriously enough, and so deserved to be censured. Or, to offer a slight variation on this theme, it frightened them because the walk might be viewed as evidence that I was a female child with an inherent character flaw who would go astray, shame my family, and disrupt the social order despite any efforts my parents might make to cultivate in me those virtues that my culture equated with goodness.

That I was able, as a child, to accurately predict my parents' negative response towards the walk, though they had never made any explicit rules against such walks or expressed any objections about such walks to me, suggests that they were as adept at transmitting their ambivalent feelings towards femaleness (for example, through such indirect methods as my mother's criticism of the clothing some girls wore and my father's intimations that I not use cosmetics when playing dress-up) as I was at receiving them. It also suggests that they themselves had been the adept children of similarly adept parents.[5]

Because I gradually came to view the discovery of my parents' imperfection as a milestone in my life, as something to celebrate as a necessary step towards coming to terms with the reality into which I had been born and with my personal potential for abandoning others, including, eventually, my own children, to protect my place in the world, I suppose it would have been understandable if at some point I had felt gratitude towards Sharon's mother for having initiated the outing that led to my discovery. I suppose it would even have been understandable if I had transferred to her some of the hero worship I had felt so unreservedly for my parents before the walk. I have never felt any such gratitude or hero worship, however, and for a number of reasons.

One obstacle to any feeling of gratitude was that the reason Sharon's mother gave for the outing (which was that a visit from two little girls who looked as nice as we did in our dress-up clothes would be a treat for her acquaintances the shopkeepers) had nothing to do with a hope that I, or anyone else, would make any important discoveries about the nature of the world as a result of the outing. Though I would not reject her stated reason as unsound in every respect and though I acknowledge that all of us can in certain circumstances benefit from seeing others and being seen, I also think that her stated reason for the outing revealed the ease, the blankmindedness, the reflexivity, with which she and her culture viewed children as objects for use, as beings whose function it is to serve and please the adult world. Her stated reason additionally suggested that she had not taken the time to personally think through her view, to consider how constrictive such a definition can be for children if it is allowed to dominate, as I believe it was allowed to dominate when I was a child and as I believe it is still allowed to dominate today.

Furthermore, because her view of us as a treat for the two couples on main street is a view society not only approves of as admirably selfless and giving but also shamelessly sentimentalizes (when it comes to generating a gush of mawkishness, few images can match that of the selfless wife and mother setting charitably off to share her treasures—her children—with those who may be less fortunate than she), I think it is exactly the sort we human beings are prone to invoke and to feel self-satisfied about. And I think we are prone to do this even though we may never have explored the image for ourselves or examined the principles embedded there, and even though there may actually be motives at work that are less than selfless, motives that, though quite human, we have been taught are base and inappropriate and that we therefore are not anxious to acknowledge, even to ourselves.

More precisely, I do not think we adults are anywhere near enough aware of our tendency to exploit children for our own use (and for the benefit of others we want to please) in the name of teaching children the importance of such things as generosity and thoughtfulness. Or, to put it differently, I do not think we have even begun to grasp our potential for feeding ourselves, and others, in the name of feeding our children. And I think our children, though we appear before them dressed ever so sheepishly in caregiver's garb, sense this unacknowledged adult tendency at a very young age indeed and that it confuses, frightens, and angers them.

In the case of Sharon's mother, I think she believed that our visit would be a treat for others and that we would have fun, but that she believed this in the unauthenticated way that often accompanies the citing of a platitude. My impression is that she had never thought about why it would be a treat for people to see little girls in dress-up clothes or about why it would be fun for us to be a treat. I also think that the motives she vocalized, though she believed them, functioned as a mask for a less socially sanctioned motive, or perhaps it was more that because she believed the vocalized motives, they quieted any wondering and created a context, a world, in which the question of a less sanctioned motive would be slow to present itself.

My sense of a less sanctioned motive arises from the fact that even as a child of about seven I was not deaf or blind to the world around me and, specifically, was not deaf or blind to the loneliness and frustration of Sharon's mother. How could I have been deaf when, on those days that I played at Sharon's house after school, I would sometimes hear Sharon's mother pleading with her husband behind the closed door of their bedroom, trying to persuade him to spend some of his free time to take her out socially, without the children, instead of spending it all to go out with his male friends? And how could I have been blind when I would see her emerge from those talks, her eyes all red from crying, her efforts to persuade her husband having failed?

Being neither deaf nor blind, even as a child, and carrying with me an image of this grown woman's loneliness, it eventually occurred to me that it may not have been her desire to show us some fun or have us share our specialness that was at the heart of her announcement that she was going to drive us downtown. In spite of what she said, she may have felt so housebound, so isolated, in her role as faithful wife and devoted mother, that when she saw her daughter and me playing dress-up, she seized upon our game as a way to secure for herself the treat of getting out of the house and having some contact with other adults, even if it was only the passersby on main street and the proprietors of the variety store and the junk shop who were her casual acquaintances. And so, though I feel sad when I think of Sharon's mother and though I denounce the concept of motherhood that denied her personal need for nurturance, I do not feel gratitude.

One irony, of course, is that it should have been a lonely and frustrated wife and mother who initiated the walk down main street. True—the initiating did allow her to escape the isolation of her house and be with other adults that one afternoon, and so probably afforded her some much-needed relief. But to my mind the initiating also placed her in the position of leading her daughter and her daughter's friend towards an adulthood as lonely and frustrated as her own. The very specialness she responded to in our being two little girls all dressed up in ladies' clothes, the very reason a visit from us could be a treat for the adults on main street, was that we were about the best evidence she, or anyone, could have given them that the world would continue as they knew it (or as they imagined or wanted it to be), that another generation of little girls were grooming themselves to step into their mothers' shoes and were doing so as nonreflectively as they woke up each morning and fell asleep each night (Russell 1983, 82–83).

And in our girlishness, our "littleness," our newness, we also made it possible for those who were disappointed in their own lives to dream again through us, to tell themselves that their lives were the exception, that though the dream had not worked for them, it would work for us and that our success would be their compensation or, for those who may prefer it, their consolation. That children, given the room, might choose to dream their own dreams, to become something more creative than the protraction or the compensation of their elders, is not an idea that would readily occur to elders who regard themselves (have been taught to regard themselves) as possessing the one true value system and who therefore are quick to equate their own protraction with the ultimate good.

Another obstacle to any feeling of gratitude was the tremendous anger I felt towards Sharon's mother for dismissing my resistance to the outing so cursorily. She not only did not respect me enough as a person to acknowledge my feelings or to try to understand them, but she also took it upon herself to tell me how I felt and how I would react by saying that of course I would want to give the outing a try (giving the outing a try was the *last* thing I wanted to do) and that the outing would be fun (though it turned out to be a revelation rather than my ruination, it was not *fun*). Neither was she sensitive to my position as a child who was a visitor in her home and who was temporarily in her care, and whose parents might have created a very different home world for their children than she had created for hers. She seemed, that is, to have no sense that I might be experiencing a conflict between her expectations of me and my family's and no sense of how children can be wrenched when they are asked to embrace, on a moment's notice, values that directly contradict those that they have been trusting in for all of their lives.

Something else she seemed not to have discovered was that the wrenching can take place and needs addressing regardless of the relative merits of the conflicting values. And even if Sharon's mother had been aware of the wrenching, it would not necessarily have made a difference.[6] Following the example of any number of adults, she could have proceeded blithely, even righteously, with the wrenching, justifying her action on the grounds that it was for my own good in that it was moving me away from inferior or damaging values towards superior, sustaining ones. Which is not to say that a set of values at work in a child's home world cannot be so damaging as to require swift and decisive intervention, but only that the intervention needs to consider the quality of the child's involvement with the home world and its values.[7]

One further obstacle to gratitude was that, on reflection, the attitude Sharon's mother took towards the public eye appeared as narrow or one-sided as did my parents'. If their attitude could have been termed too Sartrian in its preoccupation, its near obsession, with shame and the power of the other's look to rob us of our place in the world, then her worldview seemed too unsuspecting or ignorant of this power.[8] Probably the most forceful evidence of her view's narrowness was that my parents, who, in a sense, became my public when they heard about the outing, did greet the news negatively—with shock and disapproval. Additional evidence was the negative eye I turned on my parents after overhearing them discuss my walk. And there was also the negative eye my mother turned on the styles worn by some of the girls we would see when we were out and about and the negative eye my father turned on cosmetics in the context of my games of dress-up.[9] Though my reception on main street may have revealed my parents' fallibility, it did not mean that the people who had seen me, or others who could just as easily have been present that day, were incapable of shock and disapproval, or of trying to cast out those who seemed to them to represent a threat, but only that in that one instance, for any number of possible reasons, they had actualized their capacity for affirmation or, at least, for outward geniality.[10]

In addition, the attitudes of both Sharon's mother and my parents towards my walk suggested an absolute or unthinking confidence in the transparent rightness of their own perspective that did not encourage gratitude. Evidencing no desire or any sense of the need to question their own values, to examine their own motives, to seek to understand the sources and implications of their own perspective and the perspective of those around them, they were at a disadvantage when it came to giving me the sense of security, the trust, that comes from knowing that those in authority remain open to question from all sides and to the possibility of their own error, in other words, the sense of security and trust that comes from knowing that those in authority, though imperfect, seek a human truth.

A second irony embedded in the story of my walk is that it should have been a discrepancy between the perspective of Sharon's mother and my parents that led me to begin examining the values of my world. Though Sharon's mother assumed that the public would see in Sharon and me the promise that its way of life, its values, would survive through us, and though my parents assumed the public would see in us a threat to that promise, both Sharon's mother and my parents were caught up in the effort to raise the good, compliant daughters who were so central to the survival of those values and that way of life (Russell 1983, 82-83).

A last experience I want to mention is one linked in my mind to the experience of the afternoon spent playing dress-up. Bringing me one of the two great muses of my early years, this experience occurred between the ages of four and eight (I would guess at five or six), after I had moved from the house in the city where I was born to a house in the country. Although my grandmother and mother say that when I first moved to the country I was afraid of everything—the insects, the weeds, the noises, the smells, the textures—my fear had disappeared so that I reveled in my country setting by the time my muse arrived, which happened one day while I was taking a bath.

I had been sitting in the tub as it filled up, enjoying the feeling of warm water lapping against my body, when suddenly a small green tree frog (small enough to fit easily in a child's palm) poured forth from the faucet with the water and began to swim around me. That such a thing was possible, that the plumbing had not achieved one of its intended separations, and that this frog and I should meet in such an unlikely setting was the first thing, besides plain joy at the beauty of the swimming creature, that delighted me. Though there are plenty of things I would not have liked to see pour out of the faucet, and though I do appreciate the technology of plumbing, I nonetheless found it exhilarating to discover that nature was less governable, brasher, than civilization had anticipated.

My second delight was that so small and soft a wild creature, once it had infiltrated the plumbing, could have survived life in the dark world of those pipes to emerge swimming in my bath.[11] My imagination was immediately and forever captured. Ecstatic, I called out to everyone, "Come see, come see what has come out of the faucet!"—or something very near to that. My home world, though it may have been the sort to panic over the news that I had walked down main street in ladies' clothes, was not the sort to panic at the appearance of that frog and supported me in my delight, a support for which I thank that world and am glad.

As for the frog, it turned out to be just that, a frog and nothing more—not a prince, a wizard, a knight, or a fairy godmother in disguise—and so it could not speak to me in words or rescue me from life's hardships and confusions by brandishing a sword, waving a magic wand, or offering a royal hand in marriage. Even so, I believe that the sight of that small wild creature emerging from the bathtub faucet became a guiding image in my life. Inspiring me to persist in my puzzling, the image has said to me again and again, "If a small green tree frog can emerge from a vast complex of metal pipe to swim gamely in your bath, then so can you emerge from the maze that is the world into which your birth has cast you and live gamely in whatever place you find yourself."

Finally, lest some see in the image of the tree frog an argument for leaving children to find their way without the benefit of support or sympathy, no matter how confounding the maze or how lost the child, the argument being that any person can emerge from any maze without the benefit of help if he or she will only try, I would like to add that I do not see in the image any such argument. Instead, I view the appearance of the tree frog in my bath as an advantage, one afforded me by circumstance, rather than through any effort of my own, and one that I do not believe circumstance affords equally to all. In addition to this providence of circumstance that I enjoyed,

I think it is important to keep in mind that I grew up in a family that was accepting of natural creatures rather than hostile or superstitious towards them and that the tree frog appeared at a time when I was disposed to welcome it, that is, at a time when my fear of my country setting had been transformed to wonder.

Though I treasure the memory of that frog's appearance, and though I believe that personal effort is essential to the health of the human spirit and that too much support can wound as surely as too little, I also think that effort derives from perception as much as or more than perception from effort. I would not, therefore, want to entrust the well-being of children, mine or anyone's, solely to circumstance and personal effort, but would argue for a nurturing, respectful guidance that extends support and opens itself to otherness. Nor would I want to glorify my own childhood, or any one person's, by choosing it for all children or overgeneralize it by failing to consider the uniqueness of the individual life history and the ways in which such things as the chance event, timing, personal readiness, and the worldview of those who bring us up can influence our ability to find our way—our ability, for example, to recognize in an event such as the tree frog's pouring forth from a bathtub faucet a guiding image, a creative muse.[12]

On the contrary, I believe we need not see, in the histories of those who persist through lostness to find direction, a rationale for dismissing as inferior, unworthy, or lazy those who are experiencing impasse or futility. I also think that instead of resting defensively with such dismissals, we could rest more freely in a world in which we take the time to share with each and every child such images as my image of the brash and gamely swimming tree frog. In like manner, I see this as a world in which we invite these same children to share with us those images that have captured their imaginations, not only those images that I have in my six chapters presented—the wolves, the sharks, the piggies and piranha, the houses of brick and sticks and straw, the cedar chest that stores the celery green chiffon, the polliwogs, the breaking wave, the account book that bewilders, the preschool teacher who leads the children's circle time, the mother who stands the daughter of her dying friend upon a chair so she can reach the counter, the father who walks with his son along a riverbank, the grandma who passes down a photograph depicting life and death and possibility—but also those images to be revealed by children we have yet to see and hear and come through time and care to know.

To prepare for this sharing, a sharing that would call on our capacity to teach as well as our capacity to learn, I think we could ask ourselves the kinds of questions that would help us understand the sources and the implications of the mazes into which we have been born and into which we birth our children. Such questions could help us gain our bearings, name our fears, separate our dreams from the dreams of the great diversity of children in our care, and give us a fair chance of guiding them towards their own emergence. Though we often refer to them in the possessive, children do not belong to us but to themselves.

Notes

Chapter 1. A Sky-Blue, Orange-Warm Picnic

1. Because it is so easy to equate a *child*-crisis with a childish cri-sis, I want to note the oversight in applying *childish*, in its negative connotations, to children, *childish* being a word more appropriately applied to adults behaving immaturely. I guess my concern is that in our everyday dealings with children we seem to define behavior that arises naturally from what it means to be a child as "childish," and then, having defined natural behavior negatively, we feel justi-fied in becoming impatient with it.

2. The conversation is as close as memory can make it to the one David and Mark had at the picnic. One issue it will doubtless raise, an issue touched on in the preface, is that an argument over hot dog and hamburger buns in the plentiful world of the picnic is a triviality, and that my attention to it reveals a gross insensitivity to the really crucial issues of our time. My being David's mother will no doubt further erode my credibility for some readers, prompting them to dismiss my attention to the conflict as doting or precious.

Although the scope of the present work limits a full response to this criticism (as does the fact that the issue has arisen only a few paragraphs into the book), I want to say that, in addition to agreeing that the racial, sexual, and class prejudices of our culture and the

institutionalization of oppression that they promote are truly crucial issues, I also think that squabbles such as David and Mark's
have implications for conflicts we view as anything but trivial, and
I hope that this will become clearer as the book progresses. It further seems to me that trying to teach children about inequity by
invoking "shoulds" ("you should not be fighting over hamburger
and hot dog buns when children are starving in the world") is
rarely helpful, perhaps partly because it reveals no sense on the
adult's part of the wide-ranging issues children may be encountering in a conflict as apparently trivial as David and Mark's, or for the
possibility that food per se is not what the conflict is about, at least
not for the children. My experience is that invoking these "shoulds"
tends to encourage "deaf ears" in children, rather than any comprehension of social oppression, and that there are innumerable moments that lend themselves to a revelation of the social inequity
that such "shoulds" fail to communicate.

A writer could, of course, protect herself somewhat from such
criticism by choosing a conflict in which something less provocative
than food was central. She might even justify the choice with a
comforting lie by telling herself that in hiding away the plenty of
the picnic she spares the hungry the unnecessary pain of such a
scene. This choice, however, would not change the fact that food
indeed was what David and Mark fought over. Nor would it change
the fact that I became so wrapped up in shaping and narrating the
conflict, in moving myself and the reader through the rendering of
a "triviality" towards an exploration of its implications for David
and Mark as well as for others (and, I must also admit, in recalling
the extraordinary natural beauty of that spring day), that I did not
think to acknowledge the raw cultural nerve that the picnic scene
would surely touch. That the human capacity for becoming thus
"wrapped up" in the present moment has positive as well as negative
implications is a subject for another essay.

3. Although most of us probably indulge occasionally in the
careless labeling of children (I certainly do), I doubt there is any
such thing as a "discreet" conversation in the context described in
the text. In my experience, children hear, attend, listen, reflect, and
remember with more depth than adults often give them credit for.
Why we sometimes discuss children in their presence as if they do
not exist seems to me easily explained on the grounds that these

children do not exist for us in any essential sense, at least not for the duration of the conversation.

4. My negative feelings about advertising preceded the time I spent writing commercial copy and also survived it, a point I mention because it seems important to acknowledge my involvement with a world I am criticizing.

5. The anesthesiologist, the former Dr. William Miofsky (he pleaded no contest to three felony charges in Sacramento, California, in 1979), who indulged in "discreet" fellatio, and the adults at the picnic, who indulged in "discreet" conversation, though miles apart in one sense, share the dubious distinction of affording people in their care less protection than human dignity deserves. One argument adults sometimes make is that children are oblivious. "Oh, I don't think they even hear us, and if they do, it won't really matter, because they'll have forgotten it all by dinner time" is a comment typical to this defense. Interestingly enough, a similar argument was made by various members of the public in response to the Miofsky scandal: "I don't think what he did was all that bad. I mean, how could patients under anesthetic suffer any damage?" was a not infrequent comment made when the story was in the news. However, David's behavior suggests this argument's weakness in the context of the picnic, just as the emotional trauma testified to by Miofsky's patients (as well as by recent research into the degree of consciousness of patients under anesthetic) suggests its weakness in the context of the operating room.

6. Examples in the paragraph are drawn from experiences of myself and others I know or from news sources and books. The example of the child's burning was reported in *The Sacramento Bee*, October 29, 1984.

7. The description of Brancusi derives from a photograph and comments in Noguchi (1976, 26–29).

8. Rather than as an anachronism, a laughingstock, or an idealist, I see Don Quixote as essentially heroic. For an impassioned discussion of him as a man who fought for the spirit, see Unamuno (1954, 297–330).

9. My view of artistic imagination is rooted in John Keats's reference to negative capability (1959, 261).

Chapter 2. Mark at Preschool

1. Descriptions of the preschool draw on my experiences as a participating parent as well as on the experiences of another parent or two and several children who attended the school.

2. Though I have used the phrases *as friends are wont to do* and *as a matter of course* to try to clarify my view that Laura's presence at Mark's refusal resulted from the circumstance of their being friends rather than from her determination to "stand her ground" in his behalf or anything like that, there is an interesting possibility buried by my phrasing, one that would take an essay to explore but that I nonetheless want to mention briefly. The possibility is that Laura had been assigned by the adults, or was herself assuming, for any number of reasons (her sex, her age, her status as an experienced student, her enthusiasm for the school), the role of "big sister" or "mothering person" and that though she did witness his refusal as "a matter of course," she was in a position to be walking with him in the first place because Mark's parents and her own had seen an advantage in having Mark, the overprotected son, begin preschool with experienced, friendly Laura, experience and friendliness being central to our concept of woman as helper.

3. Some readers may question my citing of four-year-old Laura as a source. I find it acceptable and should add that Laura was not only much impressed with Mark's refusal at the time, but even today, twelve or so years later, counts it as one of her most vivid childhood memories. Of course, the depth of her impression and the vividness of her memory do not guarantee its accuracy, but this could be said of anyone.

4. The school used the word *job* to refer to what many of us call "toys." The choice was conscious and underscored that the "toys" were designed to be more demanding than lots of those available on the commercial market. The choice also asserted the school's conviction that children's lives are effortful in a sense that adults often reserve for themselves and in a sense that our words *toy* and *play* do not necessarily convey. I sympathize with this view and strongly agree that children's lives are effortful but also feel that because our culture conceives of *job* and *work* as highly goal or re-ward oriented, the school's choice had a drawback, which was to obscure the effortfulness of much play as a disinterested explora-

tion that is integral to creativity and that is qualitatively different from the jobs that often earn adults their income, a disinterested effortfulness that, in actuality, the school encouraged. In other words, I think that the school's effort to compensate for the misleading differentiation of children and adults on the grounds that children play (as in *easy* and *frivolous*) whereas adults work (as in *difficult* and *important*) had the side effect of obscuring the degree to which the common usage of such words as *work, play, toy,* and *job* reveals an impoverished perception of childhood and an impoverished living of adulthood, an impoverished living towards which, in the name of education, we sometimes lead our children.

5. I chose this particular job or toy because the children I know remember it as an especially popular one that they were always glad to get a chance to work with.

6. For a description of the human capacity for sharing the "thisness" of a landscape, for being "jointly present in it," see Merleau-Ponty (1962, 405–409).

7. As mentioned in note 3 above, Laura counts the memory of Mark's being carried into the classroom among her most vivid. In spontaneously relating it to me recently, she emphasized not only the great care Rita showed for Mark but also the fact that because Rita picked Mark up body facing outward and because she (Laura) had been standing right beside him, she had been full witness to the screaming and thrashing and had been greatly startled to discover that her friend Mark, or anyone, could so thoroughly dread a place that held for her the appeal of good memories from past sessions as well as the prospect of an after-recess time that would include circle time and then a free period to work-play with the jobs. Among other things, Laura's memory illustrates how seamless was the confusion or pouring together of object and meaning in her experiencing of preschool up until her witnessing of Mark's refusal.

8. Although Laura did not comment on it while relating her memory of Mark's refusal, I myself wonder, because of the upheaval she experienced at his refusal, what it might have been like to participate in circle time with so much intense resistance watching from behind and what it might have been like to be the resistant watcher peering over a fence of children. I also think that in having Mark placed behind her, Laura was in a position to experience

herself as a shield, an experiencing that relates to note 2 above and that could further develop her being cast in a "big sister" or "mothering" role towards Mark.

Here I do not mean to pass judgment on Rita's suggestion that Mark sit behind Laura but rather to suggest that the outgrowth of our actions is intricate, subtle, and not bound by our intent, and that the interplay between categories (for instance, the categories "big sister," "mother's-teacher's helper," "friend," "hero," "martyr," "savior," "victim") is far swifter than reflection and forever outstripping control and systematization. In Mark's case, we could view Rita as living a relatively new form, we could label the form "children are persons" ("children have dignity"), and we could say that the living of this new form prompted her to leave Mark's arms and legs free while she carried him into the classroom. We could also say that the new form prevented her from forcing him to sit in the circle and instead prompted her to suggest that he sit behind Laura. But while living a new form in relation to Mark, Rita placed Laura in a position that could support the old form of female child as teacher's helper, a form that can function like the constrictive tracks of modern schooling, by directing Laura towards a role of eternal subordination or apprenticeship, a role that does not encourage dignity.

9. See Straus (1982, 45–48) for a discussion of human beings as historical beings whose "experiences are not arbitrarily interchangeable" (47).

10. It was Mark's physical safety that so concerned his mother. Although vigilantly monitoring his physical exploration when he learned to crawl and walk, she was quite liberal about intellectual and emotional exploration, insofar as these are separable from the physical. But no one made this distinction during the years her children were small. Instead, she was simply typed as overprotective.

11. To prevent a wrong impression I should add that though Mark's parents introduced the idea of preschool to Mark, the idea was suggested to them by friends and family, whose stated motive was "the good of Mark" but who also seemed to enjoy demonstrating to the novice mother that she had a lot to learn.

12. A perception of the mother as a stifler of exploration also figured in Mark's mother not accompanying him into the classroom

on the first official day of preschool; the school felt that Mark would be better able to settle in without her. The possibility that her presence might have helped Mark make the transition to preschool was not explored.

13. Laura also created an imaginary friend about this time, as did her brother, David.

14. Though it will not become my focus, one point Mark's mother and I discussed regarding the timing of his refusal was that the prospect of preschool could have seemed too distant to be a threat until he actually visited the school.

15. In my envisioning of orientation day, I could be compared to David in Chapter 1: we both had spun out a scenario for an event and were distressed when a participant did not comply so that we could actualize our vision.

16. By emphasizing his mother's position as the one who had to contend with Mark's resistance, I don't mean to ignore that he also had to contend with her insistence. Instead, I want to suggest that, as the person most with him, she was in a position to know him more intimately and comprehensively than were the other adults in his life.

17. Some readers may object that my description of Mark's emotion is melodramatic and that it puts words in his mouth. It does put words in his mouth, but in an effort to suggest the emotions Mark could have been experiencing and to work against an adult tendency to dismiss strong emotion in children too young to fully articulate it. I also think that our tendency to dismiss strong emotion in children is connected to our removal from it (to our culture's radical differentiation of childhood and adulthood) and to our conception of childhood experiencing as negligible for the very reason that we have convinced ourselves it is something we leave behind or outgrow. Our inability to remember much from childhood helps us here, among other things making it easier to walk away from the child's emotion, which we tell ourselves the child will soon forget, as if forgetting an emotional experience were synonymous with being freed of its impact. To those of us who dismiss childhood emotion by pointing to the resilience of children instead of to the forgetfulness of children, I would say that even among those children who eventually appear to thrive in a situation they

once resisted, as Mark eventually did at preschool, the experience of thriving does not necessarily cancel out the memory or the impact of having been rendered powerless. Nor do I think it would be a good thing if it did, mainly because I think the experience of powerlessness is an essential experience of childhood, and of humanness, and that instead of burying it we need to help children, ourselves, and each other remember and come to terms with it.

18. Because preschool (and similar social institutions) is designed to be of use, its relationship to Schachtel's set of questions is slightly different than the relationship of, say, a tree, a bird, or a human being. Even given this difference, however, a school can still be perceived allocentrically or autocentrically, and so Schachtel's questions remain pertinent.

19. I should probably qualify Mark's perceiving by saying that in order to ask how he could protect himself from the school he must already in some sense have asked who or what the school was.

20. *Separation anxiety* is John Bowlby's term (1960, 89–113), following Freud. *Strange situation* is Mary Ainsworth's term. See, for example, Ainsworth et al. (1978).

21. I am not arguing for or against the view that Mark should attend preschool but am pointing out that the adults held the view before and after his resistance emerged.

22. It could be argued that my discussion of the credibility of women and mothers is full of contradictory concepts. I do not think, however, that these concepts are contradictory so much as that they suggest the conceptual grab bag we have at our disposal when it comes to our view of women, a grab bag which may to a degree suggest the complexity of women, or human beings, but which we also rely on to provide us with whatever concept we may need at a given moment to manipulate women according to our perspective. Focusing on a mother's relationship with her child as predominately physical can facilitate our denial of her capacity for offering spiritual and intellectual nurturance; focusing on a mother's preoccupation with her child's physical safety can facilitate our denial of the very same mother's capacity for insight into her child's mood or worldview. By attending to one facet as if it were the whole, we obscure the woman's or the mother's full potential.

23. The word *happened* makes the process sound passive, whereas on some level it must be very active. Maybe we characterize it with language suggesting passivity because the process is invisible to our way of looking. Or maybe we characterize it with such language because it occurs while our attention, our focus, is elsewhere (for example, on mowing the lawn, frying a chop, peering through a microscope, or singing a song) or because such happenings fall outside what we have learned or been taught to verbalize.

24. Though Mark's mother appears in some silent part of herself to have worked on the puzzle of Mark's resistance to preschool, she does not seem to have worked, in that same part of herself, on the puzzle of her overprotectiveness, on the possibility that it, too, may arise from some concrete ground. She does agree that she overprotects and that it is not good for Mark, but she does not try to fathom it in relation to her own life history or ask herself if it is good for *her.* Instead, she seems to accept it or resign herself to it as something that comes with the territory of her self, or her world. In her inattention to her own self, or her own world, as puzzle, she reminds me of many women I have met or read about (including, at times, myself). Mark's mother and her peers work gradually towards the championing or "saving" of others, but their championing suggests a fractured perception in that, though they may seek comprehensiveness in the embracing of the outsider or "needy" one, they ironically do not embrace themselves as women who are persons who also deserve attention and inclusion. I would compare such a perceiving to that of a person who is asked to draw a family portrait and excludes herself.

Though in the text and thus far in this note I have presented Mark's mother as pursuing Mark's well-being rather than her own well-being or her own self-interest (here I would distinguish between well-being and self-interest by saying that well-being opens itself to the whole truth whereas self-interest closes itself to the whole truth in order to avoid pain, to preserve an "is," or to save face), I do not want to sentimentalize her depiction or suggest that self-interest could not figure in her pursuit. Her pursuit of something that would encompass the gap she sensed between her past and present experience of Mark could theoretically be motivated by any one or more of the following: his self-interest, his well-being, her own self-interest, her own well-being. In addition, any combination of these would itself be infinitely variable depending on the propor-

tion of the motivations and their fluctuation through time. Exploring even a couple of the combinations would probably enlarge our
understanding of the caregiver-child relationship as a relationship
between complex persons rather than between performers of stereotypic, rigidly bound roles. However, this exploration is beyond
my present scope.

25. I am assuming that cement block and brick are enough alike
for Mark to perceive them as equivalent or nearly so.

26. My examples intentionally suggest that the familiar and the
new can powerfully attract us, but there are a number of possible
implications I would not accept. First, even if I had been attracted
to the connection solely because of its novelty, the connection could
still be accurate. Second, even if my response had involved the
connection's touching something in my own life history, it would
not necessarily follow that I was "projecting" in the narrow sense of
that term. Instead, the connection could have touched my own life
history as well as Mark's, and my response could have involved the
comprehension that the connection "felt right" not only in relation
to my knowledge of Mark but also in relation to my own life. Rather
than something strictly novel or narrowly projective, Mark's experience could thus have been a specific instance of a broadly human
kind of experiencing or, at least, of a broadly human kind of experiencing within a given culture as context. One reason I introduce
context is that I do not want to ignore the distinction between saying,
on the one hand, that human beings are beings who in essence *are
capable of* recognizing or being touched by shared experiences and,
on the other, of saying that human beings are beings who in essence,
or by definition, actually share a certain set of experiences.

27. Rather than crossing the boundary in the parent's prescribed
capacity as taxi-person or open-house attendee, I mean crossing the
boundary of the school's daily content and form, and I also mean
crossing the boundary between our adult perspective on that daily
content and form, and a *given* child's perspective on it.

28. I believe I pulled back from the agitation because of its
intensity and then used the intensity to justify my pulling back. My
intense response frightened me, and so I dismissed it as the weakness of a moment in which I had let a child's silly fearfulness get
under my skin. To be so agitated is a very unadult and irrational
way to behave, I probably told myself, a telling that could have

increased my susceptibility to any recipelike explanation for Mark's behavior that came my way. Here I would have been acting out of self-interest (closing myself off from the fact of my own fear), as I have distinguished those terms in note 24 above.

29. I do not think our culture sufficiently recognizes the scope of the work and play children become involved in on their own, an idea touched on in note 4 above. In the case of Mark's resistance to preschool, though the adults did consider aspects of his life that they felt required attention (the need for friends his own age), no one thought to look at his life previous to enrollment in preschool to see what tasks or "homework" might already be engaging him.

30. Mark's mother is certain that Mark was familiar with a book version of "The Three Little Pigs" and knows that he was read to from the Volland collection, and also that he poured over this collection on his own, but she doesn't have a particular memory of the reading of that version or any other. It is of course possible that he heard a book version other than the Volland. This circumstance has left me with a number of possible approaches. Because the Volland version was in his home and because discussing two versions allowed me to explore, concretely, the question of discrepancies between versions, I chose to include both the Volland and the Disney. Also, a discussion of two versions allows the reader to project a discussion of a situation in which Mark was exposed to only one version, to some other version entirely, or to more than two versions.

31. In this chapter I am not arguing for or against reading fairy tales, fables, or any category of story to children but rather am trying to trace one child's involvement with one story in two versions and to suggest possible ways in which the child's specific situation influenced the meaning of the story for *this* child.

32. My discussion of Mark's repetitious listening to "The Three Little Pigs" is rooted in Schachtel's ([1959] 1984) comparison of Freud's concept of the repetition compulsion and Schachtel's view that repetition is central to exploring and assimilating our surroundings (259).

33. One possibility is that Mark was genial when he felt in control of the story or had come to terms with some aspect of it and that he glowered when the story in its two versions threatened his

sense of place in the world or exhausted him with its complexities. In other words, like many adults, Mark glowered when he had had a bad day "at work" and was genial when he had had a good day.

34. In his discussion of a child's grasping of a story, Schachtel ([1959] 1984) acknowledges the influence of Heinz Werner (1948).

35. Although Schachtel distinguishes between the adult's way of comprehending a story and the child's, he also points out that an adult is in a position comparable to the child's when the adult takes on "an object of *similar significance*" ([1959] 1984, 262), and he offers a work of art, music, or poetry as an example. That the comparison between adult and child is a comparison and not an equation seems evident in light of Schachtel's observation that an adult's grasping of a story rests on "a quite different, much more abstractive kind of perception and understanding" (260) than a child's.

36. Counterexamples in which a change in a story would not upset children, and might even relieve them, are conceivable but would be tied to a child's life history and would qualify rather than contradict Schachtel's point. I also think that adults who themselves are not unduly threatened by change, but who are at the same time sensitive to its presence as well as its capacity to harm, could guide a child encountering change (for example, several versions of a story) towards an understanding of it that could enlarge a child's sense of well-being. Of course, a culture's attitude towards change and unpredictability would affect an adult's attempt to provide such guidance.

37. The absence of illustrations on a record could explain the inclusion of detail. But the distinction is still important because even given the illustrations in the Volland edition, which do impart a lot of detail not included in the written text, the Disney version is much more verbally elaborate than the Volland.

38. One way Mark might resolve the problem of the two versions would be to reject or "let go" one version altogether and designate the other as the favorite, "real," or authoritative one. Or he might select out elements of the two versions into a third story that he remembers as "The Three Little Pigs," or perhaps integrate the elements of both versions into a single story. He also might allow lots of variation so long as the story retained the essentials of a wolf (or, depending on his ability for and attitude towards gener-

alization and abstraction, any wolflike villain), three little pigs (or other vulnerable creatures), a house of straw and a house of sticks (or other vulnerable dwelling places), and a brick house (or some other impervious dwelling place).

39. See Straus (1982, 90) for a comment on revision of the past as "conversion-experience."

40. My discussion of Mark's experiencing of "The Three Little Pigs" as his own story is rooted in Chapters 2 and 4 of Straus (1982), especially pp. 31–32, 36–38, and 77–84.

41. I have distinguished between possession and exercising of language sophistication because it seems misleading to assume that a child who does not exercise a certain knowledge of language in a specific situation does not possess that knowledge. The failure to exercise the knowledge could arise not only from an unwillingness or refusal but also from the fact that the child does not recognize the situation as one in which the knowledge is applicable. Here it would be the child's way of classifying the situation (or the knowledge), rather than the absence of applicable knowledge altogether, that prevented application.

42. That Mark did not announce a recognition doesn't mean there was none. The verbally inarticulate nature of the recognition or a fear of being labeled "silly," for example, could have prevented announcement.

43. In contrasting the contexts in which listening to a veiled story and listening to the Volland edition of "The Three Little Pigs" take place, I do not mean to deny that we are generally receptive to the idea that stories stimulate children's thoughts and feelings. Rather, I want to suggest, first, that stories categorized as "classics," although themselves projections of a sort, are stories we often take for granted and, second, that our confidence that the child we read them to will experience them as other children do, or as we ourselves did, can blind us to a divergent experiencing even as we witness it. In a very different context, we might compare M. Jacobs's (1968, 35–36) discussion of J. H. van den Berg's observations on the blindness of early anatomists to the actual structure of the human body revealed by their dissections. For example, the sixteenth-century father of anatomy Vesalius numbered five blood vessels in the human liver when there are actually two, an error of perception van

den Berg ascribes to early anatomists' perception of the human body they dissected in terms of what they already knew about the bodies of animals.

In yet another context, we might consider the student response to an American short story I once assigned to an English class. In the story, mainstream Americans celebrate the Fourth of July enthusiastically while a number of Native Americans withdraw and get drunk. Evidencing a "classic" response to the story, a white student asked why the Native Americans had behaved so strangely, and when several fellow white students murmured that they'd wondered about that, too, it was one of only two Hispanic students in the class who responded. He did this by asking his classmates if it had ever occurred to them that Native Americans might not be all that keen to have the Fourth of July roll around because it reminded them that the celebrators had as good as stolen America from them. His comment brought a "Gee, I never thought of it that way before" look to the face of the class and opened the way for an important class discussion. It also suggested an important role for public school courses focusing on works in the humanities that point up the limitations of traditional or "classic" ways of seeing.

44. In my experience, our emphasis on the child's need to learn to distinguish between fantasy and reality is sometimes exaggerated enough to obscure a child's effort to "reflect" on or make sense of life as a story that unfolds. It also seems to me that what we label as a child's blurring of fantasy and reality and often judge by definition to be a problem is sometimes not a problematical blurring but instead a profound sensitivity to or insight into an aspect of reality that is, for any number of reasons, invisible to the adult. Also, if fantasy play can move a child towards an understanding of the world's complexity that adults have learned to move towards through verbalized reflection and if a child's imagination can break out in all directions when life is revealed as an object that unfolds through time and space, then such a breaking out might be mistaken for an inability to distinguish fantasy from reality.

45. To keep the record straight, I should add that even though the phrase *third little pig* functions much like a name in both versions of the story, in the Disney recording, the third little pig, after building the brick house and discouraging the wolf with the kettle of hot water, is characterized by the narrator as a smart little pig whose name is "Practical."

46. The pull Mark might feel towards an identification with the third little pig is comparable to the pull any child (or adult) born into an elite family, group, or class might feel. It is also a pull that we could take up much more explicitly in our nurturing of children, both at home and at school. That this taking up would require us to first come to terms with the pull towards privilege in ourselves seems almost too obvious to mention.

47. Compare Mark's potential for choosing the role of brother's *keeper*, and for interpreting the role as heroic, to Laura's potential, discussed in notes 2 and 8 above, for choosing the role of mother's *helper*.

48. I would not deny that the demands of earning an income and providing for the physical needs of children can leave adults with little time or energy for encountering the intellectual, emotional, and spiritual needs of children. I would, however, argue that the problem of time and money that many parents (especially single parents, usually mothers with low incomes) and others in charge of children (especially teachers) face reflects our culture's social consciousness as one that does not value children for their own sake, that takes the art of nurturing shamelessly for granted, and that places the welfare of those who nurture in direct opposition to the welfare of those who are nurtured. And I would qualify my argument by saying that, even in situations where time and money are not an issue, the intellectual, emotional, and spiritual encountering between adults and children is often impoverished. Even for those of us who have the time and money, it is difficult to nurture children in ways we ourselves were not nurtured, are not being nurtured. It is also difficult to try to know another person, a child, if we ourselves were not known as children, are not being known as adults. And it is especially difficult if we have sought time and money as substitutes for nourishment and as insulation from the call to know and be known.

49. The adult capacity for accommodating him- or herself in the name of a child seems to me boundless. One unfortunate implication is that this capacity fogs the whole area of education and makes it difficult for the inexperienced educator who genuinely wants to understand and nurture children to distinguish the accommodator who misleads from the wise elder who guides. That the accommodators think of themselves as wise elders and that any one person can be part accommodating and part wise only makes the distinction more difficult.

50. My reference to free speech and censorship is not meant as an argument for or against either. I only mean to suggest that our allegiances sometimes express themselves very powerfully when we are least aware of their expression and that it can be clarifying to recognize and sort through the depth and breadth of their power, that is, to directly face their God-likeness and question it instead of averting our gaze out of a fear of going blind.

51. Schachtel ([1959] 1984) discusses shifting perceptual modes from a slightly different standpoint. See especially pp. 214–220.

52. Although Mark's resistance to the "familiarity" of preschool is at bottom a resistance to the ultimately strange situation of death, I don't think the adults in Mark's life conceived of even a remote connection between preschool as a strange situation and death as the ultimately strange situation. I am not saying that such a connection couldn't be made (I think it could) but that the adults did not make it and that it would therefore be a gross equivocation to point out the connection and then assert that, given the connection, their analysis had been accurate after all.

53. Admittedly, it can be difficult to sort out when to intervene and when to let a child be. My feeling is that decisions to intervene and decisions to let be involve judgment and that, instead of searching for a recipelike list of foolproof rules, we need to educate ourselves and our children towards making creative judgments.

Chapter 3. David at Home

1. While working on Chapter 3, I discovered that David, now fifteen, had quite a few memories about the actual writing of his autobiographical essay, particularly about his reasons for including some of the content. Although incorporating his memories into the text would have been digressive, I want to mention a few of them here and there in the notes to Chapter 3. I especially want to note memories suggesting that David's perspective (as he remembers it) while writing his essay was in certain respects quite different from the perspective readers, including myself, might infer if they had only the contents of the essay or the excerpts I will be quoting. Because my work relies so heavily on memory, I also want to mention in these notes an example or two that demonstrate both the

precisions and imprecisions of memory. One memory concerns a discrepancy between David's memory of the assignment his teacher gave and the actual contents of the essay when I finally found it in my filing cabinet. According to David's memory, his teacher told the class to write about their lives from birth to death, and David assumed he had ended his essay by documenting his death. Only as we talked did the illogic of such an ending strike him, and when we found the essay, we saw that it ended when he was eighty and still quite active.

2. David volunteered that he had read about the connection between time of birth and the ability to see ghosts in a children's book on the supernatural that he had checked out from the school or public library.

3. In addition to touching on the human capacity for discovering the hidden, I think David's reference to his time of birth could also be an attempt to account for situations in which he experienced his ability to perceive something in his world that those around him did not perceive, or at least did not appear to David to perceive. In other words, I think that when David noticed something that others seemed not to see, he may have interpreted his perception as a special or distinguishing one and, in trying to make sense of his special "power," may have attributed it to his time of birth and to the theory of comparative powers or potentials among human beings that it implies. Despite the crudeness of the theory itself, it seems to me that David's urge to theorize about the differences he perceived among people was not so different from the urge of adult theorists in general. For that matter, I suppose the theory itself is no cruder than some of the theories we adults conceive.

David's reference to his ability to see ghosts also raises interesting questions about how he, and other children, as well as the rest of us, experience such "specialness" when we perceive it in ourselves, or when others perceive it in us, questions that have important implications for education. Depending on a child's situation at a given moment, he or she could experience the specialness as, at one extreme, distinguishing or, at the other, alienating, and as anything from a gift to a curse. Superficial as such theories are, they have the attraction of providing ascribers the security of a base from which to articulate their perceptions, at the very least to themselves.

4. An explanation David volunteered for his emphasis on his future was that as a fourth grader he had had most of his life still to live.

5. One general comment David volunteered about the adult achievements he described was that many of them had to do with fame, wealth, and good deeds. He said he could remember that though adventure and exploration of the unknown had been what really mattered to him, and though in fourth grade he had not thought of fame, wealth, and good deeds as routinely associated with a career in marine biology, he had "thrown them in" anyway because, first, his own family was not rich or famous and so had provided him with little experience in these areas, because, second, good deeds were the kind of thing everyone talked about as being important, and, third, because the speculative nature of the essay had given him the opportunity to define a career in marine biology in any terms he pleased and without regard to any conceptions he may have formed about the typical nature of such a career in actuality.

6. Between the ages of about six and eight or nine there was no television in David's home, and so his viewing would have been limited to programs watched elsewhere.

7. The phrase *flash back* is not quite right for what I want to convey, but it is better than the other obvious choice—*recall*—because *flash back* suggests being thrown back into the past rather than calling the past forward into the present.

8. Actually, the image David had of piranhas was quite common, and it is only relatively recently that this image has been challenged through research. For an example of the kind of article that could have been a big help to David when he was seven, see Ola and D'Aulaire (1986, 31–35).

9. The adjective *play-filled* is not meant to gloss over the fact that in their play children can take up and try to gain an understanding of the same sorts of serious or philosophical questions that concern adults.

10. See Straus (1982, 34) for comments on the transformation of an individual's world in the context of the shocking experience.

11. Here I am not assuming that participation according to the expectation of others would *necessarily* have prolonged or intensified

his fear or have prevented him from experiencing *any* joy in such participation. What I am suggesting is that such participation would have alienated him from his own emotions.

12. In relation to David's shame, compare Sartre (1956, 260–281) and Straus ([1966] 1980, 222–223).

13. David's characterization of some of the "scary parts" as too horrible to tell about suggests a category of material we could label "abhorrent" or "unspeakable," a category we could add to "story material," "research material," "confidential material," and "inconsequential material," which I discussed earlier in the text.

14. Here I do not mean to equate personality and life history. I used them both because I think that in the one incident at the club David interpreted individual behavior in terms of personality traits of a fairly static quality, whereas it would also have been possible to interpret behavior in terms of life history as an ongoing and less static or predictable venturing in the world. Of course, the term *life history* could connote predictability if we regarded history or the past as narrowly or mechanistically determining of the present and future.

15. Although the most obvious explanation for David's not telling Samuel or me about his fear is that he did not want to risk our ridiculing him, it is also possible that he was afraid that even if we did not ridicule him, we would experience his fear as story material and tell it to other people and that among those others some might ridicule him or make him their "laughingstock." Ironically, story material is exactly how I did experience David's fear, as is evidenced by my telling about his fear in this chapter. When I pointed this out to David, his comments suggested that the kind of storytelling he would have dreaded was that in which the child's trial becomes a matter of amusement or entertainment for others, a tale telling in which the child's emotion is treated as inconsequential and amusing because the source of the emotion is perceived as ludicrous by the tale bearer.

16. Although it is too complex a matter to take up in this chapter, I think David's focus on inconsistency may have arisen in part from a desire for predictability and that to a degree he confused consistency and predictability, a confusion that I think is "normal" in our culture. One implication of confusing the two is that we undercut the possibility of choice among alternative actions.

17. Not having seen the Tarzan movie, I will be relying exclusively on David's memories.

18. Although I respect David's observation (and similar observations by others) that what we can imagine is sometimes worse than a graphic depiction could be, I would guess that our imaginings are rooted in the concrete, in our imaginative transformation of our experience of the world, and that the "worseness" of what we can imagine is linked partly to the fact that our imaginings are born out of our own life history and so by definition can be tailored to horrify us specifically. The worseness could also be partly caused by imaginings that remain somewhat nebulous or elusive so that we never have a chance to fully meet their glance and accustom or familiarize ourselves with their "look."

19. In the Hardy boys series, Aunt Gertrude, who lives with the boys, is foil or alter ego to the boys' mother, Laura Hardy. Whereas Laura Hardy defers to her sons' adventures but worries silently, Aunt Gertrude voices these worries. She is the "mother hen" or sharp-tongued "dragon lady" stereotype of the overprotective parent who, deep down, is proud of her "sons'" adventures.

20. As in my discussion of Mark's fear of preschool in Chapter 2, my discussion of David's fear of piranhas and his bath is rooted in Straus's (1982, 31–32, 36–38, 77–84, 90) concept of first-timeness, the sudden, subjective readiness, and also in his comments on the repetition of anxiety that can follow a shocking experience.

21. See Merleau-Ponty's (1962) theory of the body.

22. Straus (1982, 79–80) has influenced my comments on the role of the child's life history.

23. The monkey's transformation from ferocious to friendly, though powerful as is, becomes more so if viewed metaphorically as dramatizing the emotional transformation children see their parents, and others, including themselves, go through day in and day out. In reading the description of the "hideous-looking simian" I could see myself on those days, particularly during the early years, when I mothered out of anger, fatigue, and confusion.

24. When I say that we sometimes have only the most limited knowledge of our children's worlds, I do not mean to imply that we should become watchdogs of their lives, violating their privacy and

intervening at every turn so that they feel as if they are under surveillance.

25. For those of us who readily or "automatically" perceive the difference between the situations faced by Tarzan and the Hardy boys, my example may seem weak and unconvincing: that is, it might seem implausible that anyone, even a child highly focused on one aspect of a situation, would fail to discern that if Tarzan were in Frank and Joe's place, he very likely would not dive, and if Frank and Joe were in Tarzan's place, they very likely would put their arms back in the water. In my opinion, such readers overgeneralize from their own ability to penetrate the difference between these two particular situations. If they were carefully to review their own life histories, I think they would find instances in which they had missed a distinction that was obvious to others.

In addition, some may object to my argument on the grounds that because Tarzan and the Hardy boys are different people with distinct life histories, they may not, when placed in each other's situations, adopt each other's strategies. My comment would be that though Tarzan and the Hardy boys would not necessarily adopt the other's strategies, these other strategies are in keeping with their general parameters of behavior and in no sense mutually exclusive or contradictory. And I would add that my argument is not intended to present either the Hardy boys or Tarzan as rigidly determined by life history or as confined to the choices they have made as dramatized in their respective narratives. I think that Frank, Joe, or Tarzan, insofar as they represent real human beings, could each try a different strategy, either in the context of their own story or in the context of the other's. A different strategy, however, would still express their life history in some sense.

26. An effort to secure peace of mind in the face of a monster-creature by maintaining a safe distance would not be unique to David, or to children. For a brief but refreshing account of the brown recluse spider as a "scary beast" that we ourselves have created, see Sue Hubbell (1983, 40–43).

27. Compare Sartre (1956, 260–281) and Straus ([1966] 1980, 222–223) in relation to David's contrasting of his bathtub and a public swimming pool.

28. The idea that piranhas would come up through the drain admittedly also involves the question of size, but it is a different one than the question of piranhas being able to fit in the bathtub.

29. In his denial of eccentricity and his citing of horror movies, David again demonstrated his susceptibility to the concept of 'normalness'.

30. My phrase echoes Shakespeare's phrase "imagination bodies forth."

31. See Schachtel ([1959] 1984, 137–138, 160–163, and 309–314) for a discussion of infant perception and body memory.

32. See Dora Russell (1983, 82–83), in which Russell comments that having children is motivated by the parents' desire to escape death.

Chapter 4. But What of Laura?

1. The distinction I've made between minor fictional characters and real people seems workable, although I agree that even minor fictional characters do not always respect the boundaries of what is written and tend to "exist" between the lines and off the page in the passages cut, in the fantasies of the writer and readers, and in the lives of the real people who have influenced the writer's perception of human beings.

2. In writing about children, I was repeatedly frustrated by having to order my focus through time and the limits of consciousness instead of being able to attend to all the children simultaneously. As I attended to one child, I kept hearing the call of the other children and was irritated at not being able to give each child what he or she seemed to need *when* it was needed and also at not being able to explore the implications of what I might be saying about one child for other children. To the extent that the limits of time and consciousness are part of the human condition, my frustration was frivolous. Though infinitesimal by comparison, however, my frustration made me think of the traditional public school classroom with its large number of students assigned to one teacher, and I concluded once again what I have often concluded before, which is that the public at large does not particularly value its children or its

teachers; given the kind and number of compromises teachers and children must make to survive their ratio and the fact that the public itself has chosen (or at least tolerates) the ratio, how could the public value them?

3. Laura was, of course, present during the weeks I worked on David's story and talked with him about his fear, and I think this may have been one factor in her eventually opening up and talking as much as she did about her own story. That I worked on both their stories for weeks, getting down my own memories and thoughts, before beginning to talk with them in any great detail may have also been a factor in that my typing away at their stories day after day drew their attention, and they would wander in and out of my room, observing me at my work.

4. See Grumet (1988, 77–94) for a discussion of the complex relationship between visibility and privacy required to sustain creative teaching.

5. There were exceptions to the rule of primary graders remaining in the homeroom. Three programs that took some primary children out of the home classroom were the speech, reading, and gifted programs. For children participating in any of these programs, fourth grade could have meant an increase in, rather than the first experience of, leaving the classroom.

6. My feelings about the gifted programs offered by many public schools are so ambivalent that any reference to Laura's participation in these programs makes me want to air my ambivalence in a detail the present context does not allow. For now, let me simply say that the presence of these programs seems to me rooted in a long history of inequity in public schooling and that the bad feelings and tensions the programs generate among students, teachers, and parents are yet another indication of the inadequacies of our system and theories of schooling.

7. Because I am arguing that Laura's illness was not part of a pattern of irresponsibility, an important question is passed over. The question involves our concept of irresponsibility and our tendency to use it as a catchall category for all those children who do not conform to our image of what a child should be at some given time and place. It seems to me that we also often view irresponsibility as something bad that must itself be corrected rather than as a

sign that some aspect of a child's relationship with the world is distorted or as a sign that our own attitude towards the world, as represented by its children, is distorted—for example, is too commandeering.

8. See Grumet (1988, 31–58) for a discussion of the historical and psychoanalytic influences on the quality of trust that exists between mothers and teachers.

9. In quoting Foucault I am not implying that we should abandon examination or swear off making judgments but rather that we increase our awareness of their potential for abuse. Also, I do not think that classification requires a normalizing gaze. At its most basic, classification seems to me to require the ability to perceive difference, which need not involve a normalizing gaze.

10. See Schachtel ([1959] 1984, 279–322) for a discussion of the development of perception from childhood to adulthood as a conventionalizing process.

11. I am not arguing that mothers and teachers are never themselves examined but that examining the performance and values of others can become a way of avoiding the need to examine our own values and performances.

12. I know that fine distinctions can be tiresome, and yet this is not always because they are irrelevant but sometimes because they ask us to consider what has previously been hidden or overlooked and so require us to expend a kind of energy we may not be used to expending.

13. There are several situations in which I could have complied with the conference as originally conceived. I could have been unusually busy or tired and not thought out the implications discussed in the text, I could have accepted the school and the teacher's authority as expert with an implicitness that elicited faithful, nonquestioning cooperation, or I could have been so well schooled when it came to following directions and so well brought up when it came to our culture's "table manners" that I could have experienced Mrs. Matthews' closing comments as equivalent to a teacher instructing me not to forget my homework or to a person at table asking me to "please pass the butter," in which case I would have complied conscientiously, graciously, as a matter of course.

14. A more positive outcome of Laura's doubting of her own perceptual powers would have been the formation of a puzzle about the nature of the world, a puzzle she would work on as she grew up.

15. If we can find no other reason to be honest with our children, it seems to me we would do so because mutual honesty is one way we can help ensure that the choices all of us make are informed by a knowledge of reality as currently understood rather than by some fantasy we promote.

16. My relationship with Mrs. Matthews could be compared to David and Mark's relationship in Chapter 1. Just as David was disconcerted when Mark took a view of the hamburger rolls that was not in keeping with David's script for the picnic, so could Mrs. Matthews have been disconcerted by my remark about Laura testifying against herself and so could I have been disconcerted by her remark about Laura's absence.

17. A third important reason for including children in conferences is to give them a chance to discover that the world need not end if the parent glimpses the child's school self and the teacher the child's home self, and so forth. Of course, revealing our various selves to audiences other than the intended one could create anxiety in any of the participants, which is why I think it is important to acknowledge and talk with each other and with children about how the boundaries of our world can create behavior patterns that are highly specific to given times and places.

18. Although there are times when it is entirely appropriate to defer to another's knowledge and in doing so to affirm our capacity to place faith in and trust another human being, it is also true that deference can be foolish and that recipes about when to defer are not easy to come by.

19. My quoting of Grumet oversimplifies her tone, particularly in relation to her use of the word *devoted*. As I read her, she is at one and the same time underscoring the sentimentalized viewpoint the nineteenth century took on motherhood (the century promoted a concept of the "devoted mother" that was incompatible with the complexity of what it means to be a human being) and the rejection of that viewpoint by twentieth-century social science. In addition, she takes issue with the attitude that twentieth-century social sci-

ence has taken towards the mother. In quoting her, I wanted to focus on her criticism of the twentieth-century attitude but had no intention of endorsing the nineteenth-century sentimentalization or of implying that Grumet endorses it.

20. In some cases I think the stigma attached to quitting arises from an unnecessarily harsh concept of responsibility, one that leans towards equating commitment with martyrdom. When we teach responsibility, I think it would be helpful if we took the time to acknowledge that some people and some jobs are a poor match and that to be responsible need not mean—in fact, in my opinion should not mean (except in certain circumstances too complex to describe here)—sticking with a job that makes one *essentially* miserable. Although I am oversimplifying, I think there is enough work to be done in the world for all of us to have jobs that satisfy us and, furthermore, that the work no one wants or that is deadening should be shared by all. I also think it is too bad that some of us have what appears to be a perverse desire to make sure our children's lives are as dreary and as joyless as our own have been and equally too bad that the power of our imaginations should be turned towards creating mythologies-philosophies whose impetus seems to be the rationalization of joylessness.

21. For readers who may view my uncertainty in the teachers' lounge as a personal reaction not based in the reality of the school and therefore not comparable to the uncertainty the children sometimes felt, I want to say that my feelings had a firm basis in the general reality of the public school as well as in the specific reality of Laura's school. Generally, my feelings arose from my sense that we all need a place where we can work in some privacy, without the frustration of constant or unexpected interruptions from all that is peripheral to our work and that, in addition, elementary school teachers, because they spend long hours working with large groups of children, also need an on-site getaway where they can take a break. In keeping with this sense, I had, as a volunteer parent at Laura's school, made a point to respect the privacy of the teachers' lounge and also to cross the slightly different boundaries that formed the classrooms as well as such places as the secretary's office, the principal's office, and the school kitchen according to the requirements of my work. Consequently, the lounge was a strange place to me. The only qualification I want to add is that in acknowledging the appropriateness of a private place like the teacher's lounge I am

not ruling out its potential to inhibit a much-needed openness and communication between teachers, parents, and students.

My feelings about the lounge also had roots in specific events at Laura's school. An example involving another library volunteer makes clear that the staff valued the privacy of their lounge in respect to parents as well as students. This volunteer, a mother, got into the habit of taking frequent coffee breaks in the teachers' lounge. Finding her presence a strain, the staff asked the librarian to explain to the mother that the breaks were inappropriate.

A second example concerns interactions between the children and the staff at the door connecting the library to the lounge. In my experience, these interactions fell into several categories, one of which included children who made every effort to respect the boundary of the lounge and who, when they did approach it, approached uncertainly. On entering the library in search of a staff member, these children would usually ask the librarian or a volunteer if she had seen a particular staff member. If the staff person was in the lounge and if the children did not have *official* business to transact, they would usually say something like "Oh, she's in the teachers' lounge. Well, we can't bother her in there." On the other hand, if the children did have official business, they might state it to an adult and sometimes even also ask if the business seemed important enough to make it okay to knock at the lounge door. Having reassured themselves that the business was official, the children would knock at the door, and, more often than not, the staff member answering the knock would maintain a distance or coolness (sometimes also remarking that the lounge was generally off-bounds) until the children made clear that they had legitimate business.

22. The issue of report cards for primary graders was controversial in Laura's school district. Although many teachers and parents were opposed to these cards and although district policy towards them fluctuated, during Laura's primary years the cards were required, which meant that once they were handed out, usually at parent-teacher conferences, it was up to parents to decide what to do with them. My view was that the cards were real and needed to be openly shared, but I also could not help but notice, given the family intimacy that grew up around this sharing at our house, the way in which the sharing of an aspect of reality gradually attaches us to the aspect, even though we may not approve of it, as well as

to the sharing. Eventually, we begin to hold tight to the aspect (in this case a report card) even when an opportunity arises to get rid of it, and we seem to forget our power to build new intimacies around aspects of reality that we truly value.

23. I know it could be argued that Laura's relief arose from having successfully hidden her irresponsibility from her mother, but this is not an argument I would make in this particular case.

24. I am not arguing that Mrs. Matthews' view of resignation necessarily reflected her opinion of Laura as a specific child, although it could have, but rather that Mrs. Matthews may have viewed resignation as a possibility open to any student in Laura's situation.

25. I did not make a judgment about whether Laura's play became less intense after the conference because I have no memory one way or the other.

26. Laura's remark "I couldn't even fit the numbers in the spaces!—there wasn't enough room for me to write!" and the conclusion she immediately drew from her remark—"and so it was a totally confining book"—broke forcefully through her description of the alternative accounting system she was describing. The breaking through and her conclusion suggest the way in which dialogue can sometimes reveal bits and pieces of information that can help us crystallize a communicable viewpoint as opposed to one that we may be able to feel and live but that we cannot spell out to ourselves or to another.

27. Using the letters *a* and *b* to distinguish between the points about the book's spacing and its logic was Laura's organizational device, not one that I added.

28. In comparing herself as treasurer to an adult who is miserable at work, Laura may seem to contradict what I said earlier about experiencing a rigid boundary between the adult's world and the child's. But my earlier comment was about the nine-year-old Laura, whereas Laura's comparison was made as a sixteen-year-old. And even if there had been no age gap, she could have experienced the boundary as rigid in some respects and fluid in others.

29. A wholesale condemnation of dependence as negative seems to me an extreme oversimplification and one that recalls an argu-

ment from Chapter 3. The argument was that when we abstract human behavior from situations and attach a positive or negative value to the abstraction (rather than to the behavior in a specific context), we overlook complexity and underestimate our full potential. In Chapter 3, I argued that David may have felt torn between the two dictums "Look before you leap" and "He or she who hesitates is lost," and in Chapter 4 I am arguing that Laura may have felt torn between her desire to live the absolutely positive value she perceived that her culture placed on independence and the absolutely negative value she perceived that it placed on dependence or a need for help.

30. When I say that the disfavor was more "than she could bear," I do not mean to be melodramatic but want to emphasize that though Laura did not literally die from the disfavor, neither did she survive it intact. My reason for wanting to make this point is that I think adults are prone to cheerily cite a child's "survival" as evidence that the child is okay and to ignore the issue of the emotional or spiritual damage that may have occurred during the effort to survive. Here I do not mean to deny the potential of adversity to strengthen us, but I do mean to assert its potential to injure us as well.

31. There is a point about Laura's notes that has been nagging me, but I cannot get it straight in memory and so have not included it in the text. I seem to remember that the subject of the notes came up at my conference with Mrs. Matthews, but, interestingly enough, I can't recall whether she referred to them as evidence that Laura always looked for the easiest way to execute her duties or as an example of the staff's effort to support Laura.

32. I want to make two comments about Laura's description of her relationship with the school principal. The first relates directly to Laura's statement that the school principal may have regarded Mrs. Matthews as a woman who was going to "get" him. Although Laura's remark could be dismissed as projection, the fact that Laura saw this as a possible relationship between teacher and principal could have arisen from a perceptiveness gained from her own difficult relationship with Mrs. Matthews. Laura's view could also have arisen from her ability to examine and classify in the sense that she could have recognized that forgetting to buy Popsicles was the sort of thing (or category of thing) that Mrs. Matthews would have

criticized. Once Laura had recognized this, she could have seen a comparison between her teacher-advisor's and her principal's relationship and the teacher-advisor's and her own relationship. In other words, Laura's "projection" could have drawn on her capacity for metaphor and could have been to an extent accurate as opposed to distorted.

The second comment is that in my effort to establish that Laura felt oppressed by Mrs. Matthews' attempts to guide her, I have offered support that itself introduces important additional issues, issues that I would like to pursue but that exceed my present scope. One is the way the relations between principal, teacher, and student recast the traditional relations between father, mother, and child. For a discussion of this recasting, see Grumet (1988, 31–58). Another related issue Laura's description introduces is the way a dissatisfaction with or a straining against the traditional family relations in nonfamily settings can enmesh us in power struggles that prolong the very relationships we strain against, especially when the straining is "blind"—not informed by a knowledge that the traditional relations have been recast. Finally, I want to say that in relating Laura's experiencing of Mrs. Matthews and the principal, I am in no sense endorsing or generalizing the view that the teacher is the villain and the principal the good guy. Although I would like to take up my objections to such a view in detail, to do so would take me too far afield from my central purpose before returning me to it.

33. Here I do not mean to imply that only an adult who knew Laura well could have raised the possibility that she had been mislabeled; actually, I think any adult of a certain attitude—even a complete stranger to Laura—could have raised the possibility.

Chapter 5. When Daphne Was a Girl

1. Viewing the stranger as suspect is nothing unusual, something E. Straus touches on when he says, "The stranger, of course, is a perfect expression of the public threat of invasion to immediate experience" ([1966] 1980, 222). But the stranger also can represent a rescuing figure who makes immediate becoming possible. On the one hand we have Bluebeard and Baba Yaga, and on the other, Glinda the Good and the Lone Ranger. Why Daphne's teacher per-

ceived the school friend as a prospective villain rather than hero I'm not sure. Nor do I know to what degree his concern was motivated by an authentic desire to protect Daphne from harm and to what degree by the possessiveness that sometimes marks the father or father figure's attitude towards his daughter's virtue.

2. The irony of such waving was suggested to me by Stevie Smith's poem "Not Waving But Drowning" (1962).

3. Some may be surprised that Daphne and Glen would have been playing hide and seek at fourteen and almost sixteen, but in their time and place it was not unusual.

4. I have said that Daphne categorized the initial assault as something that could not really have happened, but I am not implying that she was living under the influence of a personal fable, mainly because she did not comprehend sexual abuse as something that could happen to anyone, let alone as something that could happen only to others. If her conception of reality had encompassed sexuality and sexual abuse, however, I think her view of herself as a spirited tomboy could have given rise to a personal fable.

5. A tangent point I have not taken up in the text is that the "bad dream" and "fluke" categories may have been aids to a rationalization of the molestation and that even from the first assault Daphne felt compelled to keep silent and resorted to the categories as a way to avoid encountering her fear of future abuse. Another point I have not pursued in the text is that the categories "bad dream" and "fluke" are themselves distinct in their implications about responsibility for the molestation in the dugout. A dream would have been Daphne's creation, so to speak, and so something she could have felt personally ashamed of (especially given that her religion classified bad thoughts as sinful), whereas a fluke experience would have been Glen's creation and as such more easily viewed as his responsibility, if anybody's. Here I am not suggesting that Daphne would have sorted through these implications logically but only that they may have been part of a nonverbal undertone or "murmuring" that contributed to her upheaval.

6. While attempting to articulate the complex set of influences motivating Daphne's silence, I may be giving the impression that her experiencing of the various hopes, fears, and pressures was part

of a clear-cut sequence, which would be misleading. Instead, her experiencing was at times marked by a running of the gamut of hopes, fears, and pressures in a moment.

7. I do not mean to suggest that Daphne had been influenced by only one version of the heroic tradition but that her view of parents and adults as protectors suggests the influence of a particular version. I think she had been influenced by at least three versions of the tradition: the tradition of hero and victim as played by different people, with the hero in the active role and the victim in the passive; the tradition of the hero as the rugged individualist who "toughs out" adversity; and the tradition of the hero as martyr.

8. Although Daphne was a spirited, independent tomboy, she was also literally a girl, and I think this would have increased the likelihood that on one level she would have experienced the molestations (which made her femaleness about as inescapable as anything could) as overwhelming.

9. I am not advocating rash heroics and am aware of the great threat to physical survival faced by many victims of abuse. What I am advocating is a shift in the way many of us have been taught to perceive ourselves, a shift that would enable us to make decisions about risk-taking on the basis of our full potential rather than a sliced potential.

10. Daphne's desire to be given express permission not to suffer Glen's attacks recalls the way she would rub Glen's father's back, even if he fell asleep, until someone specifically told her she could stop. I think her behavior is worth serious thought as an example of how thoroughly some children experience the world, or have been taught to experience the world, as a place where their role is to await instructions from "boss" people or "boss" ideas.

11. Why Daphne's mother and Glen's father kept silent I don't know. Despite the immense discrepancy implied between Daphne's and the adults' experiencing of the bedroom scene, all of the following seem possible: (1) they dismissed the scene as an instance of "playing doctor," (2) they assumed they had made their point merely by appearing at the door and need not follow through, (3) Glen's father had spoken to him and, receiving Glen's assurance that there would be no more such scenes, had informed Daphne's mother that everything was under control, (4) the adults decided after the fact

that they couldn't really have seen what they thought they had seen, (5) the adults did not (contrary to Daphne's impression) see the molestation, and (6) the adults did not acknowledge what they had seen.

12. By initial text I don't mean the early rough or in-progress drafts of each chapter but the text of the full manuscript draft completed in 1989.

13. The history of Daphne's reference to the gun is worth noting. When Daphne first spoke about the gun, she said that it had been in evidence during some of the medications. But when we reviewed the text together so that I could eliminate any errors of content that an imperfect listening to her story might have generated, she said that her memory of the gun was vague and that, in talking to her psychiatrist about it, they had decided that the memory could have been distorted and that it could have been a general fear of her father's guns and not the actual presence of a gun that was the source of the "memory." During Daphne's recent qualifications, however, she said that though she was afraid of her father's guns, the reference to the presence of a gun during the medications was strictly fabrication.

Also worth considering is that the issue of a consciously fabricated or embellished molestation complicates the issue of fantasized molestation. A note that I included in the initial text is pertinent here and ran as follows:

> Given Freud's theory of childhood sexuality and femininity (Freud 1966, particularly pp. 576–599) and the multitude of controversies surrounding it (for example, one relatively recent controversy was sparked by *Assault on Truth* [Masson 1984]), some readers will doubtless raise the possibility that Daphne's recollection of abuse from early childhood was a fantasy. Although there will obviously be cases in which the status of alleged abuse cannot be absolutely confirmed, I think that mistaking a fantasized sexual encounter for abuse would be quite rare, even for a child between the ages of three and six, and that it has not occurred in Daphne's case. Furthermore, I do not think that Daphne's initial effort to dismiss Glen's abuse as a bad dream compromises my position. For one thing, I think that even young children are better at distinguishing reality from fantasy and dream than we may think, particularly when the reality experienced is first person and involves the sense of touch. On this same point, I think that children,

and others, would be more likely to have difficulty distinguishing a first-person reality from a first-person fantasy or dream when the fantasy or dream dramatized a real event from the past and that though the details of memories from early childhood may be vague and even inaccurate, such memories are usually accurate in their core. For another thing, Daphne's initial effort to dismiss Glen's abuse as a bad dream arose not out of the dreamlike quality of the initial molestation but out of her belief that what she was experiencing through her senses as *real* was actually impossible. Though there is much more to be said on this issue, it is too complex to pursue in this context. In fact, I have rewritten this note any number of times and, still finding it a gross oversimplification, am on the fence about whether or not to strike it altogether.

14. In commenting that Daphne's craving for protection alone qualified her for professional help, I may give some the impression that I reduce such help to the providing of protection, which I do not. Instead, I think her craving for protection suggested an essentially distorted relation to the world that therapy, given its relatively secure setting, could help her explore and recreate.

15. The series of modifiers *insufficient, undeserving*, and *highly vulnerable* may strike some as redundant. I see the modifiers as distinct, however, and would be quicker to criticize their presentation as a coordinate series on the grounds that such a series glosses over the complex relationships possible among these modifiers than I would be to criticize the series for redundancy. Taking the distinction between *insufficient* and *undeserving*—even if we grant the *insufficiency* of femaleness, or any other "ness" we care to name, which I am not here doing, it would not follow that femaleness is undeserving, unless of course we were to assume that merit is a function of sufficiency. Turning to the distinction of the modifier *highly vulnerable*, though it certainly could be argued that vulnerability is a function of insufficiency, vulnerability can be artificially increased when we accept such assumptions as that merit is a function of sufficiency and then proceed to found our culture on them. In other words, when we define insufficiency as undeserving, we can increase vulnerability by withholding anything (on the grounds of undeservingness) from love and respect to goods and services. Although I haven't the space to argue it here, I think that in our culture this assumption is widespread (although inconsistent) and

rooted in a fear of death that goes far beyond a healthy desire for physical survival.

16. The explorations from my own childhood that I shared with Daphne (in the hope of easing any self-consciousness she might feel) when I initially introduced the topic of sexuality evidently did not make it any easier for her to speak about this topic. However, those who have suffered childhood sexual abuse might be less likely to speak up about childhood explorations out of a fear that the admittance of voluntary exploration would discredit the experience of abuse. Such a fear seems generally reasonable given the skepticism, nonchalance, and even glee that sometimes greet stories of sexual crimes such as rape, especially rape in which rapist and victim were acquainted (date and spouse rape, for example) and the rape of those typically viewed as less than model citizens (prostitutes, for example). In addition, Daphne's long history of pronounced physical modesty also suggests that the topic of sexuality could be so excruciating to her that the few explorations I shared would have been powerless to ease her self-consciousness.

Two additional points need mention. One is that Daphne's father had taken for granted that all his children would be boys and that Daphne not only had known this (one of her father's favorite stories had been to tell about how sure he had been that he would have all boys, how surprised he had been to have girls, and how unexpectedly wonderful having girls had turned out to be) but had concluded when quite young that being born female and having no penis had been an error. Whether she concluded this before or after the ambiguous interactions with her father, she does not remember. The second point is that though Daphne has come to view her tomboyishness as rooted primarily in her desire to protect herself, she also makes clear that her tomboyishness allowed her to explore aspects of the world and develop friendships that would have been closed to her had she been a traditional girl. Adding complexity is that during our talks Daphne twice or so observed that her fear of her father had coexisted with a sense that he had a real liking and regard for her.

One qualification of Daphne's attraction to the male world is also in order. The view that she sought out male company in an effort to perfect her playing of a male role need not imply that she was conscious of her effort, as an actress researching a role for a movie or a play might be conscious, but rather that a nonreflective attention to or an absorption with the male way of being would have been implicit in her gravitation towards the male "corner" as a place she hoped would provide protection from sexual abuse.

17. Having said that my intention is not to plumb the ambiguities, I should add that one of my earliest responses to the news of Daphne's embellishments was intense anger accompanied by an urge to become inquisitor and "have at" the truth and that another was an intense curiosity and desire to have the puzzles of her story solved.

18. Following her crisis, Daphne affirmed as unequivocal Glen's molestations. Along with this affirmation, however, she expressed, when annotating the initial text, two reservations about those pages in the initial text dealing with the abuse by Glen, both of which led to my revising some diction. One involves pages in the current text (200, 206, 219) that refer to a psychological state that Daphne said she sometimes experienced during the period of her abuse by Glen and also at other times in her life—for example, during the weeks immediately preceding her decision to seek therapy. Whereas in the initial text the state was referred to by the terms *trance, hypnoticlike state,* and *mental lapse,* in the current text the terms used are *time loss* and *psychological distancing,* a change I chose to implement as a result of Daphne's annotations. To explain further: in annotating those pages of the initial text referring to this psychological state, Daphne made a number of comments. Specifically regarding the term *trance,* she wrote, "The trances are a confusing part. In the last molest it occurred to the best of my recollection." Commenting on the term *mental lapse,* she wrote, "confused about that definition (an interruption in thought or time then yes)," "I lost track of time, don't believe it was a true lapse," and "not sure *lapse* [my emphasis] is the right word." She also wrote that *lapse* "may not be right reference word." In further commenting on the word *trance,* she wrote, "*lost time* [my emphasis] more accurate than actual *trance* [my emphasis] although the lines are grey. A refusal to believe what had happened, a deep denial and disbelief and desire to shut out."

One reason the initial terms could give Daphne pause is that they lend themselves to an inflation of experience that borders on or crosses over into the kind of embellishment and fabrication of symptoms she did effect, apparently increasingly as therapy progressed. Whether she consciously embellished her description of her psychological state during the abuse by Glen, I have no way of knowing. One thing I have noticed is that Daphne is attracted to clinical language and certain kinds of jargon, as many of us are. That she would be susceptible to the distinction of being someone who fell into "trance states" as opposed to being someone who was, say, so alarmed or panicked by the molestations that she "became distanced from her immediate surroundings and lost track of time" seems likely to me. In fairness to Daphne, however, it is probably true that because of the embellishments, she will find her communications measured against a more exacting standard than the standard we typically apply to others and to ourselves.

In any event, after weighing the pros and cons of various options concerning the questionable vocabulary and finding them all less than satisfactory, I substituted *time loss* and phrases denoting a distancing from one's immediate concrete surroundings for the terms *hypnoticlike state, trance*, and *mental lapse*. A main factor in deciding to substitute was to make the text itself as accurate as possible and thereby minimize misimpressions among readers who do not attend to back matter such as end notes.

Daphne's second reservation is over the word *vomit* to describe her nausea following the final instance of abuse by Glen. In annotating the initial text, which presented the vomiting as unequivocal ("unequivocal" was how Daphne presented the vomiting in our precrisis discussions), she has written, "I believe I vomited, for sure was nauseated." Here again arises the question of language lending itself to inflation (as well as the question of the imprecisions of memory). Because it seems better to understate than overstate, I have qualified the word *vomit* or deleted it and substituted *nausea* in the current text (see pp. 206, 218).

I also revised the pages dealing with the molestations to explicitly state that communications with Daphne were my source of information (see p. 198). Though this seemed clear in the initial text, I wanted to be sure that I had not left room for readers to assume additional sources of information.

19. On a more general level, the relation with the father and mother and other key figures could hardly help but influence a silence such as Daphne's. And here I mean these figures as an intertwining of cultural myth and real person.

20. When quoting the initial text in the current text, I have modified the use of such words as *abuse* to describe Daphne's interactions with her father with such bracketed terms as *perceived* or *experience of* so that the ambiguity of the interactions as well as an accurate initial text are both set forth.

21. Though far from satisfactory, *deviant* is the best alternative I could come up with here. Also, though my depiction of Glen is not sympathetic, I am aware that he, too, is a child with a story of his own. I am also convinced, however, that though his story might help us to understand him, it should not prevent us from protecting others from his abuse.

22. My description of the landscape surrounding the toolshed where Daphne suffered her final instance of abuse was suggested by W. H. Auden's (1973) poem "Musée des Beaux Arts."

Chapter 6. An Afternoon Spent Playing Dress-up

1. See Buytendijk (1950, 136–139) for a discussion of the self-consciousness provoked not by the shocked or disapproving look but by the indiscreet one.

2. Although it was not my impression at the time, the shop-keepers' reception could have expressed social politeness or rote warmth rather than a spontaneously warm acceptance.

3. Though I cannot remember actually hearing my mother's voice in the adult discussion and though it would have been like her to have been working in the kitchen, I have used the word *parents* because she was present that evening and because I cannot remember anyone taking exception to the disapproval. Whether I am trying to preserve some of the myth of her in this note or trying to protect her from the pain she may experience on reading this story or simply trying to place in the open as much as the present context allows, I can't say. Perhaps I am doing all of these things.

4. Children doubtless contribute to the idealization of their parents and other adults. I think, however, that we adults often initiate and foster this idealization, getting quite caught up in it when we would do better to openly communicate our imperfections, our humanness, to children. One example of the way an entire culture can

contribute to and feed on such idealization was the nineteenth century's cultivation of the sentimental myth of the selfless, devoted mother, a myth touched on in Chapter 4.

5. Because traditions can become empty in that though we adhere to and teach them, we lose touch with the values that gave rise to them, I think we need to distinguish between two kinds of adherents. The first would support the values embedded in empty traditions if they were to discover or have the values pointed out, and the second would oppose the values if discovered or pointed out. If we proceed either to support or oppose some taken-for-granted tradition without making this distinction, we may present our argument as if we have only one audience when actually we have at least two.

6. Another possibility I have not explored because it seems less likely is that Sharon's mother sensed my parents' superior attitude, was offended by it, and derived satisfaction from involving their daughter in an outing she knew would upset them. I don't see this possibility as a problem for the arguments made in the text, however, because any satisfaction Sharon's mother may have felt could have existed in addition to the other motives.

7. See Madeleine Grumet's exploration (1988, 164–182) of the double standard we apply to "other people's children."

8. By "too Sartrian" I mean that my parents' attitude reflected a way of being that recalls Sartre's definition of shame as "the *recognition* of the fact that I *am* indeed that object which the Other is looking at and judging" (1956, 261). I also mean that their attitude suggested a view of the public eye as unflaggingly a "looking" eye that is intent on negating rather than affirming, exploring, or remaining neutral and a view of the human being as a creature who, when looked at or when "on stage," is ever conscious of being looked at. This view is suggested in such statements of Sartre's as that while making public appearances "we *never* [my emphasis] lose sight of the fact that we are looked at" (1956, 281), and it is a view that is prevalent, though certainly not pervasive, in our culture.

9. Although the roots of my mother's criticisms were doubtless complex and although the criticisms did make me feel self-conscious about being female, on one level they expressed her conviction that children should not be dressed fussily or treated as dolls.

10. Obviously, I am overgeneralizing here in that the audience was made up of individuals. Even among those who could be categorized as accepting of Sharon's and my walk, there could have been a great range of views.

11. The word *infiltrated* has certain advantages but is misleading in implying a surreptitious effort on the frog's part to penetrate the plumbing. I guess I am wanting to have my cake and eat it too by appropriating the frog as symbol while at the same time retaining the plain frogginess of the creature. This is not a particularly surprising thing for me to do, however, since I think all of us should occasionally be having a slice of cake and eating it, too.

12. Straus's discussion (1982, 41, 45–48) of the "psychic series" and of human beings as historical beings has influenced my remarks about the uniqueness of the individual life history.

References

Ainsworth, Mary D. Salter, Mary C. Blehar, Everett Waters, and Sally Wall. 1978. *Patterns of Attachment: A Psychological Study of the Strange Situation*. Hillsdale, New Jersey: Erlbaum.

Alegría, Claribel. 1980. "Small Country." In *A Book of Women Poets from Antiquity to Now*, ed. Aliki Barnstone and Willis Barnstone. New York: Schocken Books.

Auden, W. H. 1973. "Musée des Beaux Arts." In *The Norton Anthology of Modern Poetry*, ed. Richard Ellmann and Robert O'Clair. New York: W. W. Norton and Co.

Barrax, Gerald W. 1980. "Narrative of a Surprising Conversion." In *An Audience of One*. Athens: University of Georgia Press.

Bowlby, John. 1960. "Separation Anxiety." *International Journal of Psychoanalysis* 41:89–113.

Buytendijk, F. J. J. 1950. "The Phenomenological Approach to the Problem of Feelings and Emotions." In *Feelings and Emotions*, ed. Martin L. Reymert, 127–141. New York: McGraw-Hill.

Cervantes, Miguel de. 1950. *The Adventures of Don Quixote*. Trans. J. M. Cohen. Baltimore: Penguin Books.

Dickinson, Emily. 1951. *The Poems of Emily Dickinson*. Ed. Thomas H. Johnson. Cambridge, Massachusetts: The Belknap Press of Harvard University Press.

Disney, Walt. *Three Little Pigs*. Walt Disney Productions. Disneyland Record 1310.

Dixon, Franklin W. 1972. *The Masked Monkey*. New York: Grosset and Dunlap.

Figuera Aymerich, Angela. 1979. "Women at the Market." In *the Penguin Book of Women Poets*, ed. Carol Cosman, Joan Keefe, and Kathleen Weaver. New York: Viking Penguin.

Foucault, Michel. 1977. *Discipline and Punish: The Birth of the Prison*. Trans. Alan Sheridan. New York: Pantheon Books.

Frankl, Viktor E. 1971. *Man's Search for Meaning: An Introduction to Logotherapy*. Rev. ed. Trans., Part 1, Ilse Lasch. New York: Washington Square Press.

Freud, Sigmund. 1966. *The Complete Introductory Lectures on Psychoanalysis*. Trans. James Strachey. New York: W. W. Norton and Co.

Gilbert, Christopher. 1984. "Saturday Morning at the Laundry." In *Across the Mutual Landscape*. Port Townsend, Washington: Graywolf Press.

Great Children's Stories: The Classic Volland Edition. 1972. Intro. by Irene Hunt. Frederick Richardson, illus. Northbrook, Illinois: Hubbard Press.

Grumet, Madeleine, R. 1988. *Bitter Milk: Women and Teaching*. Amherst: University of Massachusetts Press.

Hubbell, Sue. 1983. *A Country Year: Living the Questions*. New York: Random House.

"I'd Run About." 1980. In *A Book of Women Poets from Antiquity to Now*, ed. Aliki Barnstone and Willis Barnstone. New York: Schocken Books.

Jacobs, M. 1968. "The Shifting Existence of Western Man: An Introduction to J. H. van den Berg's Work on Metabletics." *Humanitas* 4(1): 25–59.

Joseph, Helen. 1967. *Tomorrow's Sun: A Smuggled Journal from South Africa*. New York: The John Day Company.

Keats, John. 1959. *Selected Poems and Letters*. Ed. Douglas Bush. Boston: Riverside Press.

Kincaid, Jamaica. 1986. *Annie John*. New York: New American Library.

Langeveld, Martinus J. 1958. "Disintegration and Reintegration of 'Pedagogy.'" *International Review of Education* 4:51–64.

McGovern, Ann. 1978. *Shark Lady: True Adventures of Eugenie Clark*. New York: Scholastic Book Services.

Masson, Jeffrey Moussaieff. 1984. *The Assault on Truth: Freud's Suppression of the Seduction Theory*. New York: Farrar, Straus, and Giroux.

Merleau-Ponty, Maurice. 1962. *Phenomenology of Perception*. Trans. Colin Smith. London: Routledge and Kegan Paul.

Noguchi, Isamu. 1976. "Noguchi on Brancusi." *Craft Horizons*, August, 26–29.

Ola, Per, and Emily D'Aulaire. 1986. "Piranha!" *International Wildlife*, May–June, 30–35.

Ortiz, Simon J. 1977. "Canyon de Chelly." In *A Good Journey*. Berkeley: Turtle Island.

Russell, Dora. 1983. *The Dora Russell Reader: Fifty-seven Years of Writing and Journalism, 1925–1982*. Forward by Dale Spender. London: Pandora Press.

Sartre, Jean-Paul. 1956. *Being and Nothingness*. Trans. Hazel E. Barnes. New York: Philosophical Library.

Schachtel, Ernest G. 1966. *Experiential Foundations of Rorschach's Test*. New York: Basic Books.

———. [1959] 1984. *Metamorphosis: On the Development of Affect, Perception, and Memory*. Reprint, with preface by Jerome L. Singer. New York: Da Capo Press.

Smith, Stevie. 1962. *Selected Poems*. London: Longman, Green and Co.

Straus, Erwin. 1963. *The Primary World of Senses: A Vindication of Sensory Experience*. Trans. Jacob Needleman. New York: The Free Press of Glencoe.

———. [1966] 1980. *Phenomenological Psychology*. Reprint. Trans. Erling Eng. New York: Garland Publishing.

————. 1982. *Man, Time, and World: Two Contributions to Anthropological Psychology.* Trans. Donald Moss. Pittsburgh: Duquesne University Press.

Unamuno, Miguel de. 1954. *Tragic Sense of Life.* Trans. J. E. Crawford Flitch. New York: Dover Publications.

Walker, Margaret. 1979. "Childhood." In *The Penguin Book of Women Poets,* ed. Carol Cosman, Joan Keefe, and Kathleen Weaver. New York: Viking Penguin.

Werner, Heinz. 1948. *Comparative Psychology of Mental Development.* Rev. ed. Chicago: Follett Publishing Company.

Index

Schachtel, Ernest G.: and David's perception of water, 89; and the need for protection, 199, 200; and story as complex object for child, 33–34, 40, 269 n.32, 270 n.36; theory of perception, 27, 47, 266 n.18, 270 n.35, 274 n.51, 280 n.31, 282 n.10
Secretary, at Laura's school, 150, 153, 159–61
Security/predictability, human desire for, 100–101, 277 n.16; and theory, 275 n.3
Self-becoming: and Erwin Straus, 197, 288–89 n.1; and personal scripts, 162; and self-recognition, 39–40; and well-being, 115, 234, 256–57, 267–68 n.24. *See also* Daphne; David; Laura; Mark.
Self-interest, 115, 267 n.24
Self-worth, 117
Separation anxiety, 28, 51, 266 n.20
"Sesame Street," 40
Sexual crimes, public attitude towards, 293 n.16
Shakespeare, 280 n.30
Shame and guilt, 277 n.12, 297 n.8; and social norms, 73–74. *See also* Daphne; David; Mothers; Narrator's outing on main street.
Shark Lady, 59
Sharon (Narrator's childhood friend). *See under* Narrator's outing on main street.
Sharon's mother/family. *See under* Narrator's outing on main street.
Smith, Stevie, 289 n.2
Social and circumstantial inequality, 255, 259–60 n.2, 281 n.6; and oldest son, 41–42
Social order: and daughters, 249, 254; preservation and disruption of, 29; and sons, 42
Social sciences (20th century), 144, 283–84 n.19

Sons, cultural view of, 29, 41–42
Stereotypes, and caregiver-child relationship, 144, 267–68 n.24, 278 n.19
Story. *See* Narrative.
Story material. *See* Experience, as story material.
Strange situation, 28, 49, 51, 266 n.20, 274 n.52
Straus, Erwin: and conversion experience, 271 n.39; and human beings as historical beings, 264 n.9, 278 n.22, 298 n.12; and individual becoming, 197; and shame, 277 n.12, 279 n.27; and shocking experience, 276 n.10, 278 n.20; and the stranger, 288 n.1; and subjective readiness, 51; theory of human learning, 3
Swann, Charles, 224
Systems, limitations of, 94, 263–64 n.8

Tarzan/Tarzan movie, 69, 76–78, 79–82, 83, 85–86, 89, 91, 99–100, 101, 278 n.17, 279 n.25
Teachers' lounge, 148–49, 284–85 n.21
Teachers (professional): and model students, 116; performance of, 111, 282 n.11; and privacy, 281 n.4, 284 n.21; public valuing of, 280 n.2; relation with mothers, 128, 133, 145, 282 n.8
Teaching: as art, 14; and "shoulds," 259–60 n.2. *See also* Guidance (child); Nurture.
Therapy, 292 n.14
"This Is Your Life," 39
"The Three Little Pigs": as classic story, 32, 40–41, 45–46; as cultural object, 33; and house of bricks, 34–35, 36, 41–42, 43; and mortality, 35–36; and mother pig, 34, 35, 36–37, 39, 43; versions of,